Henry David Thoreau

Twayne's United States Authors Series

Lewis Leary, Editor
University of North Carolina at Chapel Hill

TUSAS 497

HENRY DAVID THOREAU
(1817–1862)
Photograph courtesy of the Concord Free Public Library

Henry David Thoreau

By Richard J. Schneider

Wartburg College

Twayne Publishers
A Division of G. K. Hall & Co. • *Boston*

Henry David Thoreau

Richard J. Schneider

Copyright © 1987 by G. K. Hall & Co.
All Rights Reserved
Published by Twayne Publishers
A Division of G. K. Hall & Co.
70 Lincoln Street
Boston, Massachusetts 02111

Map of Walden Pond reproduced courtesy
of the Concord Free Public Library

Copyediting supervised by Lewis DeSimone
Book design by Barbara Anderson

Typeset in 11 pt. Garamond
by Compset, Inc., Beverly Massachusetts

Printed on permanent/durable acid-free paper
and bound in the United States of America

Library of Congress Cataloging in Publication Data

Schneider, Richard J.
  Henry David Thoreau.

  (Twayne's United States authors series ; TUSAS 497)
  Bibliography
  Includes index.
  1. Thoreau, Henry David, 1817–1862—Criticism and
interpretation. I. Title. II. Series.
PS3054.S36   1987   818'.309   86-31826
ISBN 0-8057-7495-5 (alk. paper)

Contents

About the Author

Richard J. Schneider is currently associate professor and chair of the Department of English at Wartburg College in Waverly, Iowa. He also served as professor and chair of the Department of English and Modern Languages at Atlantic Christian College in Wilson, North Carolina, where he taught from 1973 to 1986. He received his B.A. from Hamline University (1967) and his M.A. (1968) and Ph.D. (1973) in English from the University of California at Santa Barbara. He has published articles and reviews on Thoreau in *ESQ: A Journal of the American Renaissance* and *Critical Survey of Poetry,* as well as articles on the twentieth-century writer William Gass in *Critique: Studies in Modern Fiction* and *Modern Fiction Studies.*

Preface

Henry David Thoreau is one of the most well-known and at the same time most misunderstood major writers in American literature. Armed with ample evidence from Thoreau's writings, critics have argued that he was a wilderness pioneer or a homebody, a savage or a saint, a political pacifist or a potentially violent revolutionary, a misanthrope or a humanist, a materialist or an idealist. Rather than depicting him as a complex human being, most critics have defended one side or another of each of these contradictions while dismissing the other.

There are a few studies that attempt to present Thoreau with all his paradoxes intact. They would certainly include Sherman Paul's *Shores of America,* Walter Harding's *Days of Henry Thoreau,* and more recently Richard Lebeaux's *Young Man Thoreau* and *Thoreau's Seasons.* Paul's book contains the closest and fullest study of Thoreau's intellectual development and literary achievement, but it emphasizes Thoreau as naturalist while providing only brief and inconsistent comments on Thoreau's politics. Harding comes closest to a well-balanced view of Thoreau, acknowledging in his preface that "Thoreau not only appears inconsistent—he is inconsistent" and describing him as a "very human human being" who "could be sweet, gentle, and thoughtful one moment and a stubborn curmudgeon the next." The work is limited, however, by its biographical basis and lack of literary criticism, and by Harding's tendency to downplay the darker side of Thoreau's personality. Lebeaux presents many intriguing and often convincing psychological explanations of Thoreau's inconsistencies but is sometimes limited by problems inherent in the psychological approach to literature.

The present study cannot attempt to address the problem of Thoreau's inconsistency and complexity in as much depth as these studies, but the hope is that it will provide in one volume an evenly balanced introduction to Thoreau as both a person and a writer. This book is an invitation to the reader to get to know more of Thoreau than *Walden* and "Civil Disobedience," as well as a base from which to explore and evaluate other more specialized studies of the man and his work. My thesis is that, when taken in all his complexity, Thoreau's value to us is not only as a naturalist and a political dissenter but also as a writer who, both in his public works and in the privacy of his journal, grappled with the relation between experience and writing, life and art.

Richard J. Schneider

Wartburg College

Acknowledgments

Special acknowledgment is due to Walter Harding (SUNY-Geneseo), to whose groundbreaking work every current Thoreau scholar is indebted and whose encouragement made this book possible. Gratitude is also due to Lawrence Willson (University of California-Santa Barbara), who first inspired me to study Thoreau; to Hennig Cohen (University of Pennsylvania), who provided a crucial opportunity for me to continue that study; and to Lewis Leary (University of North Carolina at Chapel Hill), who advised me throughout the writing of the book.

Like so many scholars, I am indebted to the National Endowment for the Humanities, which sponsored Professor Harding's and Professor Cohen's summer seminars during which much of my work on Thoreau was done. Financial support for research in Concord was also provided by the Southern Research Education Board. Further support in time and equipment was provided by the administration and the English department faculty of Atlantic Christian College, especially by President James B. Hemby, Dean F. Mark Davis, and Dr. Katherine James.

The following Thoreau scholars provided assistance by commenting on parts of the book in manuscript: Walter Harding, Linck C. Johnson (Colgate University), Michael Meyer (University of Connecticut), and Timothy Trask (Massasoit Community College). Their advice on matters of fact, interpretation, and style has been invaluable.

Finally, the deepest gratitude is due to my parents for providing an environment in which I could learn to love literature and to my wife Mary and my children—Eric, Heidi, and Rick—for their much-needed encouragement and patience during the writing of this book.

Chronology

1817   Henry David Thoreau (christened David Henry) born 12 July in Concord, Massachusetts, to John and Cynthia (Dunbar) Thoreau.

1828   Attends Concord Academy.

1833   Attends Harvard University.

1837   Graduated from Harvard; begins keeping a journal; teaches briefly in Concord's Center (public) School.

1838   Works in father's pencil factory, where he develops an improved method of mixing graphite; gives first lecture to Concord Lyceum; develops friendship with Ralph Waldo Emerson.

1839   Reopens Concord Academy, soon joined by his older brother John. The two brothers take a boating trip on the Concord and Merrimack rivers, and both court Ellen Sewall.

1840   Publishes first poetry in the *Dial*. First John and then Henry propose marriage to Ellen Sewall; both are rejected.

1841   Thoreau brothers' school closes due to John's ill health; Henry moves into Emerson's home as a handyman; publishes poems and essays in the *Dial*.

1842   Death of brother John from lockjaw; Henry suffers psychosomatic symptoms also; meets Nathaniel Hawthorne.

1843   Lives on Staten Island, N.Y., as tutor to William Emerson's children.

1844   Works in father's pencil factory; accidentally sets fire to the Concord woods.

1845   Builds and moves into one-room cabin at Walden Pond; begins work on *A Week on the Concord and Merrimack Rivers*.

1846   Begins work on *Walden;* takes first trip to Maine woods; spends night in jail for refusal to pay "poll" tax.

1847   Leaves cabin at Walden Pond to live with Emersons while Ralph Waldo lectures in Europe.

1848   First essay on Maine woods, "Ktaadn," published in *Sartain's Union Magazine;* begins career as a professional lecturer; studies surveying.

1849   *A Week on the Concord and Merrimack Rivers* and "Civil Disobedience" published; takes first trip to Cape Cod; death of his sister Helen.

1850   Works frequently as a surveyor; visits Canada (Quebec).

1851   Increases his gathering of scientific and technical data during walks in the woods.

1853   Takes second trip to Maine woods; first parts of "A Yankee in Canada" published in *Putnam's Monthly.*

1854   *Walden, or Life in the Woods* published; lectures in Philadelphia.

1855   First Cape Cod essays published in *Putnam's Monthly;* takes second trip to Cape Cod.

1856   Takes brief excursions to various parts of New England and to New Jersey; meets Walt Whitman in Brooklyn.

1857   Takes third trip to Cape Cod; takes third trip to Maine woods; second Maine woods essay published; meets John Brown in Concord.

1859   John Thoreau, Sr., dies; Henry takes over pencil factory; lectures frequently; speaks in Concord in defense of John Brown.

1860   Essays on John Brown published; final illness begins in fall.

1861   Visits Minnesota in search of drier climate.

1862   Dies 6 May in Concord.

Chapter One
Affecting the Quality of the Day

Henry David Thoreau spent much of his time trying to decide which was more important: life or art. In his youth he expressed the dilemma in couplet form: "My life has been the poem I would have writ / But I could not both live and utter it."[1] During his years as a struggling writer, he could thus console himself for his apparent artistic failure with the thought that his life as a social rebel, naturalist, and transcendentalist would prove a worthy example to others and that he had thus "affected the qualify of the day."[2] Later in life, however, when his scientific studies, travels, and political activism sometimes failed to have the impact he had hoped for, he consoled himself with the thought that at least his art—especially *A Week on the Concord and Merrimack Rivers* and *Walden*—would live after him and justify his life. As he wrote to a friend, "I am not worth seeing personally. . . . What am I to the truth I feebly utter."[3]

This basic conflict between life and art was to pervade his life and also to leave his readers in a dilemma. On the one hand, his best literary works continue to stand on their own. One can read *Walden* with profit without studying Thoreau's life. On the other hand, one is frequently in danger of misunderstanding much that he wrote if one does not know something about the man himself. Therefore, the purpose of this chapter is to present a brief summary of the events of Thoreau's life, as well as to dispel some of the most common misconceptions about them.

Before Walden Pond

Childhood and Youth.   Henry David Thoreau (née David Henry) was born 12 July 1817 in Concord, Massachusetts, a town that had been the birthplace of American political freedom and was to become, with Thoreau's help, the birthplace of American literary independence. The Thoreaus themselves were an independent lot. Henry's grandfather

Jean Thoreau had been a French buccaneer forced by shipwreck to settle in America, where he made his fortune as a merchant on the wharves of Boston. Henry's father, John Thoreau, expressed his independence in quieter ways, first as a struggling merchant whom his neighbors described as an "amiable and most loveable gentleman . . . far too honest and scarcely sufficiently energetic" and then as a successful manufacturer of the best pencils made in America at the time.[4]

Many critics have suggested that Henry was not much influenced by his father, but it seems more likely that one friend of the family, Horace Hosmer, was correct in asserting that "grapes do not grow on thorns" and that Henry at least derived from his father his love of books and his quiet stubbornness.[5] Richard Lebeaux further suggests that "Thoreau may well have identified with his father's values—values which could not assure 'success' in an increasingly competitive, aggressive, business-industrial world."[6]

Henry's mother, Cynthia Dunbar Thoreau, was well known (perhaps "notorious" would be a better word) as a shrewd and strong-willed woman who accepted only the best from the Concord shopkeepers and as the talkative proprietor of the town's most popular boardinghouse. Both Cynthia and her sister Maria were ardent abolitionists as well. From his mother Henry undoubtedly inherited the gift of gab, sharpness of tongue, and freedom of intellectual inquiry that were to mark both his life and his writing.

The seeds of Thoreau's love of nature were also planted by both parents early in his life, though they did not fully blossom until he was in his twenties. His parents often took their children for walks to various hills and ponds around Concord, frequently cooking supper at their destination.[7] His philosophic idealism, however, perhaps came from within. When he was a child, his mother would sometimes find him lying awake long after bedtime. Once when she asked him why he did not sleep, he replied, "I have been looking through the stars to see if I could see God behind them."[8] This early interest in God, however, did not transfer to any interest in church going. Rather he learned to hate Sundays because of the Puritan custom that required children to spend the day indoors in meditation on the Bible.[9] Throughout his adult life he refused to attend church, even though he was, in his own way, a deeply religious man.

His love of solitude also seems to have surfaced early. The other children in town were not particularly fond of him because of his seriousness (he was nicknamed "Judge") and his reluctance to join their games. [10] Much of this childhood reserve was simply part of his temperament, but some of it might have been a reaction against living in a home that was also a bustling boardinghouse offering very little privacy. Nonetheless, young Thoreau could be sociable enough when he wished to be. Hosmer, for instance, records that his brother Ben played with the Thoreau boys at every opportunity. [11] The person with whom Henry was closest, however, was his elder brother John. He was so thoroughly devoted to John, who was clearly the more popular of the two, that John's death in 1842 was a turning point in Thoreau's life.

The Thoreau boys were educated at the town's public school, as well as at the more prestigious private school, the Concord Academy. Henry proved to be the better scholar, so when the time came to decide which of the two boys would be sent to Harvard (there was money for only one child to go), he was chosen. Although he barely passed the entrance examinations, Thoreau did well enough at Harvard, ranking consistently in the top half of his class and winning several prizes for scholarship. He did particularly well in languages. Greek and Latin were required subjects that he mastered well enough to do later some capable, though somewhat eccentric, translations for the *Dial*. He also voluntarily took courses in modern languages, including Italian, French, German, and Spanish. [12]

He seems to have been strongly influenced by instruction in writing given by Edward Tyrrell Channing, Boylston Professor of Rhetoric and Oratory. Although the style of Thoreau's college essays is not outstanding, the list of topics assigned suggests that Channing nudged Thoreau into serious thinking about some of the topics that would later provide central themes of his writing: "Of keeping a private journal"; "We are apt to become what others (however erroneously) think us to be; hence, another motive to guard against the power of others' unfavorable opinion"; "On what grounds may the forms, ceremonies and restraints of polite society be objected to?"; "The comparative moral policy of severe and mild punishments"; "The ways in which a man's style may be said to offend against simplicity"; "On the flatness of being content with common reasons"; "Speak of the duty inconvenience and dangers of *conformity*, in little things and great"; and an essay on the theory of the sublime in nature (31 March 1837). [13] This list contains the seeds of his journal keeping, his nonconformity, his emphasis on simplicity in life and writing, and his interest in wildness (sublimity) in nature. His nonconformity at college seems to have been confined to theory rather than practice, however, because he was one of the minority of Harvard students in his class who did not receive disciplinary action when a major student rebellion took place at the college.[14]

Thoreau's years at Harvard were interrupted in 1836 by financial and health problems. From December 1835 to March 1836, he took a leave from school to earn money by teaching in Canton, Massachusetts, where he came briefly under the influence of Orestes Brownson, one of the most brilliant but controversial of New England theologians.[15] Later that spring, after returning to Harvard, he became ill (probably from tuberculosis) and was forced to drop out of college temporarily. He recovered over the summer, however, and by attending extra voluntary lectures was able to graduate with his class in August of 1837. It was the custom at Harvard for graduating students to have a six-week summer vacation prior to commencement exercises in August. Thoreau apparently spent much of that time in Lincoln with his friend Charles Stearns Wheeler, relaxing in a shanty that Wheeler had built at Flint's Pond. Thoreau fully enjoyed this visit with Wheeler, and, as Walter Harding has suggested, "it undoubtedly served as an inspiration for his later experiment at Walden Pond."[16] Thoreau returned to Harvard for graduation and participated in a debate as part of the commencement exercises. It is uncertain, however, whether he heard his townsman Ralph Waldo Emerson's famous "American Scholar" speech, which was delivered to the Phi Beta Kappa Society on 31 August. A letter from one of his classmates suggests that he may have gone home to Concord before Emerson's speech.[17]

With his B.A. degree in hand, Thoreau was now faced with the typical graduate's identity crisis of finding a vocation.[18] At first the choice seemed easy. Both of the older Thoreau children, Helen and John, were already established as teachers, so it seemed natural that Henry should also teach. The public school (known as the Center School) in Concord needed a teacher, so Henry applied and was hired. But the job lasted less than two weeks. During Thoreau's second week, his class was visited by a member of the school committee, who found the class too unruly and insisted that Thoreau use corporal punishment to maintain order. Obeying orders (he was, after all, under contract), Thoreau promptly took a ruler to several of his students, but that same evening he turned in his resignation.[19]

Because the nation was still in an economic depression, other teaching jobs were scarce. After reluctantly and unsuccessfully applying for teaching jobs throughout New England, as well as in Virginia and Kentucky, he temporarily went to work in his father's pencil factory.

There the practical skill he had always shown as a youth enabled him to help his father improve the quality of his pencils. After some research into German methods of pencil making, he improved the methods of mixing and grinding the graphite, thus making possible the first American pencils that equaled those from Europe and making his father's company the leader in the American market.

At the same time that he was being the dutiful son, he was also asserting his own independence at every opportunity. About this time, for instance, he changed his name from David Henry to Henry David. This change was simply an acknowledgment of his family's lifelong habit of calling him Henry, but it was undoubtedly an assertion of his own individuality as well. The community took it, along with the resignation from his teaching position, as another sign of his social peculiarity. One Concord farmer is known to have remarked: "His name ain't no more Henry D. Thoreau than my name is Henry D. Thoreau. And everybody knows it, and he knows it. His name's Da-a-vid Henry and it ain't never been nothing but Da-a-vid Henry."[20]

Transcendentalist. There were few among the farmers and merchants of Concord who understood Thoreau's unrest and intellectual interests, so it is not surprising that he developed an attachment to those who did. Later there would be Bronson Alcott, Nathaniel Hawthorne, and others, but the first to recognize his intellectual potential was Ralph Waldo Emerson. Emerson had known of Thoreau as a bright young college student for whom he had written a letter of recommendation, and Thoreau had read Emerson's *Nature* during his senior year at Harvard. How or exactly when during 1837 the two became more closely acquainted is uncertain, but throughout the next few years Emerson served as Thoreau's intellectual mentor, opening his library to the young graduate, introducing him to distinguished guests at the Emerson home, and frequently sharing ideas with him.

From Emerson, Thoreau gained both a general philosophy and specific support in his search for social and intellectual independence. Emerson was the unofficial leader of a loosely knit group of New England intellectuals (mostly Unitarian clergymen) known to the public as "transcendentalists." Transcendentalism was an American offshoot of European romanticism based mostly on the philosophy of Kant and Hegel as filtered through the works of Samuel Taylor Coleridge. As Emerson himself pointed out, transcendentalism was not new; it was simply "Idealism as it appears in 1842."[21] The transcendentalists took an essentially Neoplatonic and dualistic view of the universe, dividing it into "Nature and Soul,"[22] and classifying people "into two sects, Materialists and Idealists."[23] The transcendentalists reacted against John Locke's belief that human knowledge was acquired solely through the senses and that a newborn infant was therefore a tabula rasa, a blank slate to be filled in by the experiences of its senses.

Instead, the transcendentalists argued that there were limitations to this Lockean philosophy, which had for many years been the basis of Unitarianism, and insisted that humans were born with certain innate ideas that provided a direct connection between the child and God. For the transcendentalists, as Emerson declared, "Mind is the only reality, of which all other natures are better or worse reflectors. Nature, literature, history, are only subjective phenomena."[24] The secret of successful living for the transcendentalist, therefore, was to hold oneself above merely material concerns and to focus one's energies on attaining moral and spiritual excellence.

This attitude clearly put the transcendentalist in opposition to a materialistic society and demanded an inner strength and self-reliance that was a challenge to maintain. It meant that "whoso would be a man, must be a nonconformist";[25] that is, the individual must be willing to act on his or her conscience rather than on the opinions of society whenever the two conflicted. Such a philosophy appealed to Thoreau's nonconformist temperament and provided a framework for many of his thus far unstructured speculations, as well as a practical rationale for deviating from community expectations.

Thoreau's friendship with Emerson was crucial to his intellectual development and sustained him for many years, becoming strongest perhaps when in 1841 he actually lived in Emerson's house as a handyman. Both were strong personalities, however, and as Thoreau further developed intellectually, the relationship began to cool, until by 1850 they could no longer maintain the frank intellectual intimacy they had once shared. Thoreau came to feel that Emerson was too limited to vague philosophy: "I doubt if Emerson could trundle a wheelbarrow through the streets, because it would be out of character."[26] Emerson, on the other hand, had trouble going beyond his early view of Thoreau as a disciple who never quite found his own voice: "I am very familiar with all his thoughts,—they are my own quite originally drest."[27]

Despite eventual changes in his personal relation to Emerson, however, Thoreau was indelibly marked by his mentor's philosophy. When asked in 1853 to describe in writing what branch of science he was interested in, he wrote in his journal, "The fact is I am a mystic, a transcendentalist, and a natural philosopher to boot. Now I think of it, I should have told them at once that I was a transcendentalist. That would have been the shortest way of telling them that they would not understand my explanations" (*Writings* 9:4). A transcendentalist he would remain all his life, but he was a transcendentalist with a difference. Emerson's transcendentalism derived from his Unitarian background and his sense of a single spiritual force pervading the universe. While Emerson began *Nature* with a Neoplatonic division between Nature (including the human body) and the Soul, ultimately it was the Soul that was real to him. He was a thorough enough idealist to be able to express a "noble doubt" about "whether nature outwardly exists."[28] Thoreau, however, could not entertain such a doubt about the existence of the material world. Although he was not quite a Lockean in disguise, his belief in the reality of nature was unshakable. He chose to deal with "one world at a time."[29] For Thoreau reality consisted in the relation among God, humanity, and nature—a sort of transcendentalist trinity—each with its own integrity and creativity.[30] (It is interesting to note here that Thoreau's mother had Trinitarian sympathies even though she reluctantly remained a member of the Unitarian church during the Trinitarian separation in 1827.)[31] For Thoreau the ideal was not to be found so much beyond the material world as within and through it. Hence he came to know "Nature" far better than Emerson did.

Schoolmaster and Suitor. Although Thoreau had been temporarily frustrated in his efforts to make a career as a teacher, in 1838 he decided to start his own school, beginning first in the family house and soon moving to the recently vacated Concord Academy building. After a slow start, the school eventually became prosperous enough that he needed the help of his brother John. Together the two ran a successful and innovative program, with John teaching English and math and Henry teaching foreign languages and science. They frequently took the children for hikes and used practical, "hands-on" teaching methods, such as having the children assist in repairing the brothers' boat or using surveying instruments to teach math. Of the two, John was the more popular with the children because of his easygoing, cheerful manner. According to one of his students, Henry was "rigidly exacting—a *faithful* teacher to the parent whose child he had and to the child" (Hosmer's emphasis).[32]

Despite their different personalities, the two brothers were very close. This bond was made even firmer by a vacation they took together during the first week of September 1839. They had built their own boat and used it to travel up the Concord and Merrimack rivers to Hooksett, New Hampshire, where they proceeded by foot and stage-coach to Mount Washington. After climbing the mountain, they retraced their path to Concord. Henry always remembered this trip with special fondness and later used it in his first book to memorialize his brother.

The closeness of the two brothers was thoroughly tested, however, with the arrival in Concord of Ellen Sewall, the older sister of one of their students. When she visited Concord for two weeks prior to their boating vacation, both brothers fell in love with her. John, the more outgoing suitor, visited her in Scituate immediately after returning from the vacation. At Christmas Henry joined John and their Aunt Prudence on another trip to visit Ellen. When the two brothers were not visiting Ellen or she was not visiting Concord, as she did again in June of 1840, both sent her gifts—Henry sending some of his poems. In July 1840 John visited Scituate and proposed to Ellen. But although she at first accepted in her father's absence, her mother insisted that she break the engagement because the Thoreaus were too liberal for her conservative Unitarian father. It appears that Ellen preferred Henry anyway, but when he eventually proposed by letter in November, she was compelled to turn him down for the same reason. Ellen eventually married a Unitarian minister but remained fond of Henry throughout her life, keeping a picture of him in her house. Henry too remained fond of her and visited her and her husband several times in Cohasset on his excursions to Cape Cod. On his deathbed he is reported to have said of Ellen: "I have always loved her. I have always loved her."[33]

Thoreau's transcendentalist brand of love continues to puzzle critics. After Ellen, he seems not to have pursued seriously any other woman, although he may have been briefly infatuated with the Emersons' governess, Mary Russell, and he expressed a strong platonic attachment to Emerson's wife, Lidian. Eventually he became something of a misogynist. After attending a party in 1851, for instance, he wrote in his journal, "I derive no pleasure from talking with a young woman half an hour simply because she has regular features. The society of young women is the most unprofitable I have ever tried. They are so light and flighty that you can never be sure whether they are there or not there" (*Writings* 9:116). By that year, and probably much earlier, he had concluded that "the heart is only for rare occasions; the intellect affords the most unfailing entertainment" (*Writings* 9:168). He thus kept tight rein on his emotions and in his journal generally distanced them by speaking in abstractions.

So successful was that distancing that his contemporaries generally considered him to be uninterested in sex. Horace Hosmer said that "he did not have the 'love-idea' in him: i.e. he did not appear to feel the *sex*-attraction" (Hosmer's emphasis).[34] Others have suggested that he did feel "sex-attraction" but that it was directed more toward men than women. His works are sometimes included in anthologies of gay literature, such as Jonathan Katz's *Gay American History.* Even Walter Harding has become convinced that "there is evidence of a strong homoerotic element in Thoreau's personality—although I should add that to the best of my knowledge no factual evidence of homosexual *activity* on Thoreau's part has been uncovered" (Harding's emphasis).[35] Mary Elkins Moller is more specific in suggesting "a certain amount of unconscious erotic attraction" existed between Thoreau and his disciple H. G. O. Blake.[36]

The truth is probably that while Thoreau certainly was on occasion attracted to special people, both women and men, sex to him, as a Victorian and a transcendentalist, was simply a necessary evil that he tried to do without. In an essay on "Chastity and Sensuality" sent to Blake on the occasion of his wedding, Thoreau confesses that "the intercourse of the sexes, I have dreamed, is incredibly beautiful, too fair to be remembered. I have had thoughts about it, but they are among the most fleeting and irrecoverable in my experience" (*Early Essays,* 227). He also insists that "if it is the result of a pure love, there can be nothing sensual in marriage" (*Early Essays,* 274). Thoreau could find no love that pure in human society, so he turned to nature. Richard Lebeaux is probably correct in asserting that "Thoreau would seek purity in and intimacy with, the natural world as an escape from the impurities of humanity and of himself; by turning to nature he could sublimate whatever seemed sinful."[37] He preferred to "fall in love with the moon and the night, and find . . . love requited."[38]

Apprentice Writer and Lecturer. The Thoreau brothers operated their school quite successfully until spring 1841 when they closed it after John developed a prolonged illness. Meanwhile, in 1840 the transcendentalist group had started its own periodical, the *Dial,* which gave Thoreau his first opportunities to publish his writing. During the brief existence of the *Dial* from July 1840 to April 1844 Thoreau published a number of poems and essays in it. He also assisted Emerson with the editing, and in Emerson's absence edited the April 1843 issue

by himself. Of his *Dial* pieces, most of the poems are quite forgettable.
Indeed, among all his poems, published or unpublished, only a very
few have value today as more than glosses on certain journal passages.
Among those probably worth the modern reader's attention are "Sic
Vita," "Smoke," "Inspiration," and "Bluebirds."[39] Several of his *Dial*
essays, however, were important expressions of his early interest in
nature, particularly "The Natural History of Massachusetts" and "A
Winter Walk."

Another outlet for his ideas was the Concord Lyceum, which
through the financial support of Concord's leading citizens provided a
series of lectures, debates, and discussions each year. Thoreau attended,
lectured in, and at times was curator of this series. Its meetings were
often devoted to literature, philosophy, and the natural sciences and
thus afforded him both new information and a sounding board for his
own ideas and observations. It also provided him with a testing ground
for his own writing, much of which was originally created in lecture
form.

The most valuable source of and outlet for his ideas, however, was
Emerson. During 1841 to 1843 Thoreau received not only room and
board but also the benefit of Emerson's conversation, guests, and library in exchange for maintaining Emerson's property, doing odd jobs,
and occasionally entertaining the Emerson children. Thoreau and
Emerson shared not only a house but also tragedy during those two
years. In January 1842 Thoreau's brother John contracted tetanus from
a shaving cut and died in Henry's arms several days later. So grieved
was Thoreau that about ten days later he too began to exhibit the
symptoms of the disease, a psychosomatic reaction to his loss. That
same month Emerson's five-year-old son Waldo died suddenly of scar-
latina, adding much to Thoreau's grief.

Critics unanimously agree that John's death had a crucial effect on
Thoreau's personal and artistic development. Lebeaux convincingly
suggests that it burdened Thoreau with guilt about his competition
with John both for Ellen Sewall's hand and in their family life.[40] Harding also suggests that if John had lived his lighthearted personality
might have alleviated some of Henry's heavy seriousness.[41] John's death
also made Henry the sole male heir and thus placed on him the responsibility for the family business, which John might otherwise have
assumed. Artistically, Thoreau's interest in Indians and increased interest in nature can be viewed as results of John's death. The two brothers had often played Indian as children and gone hiking and looking

for arrowheads together as youths. Also, as Sherman Paul points out, "John was the nature lover, and Thoreau's most famous natural settings, the river and the pond, were associated with him."[42] Nature became not only a refuge from romantic rejection by Ellen but also the home of John's spirit, a place where Henry could be spiritually in touch with the person to whom he had been closest.

Thus far those interests in Indians and nature had found neither an appropriate style nor an appropriate audience. Life with the Emersons, as well as Hawthorne's arrival to live in the Old Manse in 1842, had nudged Thoreau more and more toward lecturing and writing as a career. His lecture on Sir Walter Raleigh at the Concord Lyceum had been praised, and the *Dial* had given him the pleasure of seeing his words in print even if it had not found him much of a popular audience. But despite Emerson's attempts to make Thoreau's works accessible to a wider audience, publishers showed little interest. It became increasingly clear that in order to become an author Thoreau would need to make some personal contacts in the publishing world, preferably in New York. Conveniently, Emerson's brother William lived on Staten Island and was in need of a tutor for his boys, so in 1843 Emerson arranged for Thoreau to undertake the position.

Unfortunately, Thoreau, who even in his youth was quite set in his personal habits, did not find himself compatible with William Emerson's strictly regimented household, although he did like the boys well enough. Nor did he find the city or its publishers to his liking. The book publishers were unwilling to take risks on unknown writers—a fact many other American writers, Hawthorne and Melville included, have complained about—and the magazine publishers had more material than they could handle already. The city itself—despite its cultural attractions in museums, libraries, and art galleries—disgusted him with its incessant bustle. In a letter to Emerson he describes it as "a thousand times meaner than I could have imagined. It will be something to hate,—that's the advantage it will be to me. . . . The pigs in the street are the most respectable part of the population" (*Writings* 6:82).

New York did indeed insure Thoreau's lasting antipathy for city life. By the end of 1843 he was back in Concord living with his parents, working in the pencil factory, and realizing with increasing sharpness how close to the city Concord was being drawn. In the 1840s Concord was a town in the process of losing its independent solitude and becoming a suburb of Boston. The railroad arrived in Concord in 1844, which gave Thoreau the advantage of being able to zip off to libraries in Cambridge or Boston in an hour. But it also transformed Concord from a town of farmers dependent upon each other for goods and services to a town of agricultural merchants peddling their crops to the city for cash and thus, in Thoreau's eyes, losing their self-reliance. With the advantage of hindsight, we must admit that Thoreau probably tended to idealize and exaggerate the previous independence of the Concord farmers. Nonetheless, he came to believe that if the townspeople were not careful, they would destroy what he saw as the most admirable place in the world.[43]

As Thoreau became increasingly critical of his community, it had good reason to become increasingly critical of him. Added to his childhood reputation for being a loner, his scandalously brief public school teaching career, and his name change, there was the fact that he accidentally set fire to the Concord woods. In April 1844, he went on a boating excursion up the Sudbury River with Edward Hoar. Having caught enough fish to make a meal, they pulled onto the shore of Fair Haven Bay and, in the process of building a fire to cook the fish, allowed it to get out of control. Thoreau ran overland for help, while Hoar went by boat. Thoreau eventually came upon the owner of the land, who rode to town for help while Thoreau stayed to watch the progress of the fire. With help from town, the fire was eventually extinguished, but not before it had burned a substantial portion of the woods on more than one piece of property. The town, of course, did not appreciate Thoreau and Hoar's carelessness, and the two probably avoided prosecution only because Hoar's father was Concord's leading citizen.[44] The accident was a lasting embarrassment for Thoreau for many years. Even as late as 1850 he was still trying to rationalize it in his journal (*Writings* 8:25).

The Walden Years

The smoldering anger of his community, the tedious work at the pencil factory, and his lack of privacy at home must have made Thoreau long for solitude. Furthermore, his literary ambitions had been on the back burner for too long, and he needed time to write. So in 1845 he received permission to use some of Emerson's land on the shore of Walden Pond, borrowed an axe, cleared a small piece of land, and built himself a one-room cabin. By May he was able—with the help of Emerson, Bronson Alcott, Ellery Channing, and some other neighbors—to raise the frame and roof of the cabin, and on 4 July (a date chosen for obviously symbolic reasons) he moved in. Later in the fall he added a fireplace and chimney. The cabin remained his principal residence until September of 1847.

The decision to live at the pond was misunderstood by many of the villagers and has continued to be misunderstood by many of Thoreau's readers. Even today, despite clarification by Harding and other scholars, certain myths persist about his life at the pond. One such myth is that he was attempting to escape from "real life" to mere loafing. It is certainly true that he wanted time away from the daily grind of the classroom and the pencil factory. But it is also true that he needed that time to accomplish goals that required considerable intellectual and physical exertion. His two main aims were to write an account of his boating trip with his brother and to study nature—an effort that involved long walking excursions and patient, intense observation of natural phenomena.

He was also engaged in labor that his neighbors could more readily appreciate. At the pond he occupied himself with an agricultural experiment in self-sufficiency to demonstrate to himself and to the Concord farmers that they need not give up their independence to pander to the city. He raised a field of beans (apparently the only ones grown in Concord that year as a cash crop, but not enough of them to be recorded in the town statistics)[45] which provided him with food while still allowing him to use the surplus to turn a small profit. He also earned money for necessities by occasionally doing odd jobs such as house painting, carpentry, and surveying.

In none of these activities was there anything idle or passive. As he says in *Walden,*

I went to the woods because I wished to live deliberately, to front only the essential facts of life, and see if I could not learn what it had to teach, and not, when I came to die, discover that I had not lived. I did not wish to live what was not life, living is so dear; nor did I wish to practice resignation, unless it was quite necessary. I wanted to live deep and suck out all the marrow of life, to live so sturdily and Spartan-like as to put to rout all that was not life, to cut a broad swath and shave close, to drive life into a corner, and reduce it to its lowest terms, and, if it proved to be mean, why then to get the whole and genuine meanness of it, and publish its meanness to the world; or if it were sublime, to know it by experience, and be able to give a true account of it in my next excursion.[46]

The verb phrases in this passage—"live deliberately," "front the facts," "suck out," "live sturdily," "put to rout," "cut a swath," "shave close," and "drive life"—all make it clear that Thoreau himself considered his life at the pond to be an active, energetic, even courageous one.

Misconceptions also persist about his social life during the Walden years. Some accuse him of being a hypocritical freeloader who, while pretending to be self-reliant, sneaked into town every evening for dinner with his parents or the Emersons. It is true that he did go into town for frequent dinners with his parents and occasional dinners with the Emersons. But these visits were made not because he could not feed himself or was too lonely to eat alone, but because he loved his family and friends and felt obliged to accept their hospitality when it was offered. His own preference was to attend such dinners less often than he actually did, because—as he says in *Walden*—they were "frequently to the detriment of my domestic relations."[47]

Nor was he totally alone even when at the pond. The misconception of Thoreau as a misanthropic recluse is as far afield as that about too much socializing in town. The fact is, as Harding reminds us, that "hardly a day went by that Thoreau did not visit the village or was visited at the pond."[48] His regular visitors included Emerson, Hawthorne, Alcott and his family, Alek Therien the woodchopper, some of his former pupils, and often on Sunday afternoons groups of children who came to see his pet mouse and have Thoreau reveal to them some of nature's secrets. During his stay, his cabin even became a fashionable site for group picnics and meetings of civic groups.[49] It should be clear, then, that Thoreau never intended to be either a recluse or Concord's version of Daniel Boone braving the perils of the wilderness. The quietly picturesque scenery of Walden Pond was adequate to allow him to accomplish his main goals of writing, studying nature, and proving his independence both to the town and to himself.

Nonetheless, when opportunities arose to achieve some of these goals more dramatically, he made the most of them. One such opportunity was his imprisonment in 1846, his second year at the pond, when he spent his famous night in jail for nonpayment of taxes. He had for several years refused to pay the "poll" tax, which was actually a head tax levied on every male over twenty years old. This refusal was intended as a direct protest against government inequity and as an indirect protest against the government's condoning of slavery. It seems likely that he really wanted his refusal to lead to imprisonment in order to dramatize his protest. At any rate, when, having walked in from the pond to go to the cobbler, he was stopped by Sam Staples, the town's amiable tax collector and jailkeeper, and asked to pay the poll tax, he refused once again. When Staples reminded him that his refusal might eventually lead to jail, Thoreau seized the opportunity for martyrdom by volunteering for immediate incarceration.

Thoreau was marched off to jail, where he was ushered into a cell with a man accused of burning down a barn. He looked forward to being seen as a symbol by the community and probably hoped to prolong his stay as much as possible. His mother soon heard of his plight, however, and scurried home to find a way of getting him out before he could further embarrass the family. That evening while Staples was out, his daughter took delivery of Thoreau's tax money from an anonymous donor (probably one of Thoreau's aunts). By the time the daughter informed Staples of the payment, he had already taken his boots off and was relaxing for the evening, so he decided to let Thoreau stay the night and free him in the morning.

That night, Thoreau came to the disturbing conclusion that the community really did not care about his protest, and this disillusionment became one of the motives for his essay on "Civil Disobedience," which was published by Elizabeth Peabody in 1849 in a collection of essays entitled *Aesthetic Papers*. The next morning when Thoreau was freed, he left the jail "mad as the devil" at not being allowed to continue his protest. What was to have been his loudest declaration of independence had turned out, at least for the moment, to be only a whisper.[50]

If his grand political gesture was at first rather unsettling, so was his attempt to study nature on a grander scale than Walden Pond could offer. Upon receiving an invitation from a cousin in Maine, he started north for Maine in late August of 1846 intending to explore the Maine woods and to climb Mount Katahdin, the state's highest mountain. This trip afforded him his first opportunity to see genuine wilderness and its original inhabitants, the Indians, about whom he and his brother John had read and fantasized in their youth. The Indians proved to be somewhat less interesting and wild than he had hoped. Although his Indian guide, Louis Neptune, was a capable woodsman, he was also a heavy drinker and hardly the "noble savage" Thoreau had hoped to meet. The wilderness, on the other hand—particularly Mount Ktaadn (as Thoreau spelled it)—was somewhat more than he had expected. While climbing the mountain he became more impatient than his companions and hurried on ahead to try to reach the peak. Upon reaching the tableland just beneath Baxter Peak, however, he was prevented by a heavy fog from finding his way to the peak itself. So he rejoined his companions, who were eager to get back down the mountain. The experience amid the fog on top of Katahdin was to remain in his memory as a profoundly unsettling indication that maybe there were parts of nature that his study of natural phenomena was not meant to penetrate, a discovery that was, as we shall see, both disturbing and exhilarating.

Generally, however, Thoreau's years at Walden Pond were everything he had hoped for. He wrote even more than he had expected, including an essay on Thomas Carlyle and drafts of both *A Week on the Concord and Merrimack Rivers* and *Walden*. He achieved an intimacy with nature that exceeded his expectations. And both economically and psychologically he felt he had achieved the independence he sought. Certainly his comments in the conclusion of *Walden* suggest his own satisfaction with his experiment. He had learned, he says, "that if one advances confidently in the direction of his dreams, and endeavors to live the life which he has imagined, he will meet with a success unexpected in common hours" (323). The experiment had been not only successful but also apparently quite complete, although later he sometimes seemed to wish that he could have extended it. "I left the woods," he says in *Walden,* because "I had several more lives to live, and could not spare any more time for that one" (323).

After Walden

Professional Writer, Lecturer, and Surveyor.   Thoreau's next life was not entirely new. The invitation that provided an immediate reason for leaving the pond was from the Emersons to return to live with them while Waldo was lecturing in Europe. But this arrangement allowed him to continue working toward his goal of being a lecturer and writer.

The stay with the Emersons in 1847 was to have mixed results. He enjoyed being with Lidian and the children, but serving as surrogate man of the house and father led him to full realization of Emerson's limitations as both a friend and a mentor. When Edith and Eddy began to call Thoreau rather than Emerson their father, Thoreau began to realize that Emerson was sacrificing too much for the acclaim of the European tour. That feeling increased when Lidian became seriously ill and Emerson failed to return to be at her side. These familial sins of omission, together with Emerson's failure to keep his promise to assist

Thoreau in publishing his essays, contributed to the tension between the two that eventually led to the breakdown in their friendship.[51]

When Emerson at last returned from Europe, Thoreau again took residence with his parents. Once again he was without a steady job. He did odd jobs and helped in the pencil factory, but eventually he found it possible to make a modest living by surveying and lecturing. He began to advertise himself as a professional surveyor in 1848, and that same year he began to find some demand for his lectures, which at that time consisted of drafts of various chapters of *Walden*. With the help of friends such as Hawthorne (now living in Salem) and H. G. O. Blake in Worcester, he was invited to lecture in several towns in Massachusetts, as well as in Portland, Maine. He is generally thought to have been a less effective lecturer than Emerson, but his sarcastic humor sometimes made him the more popular of the two, as is indicated by the following passages from the *Worcester Telegram:* "Thoreau was looked upon in a different light [from Emerson]. His humorous, sarcastic, but ever entertaining talks, rather than lectures, were received with more favor, but with perhaps less comprehension."[52] His writing career also began to progress even without Emerson's help. Instead Horace Greeley provided the inside help he needed to publish "Ktaadn," the first of his Maine woods essays, in *Sartain's Union Magazine* in 1848.

Since his stay at Walden, Thoreau had been trying to publish *A Week on the Concord and Merrimack Rivers*. Several publishers expressed interest in the book, but because Thoreau was an unknown writer they insisted that he bear the risk of printing costs and pay for them in advance. Lacking money for such an investment, even in his own talent, he postponed publishing the book. Then in 1849 James Munroe and Company offered to publish the book at Thoreau's expense but without demanding advance payment. Unfortunately, upon its publication later that same year, *A Week* earned him mildly favorable reviews but very few sales. He was to lose over two hundred dollars on the book and was forced four years later to take delivery of over seven hundred copies of the book into his own home, an experience he recorded with sarcastic humor in his journal:

For a year or two past, my *publisher*, falsely so called, has been writing from time to time to ask what disposition should be made of the copies of "A Week on the Concord and Merrimack Rivers" still on hand, and at last suggesting that he had use for the room they occupied in his cellar. So I had them all sent to me here, and they have arrived to-day by express, filling the man's wagon,—706 copies out of an edition of 1000 which I bought of Munroe four years ago and have been ever since paying for, and have not quite paid for yet. . . . I have now a library of nearly nine hundred volumes, over seven hundred of which I wrote myself. (Thoreau's emphasis, *Writings* 11:459)

The failure of *A Week* was a double disappointment to Thoreau, because it dissuaded Monroe and Company from publishing *Walden* as it had originally agreed to do. *Walden* was not published until five years later by which time, as Lyndon Shanley tells us, Thoreau had amply revised it, eliminating the weaknesses that seemed to mar *A Week*.[53]

Wanting to make sure that it would be as good as he could possibly make it, Thoreau took *Walden* through seven different drafts before finally submitting it in 1854 to Ticknor and Fields for publication. Between 1849 and 1854 he also presented many portions of the book as lectures or brief periodical articles, thus allowing himself more feedback and opportunity for revision. So by 1854 he had a painstakingly revised manuscript to submit, and this time he had little trouble finding a publisher. Ticknor and Fields enthusiastically agreed to publish it, and *Walden* appeared in August 1854. It sold well, exhausting most of the first printing within a year, and Thoreau was pleased finally to find himself something of a celebrity.

Naturalist and Citizen of Concord.   After his second brief residence with the Emersons, he settled into life at his parent's house. This move was in one sense an obvious retreat from the bold persona of independence that had been so important to him during the years at the pond, and it could be seen as a personal defeat of the ideal for himself that he wished to achieve. On the other hand, it seems likely that by then his family had learned to accept, however grudgingly, his unorthodox ideas and peculiar daily habits, so that the intellectual independence that was most important to him was probably not seriously threatened by living at home. He could stay with the family to which he had always been so close without having to make an issue of his independence by traipsing off to a western wilderness. He could thus avoid Emerson's error of sacrificing family life too fully for the sake of his art. Most of the time the woods around Concord were interesting enough for his purposes.

He settled into a generally comfortable life, reserving his afternoons for walks in the woods, carrying his notebooks and occasionally chatting with a special companion such as Ellery Channing (nephew of the famous preacher). Although Thoreau was fussy about walking companions, in the post-Walden years he was hardly a recluse. He was friendly with many of Concord's solid citizens, such as Sam Staples and the farmer George Minott, and had a special interest in some of the town's laborers and ne'er-do-wells, such as Alek Therien, John Goodwin, Bill Wheeler, and George Melvin. The journal suggests that he frequently enjoyed conversations and even occasional walking excursions with these men. It is also true that many of Concord's citizens thought him odd and unfriendly, but he was nonetheless one of the town's most well-known citizens and had many friends. Indeed, his melon parties were one of Concord's most popular annual social events.[54]

Thoreau was thus attracted to the town, while at the same time he realized that his most important tasks lay in the solitude of the woods. But, after applying a modern psychological test to his personality, Everett and Laraine Fergenson suggest that "as Henry walked resolutely off to enjoy his solitude, he looked back to see if anyone might be following."[55] One result of this conflict between society and solitude for Thoreau was frustration about his inability to live up to both his own and his friends' expectations. In 1851, for instance, he seems to have reassessed his life and found it wanting. In July he wrote in his journal, "Here I am thirty-four years old, and yet my life is almost wholly unexpanded. How much is in the germ! There is such an interval between my ideal and the actual in many instances that I may say I am unborn. There is the instinct for society, but no society" (*Writings* 8: 316). He knew that his friends—even Emerson—were disappointed in his lack of success as a writer, and he tried to console himself by applying an early version of the "different drummer" image that he included in *Walden:* "Methinks my seasons revolve more slowly than those of nature; I am differently timed. I am contented. This rapid revolution of nature, even of nature in me, why should it hurry me? Let a man step to the music which he hears, however measured" (*Writings* 8:316). The success of *Walden* three years later would eventually ease this frustration, at least temporarily, and seem to justify the slow pace at which his life progressed.

Walden, however, was intended to be only a beginning. By the time of its publication he had already had larger plans in mind for many years. As early as 1841 he had recorded in his journal the possibility of writing a poem of apparently epic proportions "to be called 'Concord'" (*Writings* 7:282). He soon learned that poetry was not his genre, but the idea of writing a natural history of Concord similar to White's

Natural History of Selborne persisted throughout his life. Throughout
the post-Walden Pond years he used his daily walks to record extensive
observations about the flora, fauna, and other phenomena of the Concord woods. It might be frogs, or the springtime blossoming of the
flowers, or moonlight, or the colors of the fall leaves that caught his
interest at any given time, but always the information was stored away
in the journal. The task of gathering such data was fascinating but also
impossibly long, so that it became increasingly difficult for him to see
how all of his information could ever be molded into an organic whole
to surpass *Walden.*

One effect of his attempt to know every natural fact in the Concord
woods was that his observations became increasingly scientific both in
point of view and in method. Although previously averse to killing
animals other than fish, he now occasionally found it useful to kill and
dissect a turtle or a duck. He also began in the 1850s to record charts
and tables of data in the journal. He thus gradually changed the purpose of the journal from being mostly a testing ground for transcendental thoughts to being equally as much a depository for scientific
data that contained or might eventually be transformed into such
thoughts. This change sometimes seemed to him an artistic step back-
ward, as this journal passage from 19 August 1851 suggests: "I fear
that the character of my knowledge is from year to year becoming more
distinct and scientific; that in exchange for views as wide as heaven's
cope, I am being narrowed down to the field of the microscope. I see
details, not wholes nor the shadow of a whole. I count some parts, and
say 'I know'" (*Writings* 8:406).

We can probably never know beyond a doubt whether the collection
of such data was simply an elaborate means of artistic procrastination,
whether he genuinely hoped to transform all his information into the
symbolic truths of a larger work, or whether the collection of the material had value to him in its own right. Probably all these motives
were present and at constant odds with each other, although the last
seems to have dominated his later years. By 1856 we sense that, as
Lebeaux suggests, "he was swimming in facts and had to struggle to
keep his creative vision above water."[56] By the time of his death, he
regained some of his ability to translate facts into artistic symbols in
brief essays such as "Wild Apples" and "Autumnal Tints," but his
larger projects, including a possible calendar of the seasons and perhaps
a book on Indians, never went much beyond the note-taking stage.

This conflict between scientific objectivity and transcendental subjectivity remained throughout his artistic career, and his attempt to resolve it was the source of much of his artistic energy. His whole life was an attempt to find the key to reconciling reality and art by becoming a "seer," someone who could penetrate the illusions of the material world and delve into the truth within them. Early in his career he depended perhaps too heavily on transcendental idealism, and late in his career he frequently could not penetrate beyond the surface of the facts. In 1857, for instance, he quotes the art historian Winckelmann, apparently applying the passage to his own life: "I perceive, also, that a certain delicate spirit begins to evaporate, with which I raised myself, by powerful soarings, to the contemplation of the beautiful" (*Writings* 15:243). Only in *Walden* was he able to fully balance reality and art in a sustained effort for the public eye. Later he came to a tentative scientific resolution through his study of water reflections as intermediaries between subject and object. But eventually it was in the privacy of his journal that he merged reality and art most fully by making the written recording of natural facts his main artistic task.

Traveler. Another manifestation of the conflict between life and art that complicated his studies was the conflict between his love of Concord and the temptations of travel. He was well aware of Emerson's warning in "Self-Reliance" that traveling could be a fool's paradise, so in his early years he left Concord only when absolutely necessary to seek a job, get an education, or further his writing career. He frequently insisted that all of nature's truths lay waiting for him in the Concord woods. In his journal for 1853 he writes: "I cannot but regard it as a kindness . . . that by the want of pecuniary wealth, I have been nailed down to this my native region so long and steadily, and made to study and love this spot of earth more and more. What would signify in comparison a thin and diffused love and knowledge of the whole earth instead, got by wandering?" (*Writings* 11:496–97). Despite such frequent warnings about the dangers of travel to be found in his writing, it is also true that travel held some genuine attractions for him both personally and professionally.

Concord might very well have seemed the best place on earth, but at times he also realized that it did not quite include nature in all its variety. Particularly in the 1850s, as Concord moved steadily toward becoming a suburb of Boston, Thoreau bemoaned the lack of wildness in the Concord woods. In 1856, for instance, he mourns the loss around Concord of such wild animals as the cougar, wolf, moose, and beaver and concludes, "I cannot but feel as if I lived in a tamed, and, as it were emasculated country. Would not the motions of those larger and wilder animals have been more significant still? Is it not a maimed and imperfect nature that I am conversant with?" (*Writings* 14:220–21). The incompleteness of the woods around Concord frequently led him to seek such wildness elsewhere. Throughout his life he climbed mountains in Massachusetts and neighboring states. He also sought wildness in the Maine woods, to which he made three excursions (1846, 1853, and 1857), and on the sandy shorelines of Cape Cod, which he also visited three times (1849, 1855, and 1857). What he found on these excursions we shall examine more fully in following chapters, but what he was seeking was a wildness that would prove that there was still some nature beyond human exploitation and that the human potential for living in harmony with nature on this planet had not yet been exhausted.

During the last fifteen years of his life he also traveled frequently for other reasons. In 1850 he visited Canada to satisfy his curiosity about a "foreign country." In 1854 he went to Philadelphia to lecture (with a stop in New York). In 1856 he traveled to New Jersey to survey the new town of Eagleswood. During that trip he went with Alcott to Brooklyn to meet Walt Whitman, who proved to be a kindred spirit with whom he was much impressed. There were also trips to New Bedford for occasional visits with his hypochondriac friend Daniel Ricketson. Thus despite his reputation as a homebody, he actually traveled quite frequently, if not very widely. Whatever the motives for his travels, however, he became increasingly aware throughout the years that, despite its limitations, Concord was the heart of his artistic life and his travels would always be "great circle sailing."

Public Reformer. The increase in his traveling after the Walden Pond years was undoubtedly due in part to his gradually increasing reputation as a writer, which widened his circle of acquaintances and contacts, but it was perhaps also a sign of his gradual recognition of the interrelation between the individual and the larger society. He had always been a strange mixture of private truth-seeker and public reformer, insisting even while at Walden Pond on spending a night in jail as a public protest. On the other hand, as a transcendentalist he insisted that any reform must begin in the hearts and minds of average private citizens and that the legislation of governments and the zeal of public reformers could have little impact on social ills. Of the government he says in "Civil Disobedience" that it "never of itself furthered any enterprise, but by the alacrity with which it got out of its way,"[58] and in *Walden* he speaks of "self-styled reformers" as "the greatest bores of all [his visitors to the pond]" (*Walden,* 153–54). Yet he himself was in his own way a reformer, and his very resistance to the government on issues of taxation and slavery was a tacit acknowledgment of its power. Perhaps taxation and slavery were issues on which he felt compelled to take a public stand precisely because they were so clearly threats to the individual integrity and freedom of every American, whether free or slave. His concern with the taxation issue subsided after his stay in jail when the town officials finally decided that his simple life-style hardly made him worth taxing anyway, but the slavery issue became increasingly important.

His interest in the injustices of slavery was undoubtedly due originally to his mother, who was a charter member of the Concord chapter of the Women's Anti-Slavery Society.[59] During the 1840s he actively participated in the abolitionist movement in a variety of ways. His most famous early contributions to the cause were his ringing of the town bell to announce Emerson's speech on emancipation in the West Indies in 1844 and his serving as a "conductor" on the underground railroad. But his cabin at Walden Pond was seldom if ever a station on the underground railroad, because it offered no place for a fugitive slave to hide; such fugitives were concealed instead in the Thoreau family home in town.

During the 1850s his interest in abolition intensified as the issue publicly moved closer to home. When the Fugitive Slave Law was passed, he expressed his horror only in the privacy of his journal. But in 1854, when a fugitive slave named Anthony Burns was arrested in Boston and shipped back to Virginia, Thoreau joined other Massachusetts abolitionists in protest, giving a forceful lecture on "Slavery in Massachusetts" at a Fourth of July rally in Framingham.[60]

His most intense involvement in the abolition movement, however, was his defense of John Brown's raid on Harpers Ferry. He first met Brown in Concord in 1857 when—at the invitation of Thoreau's friend (and later inept editor of Thoreau's works) F. B. Sanborn—Brown came to lecture. He talked with Brown again on Brown's second visit to Concord in the spring of 1859, and on both occasions Thoreau was very much impressed by his zeal. He admired Brown as "a transcendentalist above all, a man of ideas and principles" who was willing to risk his life for those principles (*Reform Papers,* 115). Whether Thoreau knew of the savagery Brown demonstrated in the Pottawatomie massacre in Kansas has been much debated, but a recent study suggests that he may indeed have known and simply chose to overlook it.[61] It now seems clear that Thoreau was interested in Brown both as a man of principle and as a man of action. After Brown's capture in October 1859, Thoreau spoke in his defense several times in the Boston area, delivering "A Plea for Captain John Brown" with considerable impact. He also arranged memorial services in Concord on the day of Brown's execution, and a year later submitted his brief essay "The Last Days of John Brown" to be read at a memorial service in North Elba.[62] Nor was he hesitant to back these speeches with action when shortly after Brown's capture he helped one of Brown's insurrectionists escape to Canada.[63]

His defense of John Brown suggests that there was a sense of urgency in Thoreau's life in the late 1850s. More strongly than any time since the Walden Pond years he seems to have sensed the real possibility of affecting the quality of the day and of the nation. He also seems to have identified with Brown, seeing in him, as Lebeaux suggests, "what he most wanted and needed to see in himself"—particularly "the fiery, independent man who had forsworn conventionality, no matter what the inducements."[64]

Invalid. This urgency was also intensified by Thoreau's sense of the shortness of his own life. The consumption that had first attacked him during his college years left his lungs frequently susceptible to problems from colds. In 1855 he suffered another protracted and undiagnosed illness that left him so weak in the legs that he had to discontinue for a time his daily walking excursions. Then in the winter of 1860 he contracted bronchitis, which became worse during a trip he made to Connecticut to give a lecture. Badly weakened in the lungs, he became consumptive and was confined to the house for most of several months. Doctors recommended a change of climate, so when he was well enough to travel he arranged a trip to Minnesota, which was advertised as having air that was drier and easier on the lungs. Young Horace Mann, Jr., agreed to accompany him, and in May 1861 the two left Concord by railroad and arrived in Minnesota by Mississippi steamboat two weeks later (26 May).

In Minnesota he and Mann searched for new botanical specimens, Thoreau being particularly pleased in finally seeing wild crab apple trees. The only other benefit of the trip for Thoreau was the sight of a gathering of genuine Sioux Indians in Redwood. Since the 1840s he had kept voluminous notebooks on Indian lore, but these were the first truly "wild" Indians he had seen. Unfortunately, however, Minnesota did not hold any benefits for his health, so he and Mann returned to Concord in July with Thoreau weaker than ever.

In the fall of 1861 his coughing eased somewhat, giving his family some hope that he might recover. But he soon worsened and by November was too weak to keep his journal (his last entry is 3 November). Although weak during his last months, he remained in good spirits and even managed to rework some of his lecture manuscripts for publication in the *Atlantic Monthly*. In the days before his death, when not receiving the many friends who came for a last visit, he persisted in revising his Maine woods essays for publication, a task that was incomplete when he died quietly 6 May 1862 on a bed he had made himself. During his last days he is said to have been in surprisingly good spirits, an attitude that could only have been even more cheerful had he known how many readers would eventually have the quality of their days affected by both his life and his art.

Chapter Two

The Transcendental Artist: *A Week on the Concord and Merrimack Rivers*

A Week on the Concord and Merrimack Rivers is Thoreau's most thoroughly transcendental book. It is the work of a young writer, still very much under the influence of Emerson, expressing his zeal for transcendentalism while at the same time attempting to express his own unique vision. It thus contains all the weaknesses of imitation, while displaying many sparks of the brilliant originality that marks his best work. The balance between life and art that he achieved in *Walden* is suggested but not realized in *A Week,* because the description of the actual boating trip taken by Thoreau and his brother is often overwhelmed by inserted essays on various transcendental topics. Nonetheless, as a portrait of the young man as artist, it is revealing and well worth reading, both in its own right and as a hint of the greater achievement in *Walden.*

Life

The journey described in *A Week* took place in 1839 when Thoreau and his brother John took advantage of the break between the summer and fall terms of their school to take a boating and hiking trip to Mount Washington via the Concord and Merrimack rivers.[1] They had built a boat that spring and equipped it with both oars and sails, as well as with wheels for transporting it overland. Loading it with a tent for shelter and with potatoes and melons for food, they shoved off down the Concord (Musketaquid) River on the afternoon of Saturday, 31 August. The river portion of their trip comprised five days of pleasant, mostly uneventful boating (using oars, sails, and canal towrope) and camping. It took them as far as Hooksett, New Hampshire, which they reached the following Wednesday evening.

At Hooksett they stored their equipment with an obliging farmer and on Thursday hiked to Concord, New Hampshire, where the next day they caught a stagecoach to Plymouth, New Hampshire. Friday and Saturday were spent hiking overland toward Mount Washington (Agiocochook), the highest peak in the White Mountains. On Sunday they arrived at Crawford's Notch House, and on Tuesday they climbed Mount Washington without much difficulty. Having achieved their destination, they retraced their steps, reaching their camp at Hooksett on Thursday, 12 September. After taking on provisions, they proceeded down the Merrimack and rapidly accomplished the return to Concord, Massachusetts, arriving the next night, Friday, 13 September.

Although Thoreau kept a journal on the excursion and began to work some of it into an essay as early as 1840, he seems to have gotten the idea of writing a book based on the trip only after his brother John's death in 1842.[2] In some ways *A Week* is thus an obvious memorial to John. He invokes John as his literary muse in the first epigraph of the book (3), and many of the topics discussed in the book—particularly nature and Indians—are topics that had also been dear to John. It is nonetheless a strange memorial in that John is presented only as a very vague, at times virtually invisible figure. In the prefatory "Concord River" chapter, Thoreau omits John entirely and uses the first person, saying that "I resolved to launch myself on its [Concord River's] bosom, and float whither it would bear me" (13).

In "Saturday," however, the "I" switches to "we two, brothers, and natives of Concord" who "weigh anchor" (15). This "we" persists throughout most of the actual narrative of the journey, but little clarity is given to the personality of either brother. The closest Thoreau comes to an overt memorial to John is at the end of "Sunday" in his descriptions of the two brothers' dreams. "One sailor [Henry] was visited in his dreams this night by the Evil Destinies," he says. "But the other [John] happily passed a serene and even ambrosial or immortal night" (116). This passage is a clear tribute to John's easygoing personality and Henry's admiration of it.

Nonetheless, such a vague portrait of someone to whom Thoreau was so close is puzzling. The most convincing explanation thus far is Richard Lebeaux's in *Young Man Thoreau*. He argues that Thoreau's memory of John led him to write the book as a penance for his competition with John over Ellen Sewall and his general envy of John's popularity, but that on another level, "in order to protect himself from being overwhelmed by his grief and guilt, Thoreau could write only obliquely about his brother's death."[3] Lebeaux also suggests that despite Thoreau's invocation of his brother as muse, there was "the fear that his brother refused him this service."[4] Thoreau does seem uneasy about John in *A Week,* torn perhaps between wanting to memorialize him and at the same time wanting to affirm his own worth and independence of his brother. Often the latter seems the stronger of the two impulses.

Previous attempts to establish his own merit had met with little success. He certainly had achieved no independence in his father's pencil factory, and much of the success of his school had to be attributed to John. He had, however, felt some brief sparks of independence in seeing his writing in print in the *Dial,* so increasingly his thoughts had turned to a literary career. His move to Walden Pond was thus in one sense a career move, a retreat or "strategic withdrawal,"[5] to allow him to write a major work worthy of wider public attention. It was to that extent as much an attempt to attract public attention as to escape from it. As we have seen, however, it failed to do so and was, in retrospect, of value to him primarily as a testing ground for his style and ideas.

Art

Structure.   His first major problem with *A Week* proved to be the structure of the book. It was, as Sherman Paul convincingly argues, "the first version of *Walden,* his first attempt to find a form that would express his life."[6] A proponent of romantic organic theories of art, the young Thoreau believed that the form of a work of art should grow naturally from its content. As Emerson says in "The Poet," "The thought and the form are equal in the order of time, but in the order of genesis the thought is prior to the form."[7] The trick was to find the natural correspondence between the content and the form.

The degree to which Thoreau succeeded in achieving this correspondence has been much debated. Early readers of the book tended to find little coherence in the book as a whole, even though they praised certain parts. Emerson found the narrative of the boat trip to be "a very slender thread for such beads and ingots as are strung on it."[8] Since Emerson, critics have generally agreed that the narrative itself provides insufficient unity for the many essays sprinkled throughout and have sought other ordering principles. Walter Harding summarizes: "[Recent critics] see the book as 'a search for the sacred' or 'an exposition of the Transcendental experience' or ' a defense of the American Indian' or 'a paean to the Greek gods.' Others argue that the book is unified by its structure and see it as based on the epic or the pastoral genre or the biblical story of creation or on circular imagery."[9] Such a plethora of theories about the book's structure leads Harding more or less to throw up his hands in despair and conclude that Thoreau's attempts at unity must be viewed as unsuccessful until more agreement among critics can be achieved. Nor is the confusion likely to be dispelled by a brief introduction such as this. But it may be useful to call attention to some of the most nearly convincing theories and to throw yet another twig on the fire of controversy.

The most obvious structural devices are the days of the week and the circularity of the journey itself. The two-week journey is condensed into one week to eliminate an account of the hiking part of the journey and thus give at least the superficial unity of a single boating trip. The one-week cycle of days also corresponds with the circular movement of setting out and returning home to suggest the cyclical aspects of nature and of human life. As the brothers conclude their journey, for instance, Thoreau comments that "we were rowing homeward to find some autumnal work to do, and help on the revolution of the seasons" (388–89).

Unfortunately, Thoreau's attempt at organic structure breaks down here, because the thoughts recorded on a particular day seldom have a clear relation to the events or expectations of that day. "Sunday," with its critique of Christianity is an obvious exception. Also, neither of the brothers seems to complete this cyclical journey much altered. The last essay is on silence, a quality that presumably accompanies or makes possible transcendental insight, which might suggest that the book is working toward a vindication of transcendental experience. But there is no evidence that Thoreau has been significantly changed by the trip or has had any transcendental revelation.

Thoreau himself was well aware of his problems with literary structure, as is indicated by this passage written during his stay by the pond: "From all points of the compass, from the earth beneath, and the heavens above have come these inspirations and been entered duly in the order of their arrival in the Journal. Thereafter when the time arrived they were winnowed into Lectures—and again in due time from Lectures into Essays—And last they stand like the cubes of Pythagoras firmly on either basis—like statues on their pedestals—but statues rarely take hold of hands—There is only such connexion as is attainable in the galleries. And this affects their immediate practical & popular influence."[10] Thoreau used this method of moving from journal to lecture to essay for all his major works, but in none of them is it so transparently evident as in A Week.

The metaphor of the art gallery also gives us a useful hint about the work's structure, which is based in many ways on the visual arts. As in Walden, Thoreau emphasizes in A Week the importance of being a "seer" in both a physical and mystical sense. Specifically he uses what John Conron calls "visual logic," an organization of nature description that is based on either a fixed point of view or on physical movement such as a walking excursion or, in this case, the boating trip.[11] Throughout the book Thoreau describes objects along the river as works of visual art. A fisherman and his dog, for instance, stand "like statues under the other side of the heavens, the only objects to relieve the eye in the extended meadow" (23). Many passages are organized like a landscape painting, as is this one in "Sunday": "[The air] had the same effect on the landscape that a glass has on a picture, to give it an ideal remoteness and perfection. The landscape was clothed in a mild and quiet light, in which the woods and fences checkered and partitioned it with new regularity, and rough and uneven fields stretched away with lawn-like smoothness to the horizon, and the clouds, finely distinct and picturesque, seemed a fit drapery to hang over fairy-land" (46). The organizational techniques of landscape painting—foreground, mid-ground, and background planes; lighting; framing; and spatial and color relationships—are clearly evident here.

Another art form that Thoreau may have had in mind is the moving gallery of a panorama—a series of sketches or paintings done on very long rolls of canvas that were slowly unrolled before the audience in a specially constructed and darkened auditorium, usually with narration and musical accompaniment. Such panoramas were very popular entertainments in Thoreau's day and were sometimes of such epic proportions as to depict scenes along the entire length of the Mississippi River. Although our first evidence of Thoreau's seeing an actual panorama does not appear until his journal for 1851 where he describes seeing one "some months ago" (it was actually in 1849), he was certainly familiar much earlier with smaller versions of a similar idea in the "stereoramas" and dioramas that were occasionally part of lyceum presentations.[12] In A Week Thoreau is rather like a panorama exhibitor verbally unrolling his renderings of the landscape to us, the essays serving as the colorful amplification of his topic, such as a narrator might use in a spoken presentation. He hints at this panoramic aspect clearly in his description of the life of canal boatmen, who "have the constantly varying panorama of the shore to relieve the monotony of their labor" (210).

Of course, the pictures in Thoreau's gallery are not all landscapes. Each of the essay digressions is also in a way an intellectual self-portrait of the author. The only unity to these portraits, however, is that they are all aspects of the same mind and all reflect some association, no matter how awkward, with the river. One can also move easily from this gallery metaphor to the symbolic level of the river as the river of life and each of the essays as aspects of that life. To that extent *A Week* is about "the growth of the poet's mind" like Wordsworth's *Prelude,* although the relation between the chronology of the river journey and the chronological development of Thoreau's ideas is not clear. Instead he prefers to have us meander past these self-portraits in as leisurely and random a fashion as the river itself.

Thoreau apparently also tries to imitate the meanderings of the river in his experiments with time and point of view. Our sense of temporal continuity is frequently jarred by sudden, unpredictable shifts from historical anecdotes to current topics to prophecies, suggesting that he purposely intends to break down temporal distinctions to emphasize the transcendental present—the mystical union of past, present, and future. "Sunday," for instance, begins with a description of river scenery as the morning fog clears, moves to an historical essay on the founding of the town of Billerica, and then shifts to a long essay on legends, myths, and fables.

These shifts in time and topic are also generally signaled by a shift in point of view. The personal "I," which Thoreau uses in the introductory "Concord River" chapter shifts to the plural "we" whenever he describes the river experiences.[13] In the digressions, however, he often shifts to an impersonal point of view, as if to make a Whitmanesque universal pronouncement rather than a merely personal observation. At other times he plays variations on the personal "I," sometimes using it as the voice of the leisurely traveler and at other times as the voice of prophecy.[14] The intent of such shifts is probably to downplay Thoreau's own personality in order to convey the variety of "transcendental experience itself," but unfortunately they sometimes tend to confuse rather than enlighten the reader.[15]

Thoreau's problem is one of tone as well as of point of view. He had not yet learned how to season his preaching with humor, to cajole rather than to browbeat his audience. Many modern readers continue to share James Russell Lowell's irritation at being "bid to a river party—not to be preached at."[16] Nor is there much consistency of tone throughout the book. He is congenial as a familiar essayist in the essay on fish ("Saturday," 23–38), perversely paradoxical in the essay on friendship ("Wednesday," 259–89), and overly strident in the essay on religion ("Sunday," 64–78).

It is quite clear that Thoreau intended the book to be of one piece, if only in an organic, transcendental way. As Paul says, Thoreau wanted A Week to be "unified on both literal and spiritual levels" and for "one to be adequate to the other."[17] But William Drake is also as surely correct in judging that Thoreau failed in the second half of this intention, because the essays do not "develop naturally out of the context of the experience."[18] One might also add that Thoreau's structural problem in A Week is not that the narrative thread is too thin but rather that he attempts to use too many unifying threads without weaving them smoothly enough into a single fabric.

Despite these structural problems, however, parts of A Week show signs of Thoreau's gaining structural and stylistic control of his material. He occasionally succeeds, for example, in matching form to content. In "Friday" he describes the rapid downstream journey home and comments that "the current of our thoughts made as sudden bends as the river" (339). For several pages to follow his paragraphs also make "sudden bends"; they are short, clipped paragraphs that jump rapidly from idea to idea in a brief essay on poetic genius. Later in the same chapter, the river opens "into a broad and straight reach of great length," as do his paragraphs at that point (360). This matching of form and content is a bit obvious but nevertheless a step in the right direction.

Other passages demonstrate a power and versatility in Thoreau's prose style. The essay on religion in "Sunday," despite its harshness, contains examples of his ability to create a catchy sentence: "Men reverence one another, not yet God" (65); "It is necessary not to be a Christian, to appreciate the beauty and significance of the life of Christ" (67); "Christ was a sublime actor on the stage of the world" (73); and "There is more religion in men's science than there is science in their religion. Let us haste to the report of the committee on swine" (78). This mastery of the memorable sentence was an important aspect of his later achievement.

There is also evidence of developing stylistic precision in his retelling of the Hannah Dustan story, in which he uses time shifts much more effectively than elsewhere. He begins in the past tense, describing a scene one hundred forty-two years earlier in which Hannah Dustan, her nurse, and an English boy escaped from their Indian captors by killing and scalping them in their sleep and then paddling a canoe down the very stretch of river that the two brothers were traveling. Having described the scalpings with powerful understatement, he shifts to the present tense to express his own—and encourage the reader's—identification with Hannah Dustan's predicament: "Early this morning this deed was performed, and now, perchance, these tired women and this boy, their clothes stained with blood, and their minds racked with alternate resolution and fear, are making a hasty meal of parched corn and moose-meat, while their canoe glides under these pine roots whose stumps are still standing on the bank" (322). He describes the scene with realism and power, focusing on the panorama of sights and sounds that the fugitives must have seen, but with a drastically different effect on them than on the brothers: "An Indian lurks behind every rock and pine, and their nerves cannot bear the tapping of a woodpecker. . . . Deer gaze at them from the bank; a few faint-singing forest birds, perchance, fly over with a startling clangor; but they do not observe these things, or they speedily forget them. They do not smile or chat all day" (322–23).

He concludes the story by raising it to the level of living myth, achieving his goal of conveying the presentness of the past: "The family of Hannah Dustan all assembled alive once more, except the infant whose brains were dashed out against the apple-tree, and there have been many who in later times have lived to say that they had eaten of the fruit of that apple-tree" (323–24). It is a story powerfully but simply told, which suggests that, had Thoreau not shared the New England Puritans' prejudice against fiction, he might have rivaled his neighbor Hawthorne as a writer of short stories and novels. It is also a story that presents a stark shift from transcendental generalities toward the fronting of facts, no matter how harsh, which would be one of the strengths of *Walden*.

Themes.   Although Thoreau had not yet achieved a consistently effective style in *A Week,* he had begun to wrestle with many of the themes that would later concern him. Pervading *A Week* was the biblical question that occupied the rest of his life and writing. He cites it in the essay on religion in "Sunday": "For what is a man profited, if he shall gain the whole world, and lose his own soul? or what shall a man give in exchange for his soul? (Matt. 16:26; *A Week*, 72). This text was to provide the specific theme for one of his most frequently delivered lectures and for his essay "Life without Principle."

For the young man who was still unsettled as he went to live by the pond eight years after his college graduation, the crucial question was "How can I live without selling my own soul?" All around him he saw his Concord neighbors—farmers, merchants, perhaps even his own father—obsessed with economic survival while they ignored the question of whether making money was really the most important purpose in life. Emerson's transcendentalism had offered him an alternative purpose: spiritual and artistic development. But how could one devote time to the ideal when the need to get a living was so urgent? In *Walden* he found some practical as well as theoretical answers to that question, but in *A Week* he was still working out the theory for himself. He thus spends much of the book trying to clarify the philosophical relation between the real and the ideal, the temporal and the eternal, the life of action and the life of art.

His concern with the dualism of life is announced immediately in the "Concord River" prologue. He points out that the river's Indian name, Musketaquid, means "grass-ground river," a factually descriptive name in comparison to the more idealistic English name of "Concord." Paradoxically, however, the Indian name is more likely to be eternally accurate than the white's attempt at idealism: "It will be Grass-ground River as long as grass grows and water runs here; it will be Concord River only while men lead peaceable lives on its banks" (5). He thus hints at the possibility, reiterated throughout the book, that the material world can also be the ideal.

That Thoreau's purpose is to explore the ideal through experience with the real is further emphasized in "Saturday," the first chapter dealing with the journey itself. He describes his boat as "painted green below, with a border of blue, with reference to the two elements in which it was to spend its existence" (15), the green representing the real world of matter and the blue representing the ideal heavens.

The fish in the Concord River are presented with this same symbolic dualism. He begins his essay on fish with his assertion that "it concerns us to attend to the nature of fishes, since they are not phenomena confined to certain localities only, but forms and phases of the life in nature universally dispersed" (25). He then describes each of the various kinds of fish, hinting at their symbolic import. The sunfish, for instance, uses a graceful sculling of the fins, which "is expressive of their humble happiness" (27). It is in harmony with its environment, dwelling "far from many accidents inevitable to human life" (28). The shiner, on the other hand, is less content with the seclusion of the river and seeks waters closer to the surface, "gliding its life through with a quirk of the tail, half in the water, half in the air" (30), like the brothers' boat and like the idealist himself, who seeks to balance the material and spiritual life. The fish, then, are types of people, or rather types of human temperaments, as well as, Sherman Paul suggests, "a catalog of thoughts" that Thoreau was trying to "catch" in his book. [19]

This use of nature as symbol is, of course, consistent with Emerson's view of nature as a mere hieroglyphic of spiritual truth, not as a reality in its own right. For Emerson, nature's value is almost entirely in its spiritual meaning. One's perception passes through the object as a mere medium to get to the ideal. This Emersonian view of nature is repeated at other places in *A Week*. When the two brothers kill and eat a pigeon on Tuesday, for instance, Thoreau remarks that "it did not seem to be putting this bird to its right use, to pluck off its feathers, and extract its entrails, and boil its carcass on the coals" (223). Presumably the right use would have been as Emersonian symbol. Thoreau's goal was to be able to penetrate not only physical but spiritual reality by exploring nature. In the "Friday" chapter he affirms that "surely, we are provided with senses as well fitted to penetrate the spaces of the real, the substantial, the eternal, as these outward [senses] are to penetrate the material universe" (386). The implication is that the material universe is not ultimately "real" or "substantial."

But there is also a very non-Emersonian quality to Thoreau's transcendentalism in *A Week*, which seems directly to contradict this view of nature as mere medium. Earlier in "Friday" he contradicts himself by affirming the substantiality of nature's physical presence: "The landscape is indeed something real, and solid, and sincere, and I have not put my foot through it yet" (350). Later in this passage it becomes clear that the substantial aspect of the landscape that he refers to is its apparent timelessness: "When my thoughts are sensible of change, I love to see and sit on rocks which I *have* known, and pry into their moss, and see unchangeableness so established" (351, Thoreau's emphasis). His later study, particularly on Cape Cod, suggests that nature might not be so firm after all, but for now such thoughts allowed him to blend his transcendental idealism with his temperamental interest in natural fact.

The difference from the Emersonian view is crucial. Thoreau expected to find spiritual truth *in,* not merely through, nature. He felt confident that he could "see, smell, taste, hear, feel, that everlasting Something to which we are allied, at once our maker, our abode, our destiny, our very Selves" (173). Nature for him seemed frequently to be more than mere symbol, as he suggests in the following questions: "May we not *see* God? Are we to be put off and amused in this life, as it were with a mere allegory? Is not Nature, rightly read, that of which she is commonly taken to be the symbol merely?" (383, Thoreau's emphasis). As Jonathan Bishop suggests, the last of these questions "anticipates, deservedly, a positive answer. The other questions which precede this, though . . . are . . . susceptible to a negative or at least ambiguous reply. But to the writer at the moment they must have all seemed rhetorical in the same degree."[20]

Thoreau's idea that humans could see God in nature was in fact ambivalent as well as ambiguous even as early as *A Week.* This juggling of two contradictory views of nature seems to bother many critics more than it is likely to have bothered Thoreau. He would undoubtedly have agreed with William Blake that "Without Contraries is No Progression."[21] This ability to juggle contradictory viewpoints—something akin to what Keats might have called "negative capability"—was a source of much of the vitality in his writing.[22] Carl Hovde's observation that Thoreau "valued imaginative insight more than coherent system" is thus quite accurate and important for us to remember in reading not only *A Week* but all Thoreau's writing.[23] His ability to present both transcendental and nontranscendental views of nature in the same chapter of *A Week* without apology is a case in point.

Whatever his differences with Emerson about the role of nature in transcendental insight, there seems to have been none in his view of the goal of such insight. Like Emerson he believed that a mystical, transcendent vision of reality was possible. Although we might not be able to *see* God, Thoreau generally believed that we could. *A Week* is, therefore, as Bishop suggests, "an expression of faith; a faith which the encounters described have 'to some extent' justified."[24]

One such encounter is found in Thoreau's account of an earlier climbing of Saddleback Mountain in which he experienced a mystical mountaintop vision, one very similar to Wordsworth's on climbing Mount Snowden in *The Prelude.*[25] Like Wordsworth's account, it presents essentially a night vision, although Thoreau's is lighted by the first rays of daybreak rather than by Wordsworth's moon. Like Wordsworth, Thoreau is confronted by a sudden vision of a vast sea of clouds below him: "As the light increased I discovered around me an ocean of mist, which by chance reached up exactly to the base of the tower, and shut out every vestige of the earth, while I was left floating on this fragment of the wreck of a world, on my carved plank in cloudland, which required no aid from the imagination to render it impressive" (188). Earth and clouds, the physical and the ideal, now seemed to be reversed: "It was a favor for which to be forever silent to be shown this vision. The earth beneath had become such a flitting thing of lights and shadows as the clouds had been before" (188). Thoreau, however, is much more optimistic about the significance of his vision than is Wordsworth. While Wordsworth finds the light of the moon (imagination) able to shine only a short way into the dark mysteries beyond the sea of clouds, Thoreau finds in his mountaintop vision confidence that his aspirations toward the ideal can succeed: "As I had climbed above storm and cloud, so by successive days' journeys I might reach the region of eternal day beyond the tapering shadow of the earth" (189).

This youthful confidence also pervades his wrestling with the question of vocation. Much of *A Week* consists of speculations about how one may best live a transcendental life, how to make the best use of those "successive days' journeys" toward "eternal day." Two possible paths appealed to him, one the path of the "hero" and the other the path of the "poet." His goal was to combine the two on the transcendental assumption that the greatest life is the greatest poetry, and vice versa. This mutual compatibility of the lives of action and of art is suggested by his discussion of "mute, inglorious Miltons" in the "Concord River" chapter. Along the river, he says, one might see "greater men than Homer, or Chaucer, or Shakespeare, only they never got time to say so; they never took to the way of writing. Look at their fields, and imagine what they might write, if ever they should put pen to paper. Or what have they not written on the face of the earth already, clearing and burning, and scratching, and harrowing, and plowing, and subsoiling, in and in, out and out, and over and over, again and again, erasing what they had already written for want of parchment" (68).

The obscurity and universality of so much of life's heroism and the sense of the poetry that exists in so many lives, past and present, was a major reason for Thoreau's interest in history and the many historical digressions in *A Week*. Figures such as Farwell the Indian fighter (168) or Hannah Dustan were clearly heroic, and the historical record of their adventures had the universal quality of myth. Even their most blood-thirsty actions—Hannah Dustan's scalping of her Indian captors, for instance—had parallels to poetry. "The talent of composition," Thoreau observes, "is very dangerous,—the striking out the heart of life at a blow, as the Indian takes off a scalp" (329).[26] Just as dangerous as scalping was the writer's willingness to expose his soul to the world, to strike it out at a blow (stroke) of a pen.

The Indians too were forgotten heroes and poets whose poetic life in nature, although in a sense past, could still be felt as present in the landscape. Thoreau was interested not so much in what the Indians did in the past as in their impact on the present. "Time hides no treasures," he says. "We want not its *then*, but its *now*" (154, Thoreau's emphases). Therefore, "it is the province of the historian to find out, not what was, but what *is*" (155). Thus he uses the history of the Indians, whether found in written records or in artifacts, as a point of comparison with the present. He transcribes, for instance, the letter of John Hogkins, a Penacook Indian, written to the colonial governor to request assistance in defending himself against enemy "Mohogs": "I afraid allways Mohogs he will kill me every day and night. If your worship when please pray help me you no let Mohogs kill me at my place at Malamake [Merrimack] river called Pannukkog and Natuk-kog, I will submit your worship and your power" (200). Thoreau must have delighted in the primitive vitality of such broken English—a kind of mythological originality and wildness—but the main point of the passage is to demonstrate the universality of nature in the midst of drastically changed human circumstances, as in his comments on the Hannah Dustan story; Thoreau observes that "one hundred and fifty-four years having elapsed since the date of this letter, we went un-alarmed on our way . . . seeing no traces of 'Mohogs' on the banks" (220).

Indian artifacts, which Thoreau seems to have been particularly ad-ept at discovering, could serve a similar function. In "Tuesday" he describes "a small desert" on the east bank of the Merrimack that had once been a cultivated field but had been so denuded by fishermen clearing away fishing spots that "the sand was blown off down to the ancient surface," thus exposing "the foundation of an Indian wig-wam . . . , a perfect circle of burnt stones four or five feet in diameter, mingled with fine charcoal and the bones of small animals, which had been preserved in the sand" (146). This discovery leads to no comments about the beauties of the "noble savages'" simple life, such as one might expect from a romantic like Thoreau, but rather to a contrast with the brothers' present activities—bathing and relaxing in the sun. A relatively trivial contrast by itself, it nonetheless demonstrates his interest in the ever-moving presence of time. "History," he says, "fluctuates as the face of the landscape from morning to evening" (154). Thus one task of the hero-poet is to be alert to these fluctuations and to use them in his life and writing as clues to the eternal.

Thoreau felt that the ability to take advantage of such universal perceptions depended on maintaining a transcendental perspective on life, whether past or present. As a hero-poet he had to realize his own centrality, that is, to recognize that his individual reality was shaped or even created by his own unique mind, which was part of the mind of God. Emerson had described human life as an expanding circle with the individual at the center: "The life of man is a self-evolving circle, which from a ring imperceptibly small, rushes on all sides outwards to new and larger circles, and that without end."[27] Thoreau uses this same metaphor: "Let us wander where we will, the universe is built round about us, and we are central still" (331). "The sun," he says later, "is not so central as a man" (349). This centrality implies the essentially subjective nature of transcendental reality; the world is the imaginative extension of the individual mind. This centrality could be described as vertical and horizontal, as well as circular. The hero must maintain a balance between the world of matter below and the world of spirit above. He is one "who preserves equipoise in his life, and moves serenely on his path" (307). Or, in horizontal terms, he is like the brothers themselves sailing downstream and needing "only to steer, keeping [their] bark in the middle," (317) the banks of the river representing the dangers of excessive idealism on one side and materialism on the other.

This central perspective allows the hero to approach the eternal while still dwelling in the material. On the one hand, "he lives out of an eternity which includes all time" (311–12). He can thus dismiss as unimportant most of the affairs that seem so important to lesser persons, as in his story of the king who seeks "a prudent and able man, who is capable of managing the state affairs of my kingdom" (129). The king's minister wisely responds that "the criterion . . . of a wise and competent man, is, that he will not meddle with such like matters" (130). Having few important material affairs to attend to, he will need few material possessions: "It does not cost much for these heroes to live; they do not want much furniture" (344).

Nevertheless, the hero must be capable when necessary of coping with the problems of the everyday material world as well. "Even here," he says, "we have a sort of living to get, and must buffet it somewhat longer. There are various tough problems yet to solve, and we must make shift to live, betwixt spirit and matter, such a human life as we can" (73–74). He thus finds Christ's failure to acknowledge this immediacy and reality of the material world enough to disqualify him as a hero. Despite his idealism, Christ thus "taught mankind but imperfectly how to live; his thoughts were all directed toward another world" (73).

Finally, the hero must be an explorer, always expanding the bounds of that circle of which he is the center. Although the farmer's life may be admirable enough because "it is sometimes pleasant to make the earth yield her increase, and gather the fruits in their season," he feels compelled to add that "the heroic spirit will not fail to dream of remoter retirements and more rugged paths" (55). Nor must he expect his pioneering to be followed immediately. His example will likely have impact on others only very slowly. Thus "the hero . . . will know how to wait, as well as to make haste"(128).

All these qualities are, of course, philosophical abstractions essentially untested yet by Thoreau's own experience. The retreat to Walden Pond to write *A Week* was the beginning of his deliberate attempt to mold himself into a transcendental hero. The feisty independence, the aloofness from mundane matters, the insistence on exploring the physical as well as the spiritual world, and the maintaining of a balance between them were all just beginning to develop. They would develop rapidly, however; his different drummer would speed up the cadence considerably during the Walden years.

An important part of that development from abstract to practical hero was his freeing himself from earlier role models, such as Sir Walter Raleigh. One would need to think a long while to find a role model so dissimilar from Thoreau himself. Yet he gave a lecture on Raleigh to the Concord Lyceum in 1843, revised it for publication in the *Dial* (which folded before the essay was published), and eventually used a small portion of it in *A Week*. Certainly he was not a dashing courtier like Raleigh. Yet he was in his own way an explorer and a nonconformist like Raleigh, and he wished to express his heroism in writing as Raleigh had done.[28] While he occasionally offered himself for Raleigh-like martyrdom, as in his night in jail and his unpopular support of John Brown, it was more and more as a writer that he came to see his heroism developing. It is interesting that of his essay on Raleigh the only part included in *A Week* in which he mentions Raleigh by name is a passage that praises him as a literary stylist: "Sir Walter Raleigh might well be studied if only for the excellence of his style, for he is remarkable in the midst of so many masters" (104).

The view of the writer as hero accounts for the frequency of literary criticism in *A Week*. There are extended essays on Homer and Greek myth ("Sunday"), Christian and oriental scriptures and writing of history and biography ("Monday"), Anacreon ("Tuesday"), Aulus Persius Flaccus and Goethe ("Thursday"), and Ossian and "modern poets"—including Chaucer ("Friday"), as well as many brief references to other writers, such as Wordsworth. Of these, he strongly prefers ancient writers like Homer for the timeless, mythological quality of their pioneering work. "The poet," he says, "is he who can write some pure mythology today without the aid of posterity" (60). Such a poet is "no tender slip of fairy stock who requires peculiar institutions and edicts for his defence, but the toughest son of earth and of Heaven" (340). In contrast to such tough ancient pioneers of language, the "modern" writers, such as Wordsworth or even Chaucer, seem tame and no longer to have the "bardic rage." The modern poet "only conceives the deed, which he formerly stood ready to perform" (367).

Implicit in such literary judgments were three problems inherent in the transcendental view of the hero as artist: the impossibility of matching the artistry of nature itself, the difficulty of becoming a true poetic genius rather than a mere artist, and the familiar conflict between life and art. The first of these problems could be dealt with by simply appealing to nature's tolerance of humans' inferior efforts. Thoreau knew that "Art can never match the luxury and superfluity of Nature" (318). In that sense it is futile to become a poet. Despite the limitations of human artistry, however, there is a place for it, because "Nature is prepared to welcome into her scenery the finest work of human art, for she is herself an art so cunning that the artist never appears in his work" (316). In other words, human art is one way in which nature expresses its own artistry, humans being, by Emerson's definition, at least partially a part of nature, the "Not Me." Thus the artist could adopt nature's goal: "A perfect work of man's art would also be wild or natural in a good sense" (316).

Because transcendental nature is also an expression of God, nature's purpose, and thus the artist's, is to reveal God. The poetic genius must thus be "an inspired or demonic man, who produces a perfect work in obedience to laws yet unexplored" (328), the laws of God. Poetry is "the mysticism of mankind" (328). To be a true poet and mystic was, as Thoreau already knew all too well, a tragic as well as heroic undertaking, for "there has been no man of pure Genius; as there has been no one wholly destitute of Genius" (328). The poet is thus doomed to fail in his or her highest aspirations and thus to become only an artist, one "who detects and applies the law from observation of the works of Genius, whether of man or nature," or, worse yet, a lowly artisan "who merely applies the rules which others have detected" (328).

In establishing this hierarchy of artistry Thoreau seems to be applying Coleridge's definition of the primary and secondary imagination and of the fancy in the *Biographia Literaria* in order to define his own artistic aspirations.[29] It was nothing less than primary "Genius" (imagination) that he, in his youthful confidence, aspired to, despite the odds against him. He hastens to add, however, providing the security of a consolation prize for himself, that "the Man of Genius may at the same time be, indeed is commonly, an Artist, but the two are not to be confounded" (328).

When Thoreau uses the world "artist," then, he is often damning with faint praise. He complains of Goethe, for instance, that his "whole education and life were those of the artist. He lacks the unconsciousness of the poet" (327). He lays the blame on Goethe's city-bred youth: "the life of a city boy, whose toys are pictures and works of art" (327). Here "art" is clearly a negative word implying separation from nature. This Yankee suspicion of visual art as superficial and elitist derives from Puritan associations of sculpture and painting with monarchical splendor, associations that Thoreau indirectly absorbed through New England culture.[30] Unfortunately, this suspicion also resulted in his giving too little credit to the American landscape painters of his own day, artists like Thomas Cole who shared many of his own beliefs and who used similar techniques of composition. Thoreau was distressed to see that "men will go further and pay more to see a tawdry picture on canvas, a poor painted scene, than to behold the fairest or grandest scene that nature ever displays in their immediate vicinity, though they may never have seen it in their lives" (*Writings* 8:217).

Thus while he instinctively saw the similarity between landscape painting and his own art and used the methods of painting to organize his book, he always believed that writing was somehow a nobler art than painting. "Language," he says at the end of "Saturday," is "the most perfect art in the world" (42). Language is closest to being the perfect artistic tool, because it appeals not only to the senses but to the imagination, the genius, of the reader. "Give me a sentence," he says, "which no intelligence can understand" (151). James Russell Lowell wisecracked that all too often Thoreau achieved this goal in his own writing, but the statement's meaning is nonetheless significant. What Thoreau is asking for and setting as a standard for his own writing is language that appeals not just to the reader's rationality (intelligence) but beyond it to his or her imagination.

The person who can write such sentences is, for Thoreau, the "Poet," a word he uses sometimes in the honorific sense to mean the "Genius," and sometimes in the more ordinary sense of a verbal artist (although for him the "poet" does not necessarily need to write in verse). The greatest concern of the former is a successful life, while the greatest concern of the latter is the artistic expression of life: "There are two classes of men called poets. The one cultivates life, the other art,—one seeks food for nutriment, the other for flavor; one satisfies hunger, the other gratifies the palate. There are two kinds of writing, both great and rare; one that of genius, or the inspired, the other of intellect and taste, in the interval of inspiration" (375). The true test of which kind of poet Thoreau was to become would be the evidence of how he lived his life. "The true poem," he says, "is not that which the public read. . . . It is *what he has become through his work*" (343, Thoreau's emphasis). Here he echoes Emerson's belief that "art is the path of the creator to his work."[31] Writing was thus to be a means, not an end in itself, a view that Thoreau changed significantly later in his life.

As for the poet's choice of form between verse and prose, Thoreau had already decided, despite the frequent inclusion of his verse in *A Week,* that prose was his preferred form. Although romantic writers tended to prefer verse as the higher form, Thoreau had already wisely sensed his own severe limitations as a poet and had developed a genuine theoretical preference for prose as the more stable and enduring form: "Great prose, of equal elevation, commands our respect more than great verse, since it implies a more permanent and level height, a life more pervaded with the grandeur of thought. The poet often only makes an irruption, like a Parthian, and is off again, shooting while he retreats; but the prose writer has conquered like a Roman, and settled colonies" (342).

Thoreau was able to make a few "irruptions" into brilliance in *A Week,* but he could not conquer the literary world with transcendental philosophizing alone. Ironically, by the time he went to the pond to write it, his life had already outdistanced his art. By the time he had fully recorded the theoretical program for his life, he was already transforming these generalizations about the "hero-poet" into the action of living the transcendental life in all of its practical applications at Walden Pond. *A Week* was an old skin that he was sloughing off even as he created it. It was nonetheless a necessary stage in his development, which he could not avoid and which cleared the way for *Walden,* the more fully realized and practical guide to heroic living that proved him a poet and artist in the highest sense.

Chapter Three
The Seer of *Walden*

Walden was published by Ticknor and Fields on 9 August 1854. Thoreau's comment on the event in his journal is characteristic of his reticence about letting public events intrude on the privacy of the journal: "Walden' published. Elderberries. Waxwork yellowing" (*Writings* 12:429). Although Thoreau may have been trying to keep the lid on his excitement by implying that the publication of *Walden* was no more important than the elderberries, Emerson, in a letter to an English friend later that month (28 August), suggests that Thoreau's pride in the book was evident to his neighbors: "We account Henry the undoubted King of all American lions. He is walking up & down Concord, firm-looking, but in a tremble of great expectation."[1]

Thoreau's great expectations were at least partially justified, for *Walden's* reception, though modest, was significantly better than that for *A Week*. Initially there were mostly favorable reviews and good sales, 1744 copies out of a first printing of 2000 selling the first year.[2] But it would take five years to exhaust the remainder of the first printing, and in the first fifteen years after its publication, *Walden* averaged sales of only about 300 copies per year.[3]

Although Thoreau began both *A Week* and *Walden* during his two years by the pond, *Walden* is so much the superior book that *A Week* seems like an apprentice piece. *Walden* comes as close to unifying life and art as Thoreau ever came in his published works. To emphasize that unity, the format of separate discussions of his life and art used in other chapters of this book will be omitted here.

Part of the difference between *A Week* and *Walden* lies in the order in which the two books were begun. The first draft of *A Week* was written mostly in 1845, but Thoreau probably did not start to write *Walden* until late in 1846 or early in 1847 shortly before he left the pond for good.[4] The year between the beginnings of the two books seems to have increased Thoreau's confidence both personally and artistically. As he started *A Week* he was still in retreat from the village, but by the time he started *Walden* he had successfully and pleasantly weathered a full year living at the pond. He knew the advantages of such a life, and he no longer felt defensive about it. Psychologically, as Richard Lebeaux observes, "By the end of his first year at Walden, Thoreau had finally succeeded in settling on and building a solid early adult life structure."[5] It was now the villagers whose lifestyle was questionable, and as a hero-poet who had turned transcendental theory into action, he was ready to contrast his life to theirs point by point.

The other crucial difference between the two books is in the longer gestation period of *Walden*. Although *Walden* was far enough along by 1849 for its impending publication to be announced in *A Week,* the failure of *A Week* discouraged him enough to postpone publication for another five years. By 1854, *Walden* had the advantage of being taken through seven drafts, each of which added to and refined the original version, according to Lyndon Shanley, "without destroying the fundamental character or any considerable portion of the original."[6] During the five years after the publication of *A Week,* Thoreau never abandoned his belief in nature's essential goodness and spiritual significance, but he learned to question nature more aggressively and to see it as more complex than he had found it at the pond. He also came to realize that he did indeed have several more lives to live and that the Walden experiment, while proving a firm foundation for his life and art, was only a base from which to confront other challenges. Thus *Walden* became a remarkably subtle, complex, and practical book, one that expresses his double vision of the human balancing act between spiritual and physical reality more effectively than had *A Week.*

Like *A Week,* however, *Walden* can be approached from widely varied points of view. A recent checklist of *Walden* criticism reveals that *Walden* has been described as belonging to numerous genres: extended familiar essay, autobiography, satire, pastoral, literary excursion, and prophecy.[7] Most recently it has even been described as a parody of architectural house pattern books.[8] Critics have also argued for a wide variety of literary classics as models for *Walden,* including *Robinson Crusoe, The Prelude, The Compleat Angler, The Bhagavad-Gita, The Natural History of Selborne, Gulliver's Travels,* and *Pilgrim's Progress.*[9]

Thoreau combines elements of these many models through several interwoven structural devices. The first and most obvious is the cycle of the year, which is paralleled by the cycle of the day ("The day is an epitome of the year. The night is the winter, the morning and evening are the spring and fall, and the noon is the summer" [301]). Just as he condensed two weeks into one in *A Week,* he condenses two years at the pond into one to convey the pattern of growth, death, and rebirth without unnecessary repetition. Of the events he records in *Walden,* the vast majority seem to be from his first year at the pond. He omits or only very briefly mentions significant events of the second year, such as his trip to Mount Katahdin, many details of his night in jail, and his increasing scientific studies, perhaps, as Lauriat Lane, Jr., suggests, because they were troubling experiences that would have undercut the optimism of the book.[10] Almost certainly, however, the pattern of events had already been established by his first draft, and these major events would have required extended treatment. His decision to omit them resulted in a more unified and effective book.

Another major reason for the unity of *Walden* is Thoreau's success in creating a more interesting persona than in *A Week.* In the first few pages of *Walden* Thoreau establishes this persona so carefully that the reader must become familiar with it in order to understand the book fully. The first paragraph, consisting as it does mostly of prepositional phrases defining precisely where and how he lived during the writing of "the bulk" of the book, announces that this persona values facts. This foundation in facts is also suggested by a significant difference from *A Week:* most of Thoreau's thoughts in the earlier book originate on the river, symbolically a less firm base than the cabin built solidly in the woods on the shore of a pond.[11]

More important, however, Thoreau's description of the cabin's location establishes the importance of the persona's—and by extension the reader's—assuming an advantageous position from which to view life. This position is announced as an intermediate one: it is in Concord but still "a mile from any neighbor" (3), is in the woods but also on the shore of the pond. This artistic stance is similar to the one Whitman preferred: "Both in and out of the game and watching and wondering at it."[12] Thoreau is far enough from Concord to view it with some objectivity but is still involved in it enough not to abandon all subjective attachment to it. He is in the woods but not in the wilderness. His beanfield, we learn later, is a "half-civilized" (158) field. He is also situated at the conjunction of three elements: on land, but near water, and with a plentiful view of the sky. This is the position of centrality he sought in *A Week.*

Thoreau presents himself through the rest of the book as a practical Yankee living just outside the bounds of genteel society and demonstrates a typically dry New England sense of humor based on (mostly) good-natured irony and wordplay.[13] In the second paragraph he tells us how he began the book in response to questions about his life in the woods: "what I got to eat; if I did not feel lonesome; if I was not afraid; and the like." Those asking such questions seemed to think his mode of life "impertinent"—that is, irrelevant to their lives and probably frivolous—but he argues that it is indeed "pertinent"—that is, applicable to their own situations. He says that his book will also be addressed to "poor students" (4), by which he means not only students with little money but also students who are so intellectually poor and unenlightened that they do not yet know how to live.

His subject, he implies, will be people stranger than the "Chinese and Sandwich Islanders"; it will be those "who are said to live in New England" (4). One can read this clause straightforwardly as merely locating his subject in New England. Almost surely, however, he intends us to emphasize the "are said," thereby questioning whether or not such people's activities are genuinely "life" rather than a kind of living death. Possibly the "are said" qualifier is also meant to apply to the "New" in New England to question whether their lives are genuinely new. Such wordplay was more obvious in his lectures when he could add emphasis by the tone of his voice. That he intends such wordplay in print as well is suggested by a passage from paragraph two, which he canceled from his first manuscript and which contains his intended emphases clearly marked: "Some have not come to my house because I lived *there*—others have not come because I *lived* there—and others again, because *I* lived there."[14] One critic has found sixteen examples of wordplay in just the first three paragraphs of the book.[15]

Wordplay and puns are Thoreau's initiation test for the reader. In his lecture "Life without Principle" he comments that "the greatest compliment that was ever paid me was when one asked me what *I thought,* and attended to my answer" (Thoreau's emphasis).[16] Thoreau demands such attention from his readers as well. Those who attend closely enough to his language in *Walden* will catch his wordplay and thus the full complexity of his thought; those who do not will miss much of what he has to say.

Recognition of Thoreau's wordplay also assures that the reader will enjoy the book's humor, much of which resides in puns. As Edward Galligan says of Thoreau's stance as a "comic hero," if one recognizes the comic element, "the book is a delight and constant companion; if one does not, if one assumes as most students do when the book is assigned to them that the narrator is a not-to-be-ridiculed hero, then *Walden* is a pretentious bore."[17]

Thoreau uses a wide range of comic techniques. He humorously revives clichés, as when he describes the auctioning of the contents of a dead man's attic and observes that "when a man dies he kicks the dust" (68). He tells deadpan jokes, such as the story of the farmer who claims that Thoreau's vegetarian diet is unhealthy because "it furnishes nothing to make bones with," while Thoreau notices that the farmer is "walking all the while he talks behind his oxen, which, with vegetable-made bones, jerk him and his lumbering plough along in spite of every obstacle" (9). Sometimes he succeeds with a cleverly humorous metaphor, as in his description of the village's main street as an Indian gauntlet (168).

His most successful comic device, however, is his own comic persona. He describes himself in the book's epigraph as Chanticleer the rooster: "I do not propose to write an ode to dejection, but to brag as lustily as chanticleer in the morning, standing on his roost, if only to wake my neighbors up" (title page and 84). He is what Galligan calls "the homeliest, loudest, most preposterous of birds, a rooster crowing in the morning, waking everybody up whether they want to wake up or not."[18] Remembering all the fables about vain roosters being outwitted by sly foxes, we know that this narrator, despite his admission of egotism on the book's first page, is no stuffy egotist. This unflattering view of himself is made doubly clear by his identification later in the book with another comical bird: the loon. Thoreau's persona is a narrator able to parody even his own most serious transcendental endeavors, as in the dialogue between the "Hermit" (Thoreau) and the "Poet" (probably Channing), during which the Hermit, having been interrupted in mid-meditation by the Poet's invitation to go fishing, sends the Poet off to do the dirty work of digging the worms while he resumes his transcendental meditating as if he were returning to marked pages in a book: "Let me see; where was I? Methinks I was nearly in this frame of mind; the world lay about this angle. Shall I go to heaven or a-fishing?" (224). He goes fishing.

This comic persona serves several purposes. It certainly entertains the reader and thereby lightens the preachy tone to which Thoreau had shown himself susceptible in *A Week*. That he knew he was still preaching is clear in his journal for 6 May 1851 where he says: "Like other preachers, I have added my texts—derived from the Chinese and Hindoo scriptures—long after my discourse was written" (*Writings* 8:192). But he was determined not to let preaching scare off his audience again. Comedy is thus the honey with which he sweetens the potentially bitter taste of his social criticism. He can get away with reminding his readers of what "mean and sneaking lives many of you live" (6) by joking with them about how they "have come to this page to spend borrowed or stolen time, robbing your creditors of an hour" (6). The humor is his sly nudge in the reader's ribs, as if to say, "I know what you're up to; you can't fool me." Instead of threatening his readers with the consequences of their sins, he teases them into facing their own foibles; he wants to show them not so much how *bad* they are but rather how *foolish* they are to live such misguided and inefficient lives. He is simply a fellow Yankee reminding them of their own innate wisdom and striking cleverly at their Yankee pride in their own ingenuity. Inured to being called sinful by their preachers in church, they are more likely to flinch at being called foolish. Inheriting a farm thus becomes "a misfortune" instead of a fortune and is found to lead to a "fool's life" (5). Even Negro slavery appears "frivolous" compared to the northern Puritan's habit of being "slave-driver of yourself" (7).

More importantly, the comic persona invites readers to adopt a more resilient view of life, to loosen up their puritanical seriousness and see the humor as well as the earnestness of life. Their "quiet desperation" is, from one point of view, quite serious (8). But he adds quite simply that "it is characteristic of wisdom not to do desperate things" (8), thus implying that such foolishness can be promptly remedied. The logic echoes that of the greatest Yankee pragmatist, Benjamin Franklin, who records in his *Autobiography* his attempt to achieve moral perfection by reminding himself that "as I knew, or thought I knew, what was right and wrong, I did not see why I might not *always* do the one and avoid the other" (Franklin's emphasis). [19] Franklin takes his goal seriously but at the same time seems to recognize the silliness of his oversimplification. Thoreau too invites us to take a double view of the quest for moral perfection that he proposes, so that throughout the book we must be alert for paradoxes and double meanings.

Within the first few pages of the book, then, Thoreau establishes a clear picture of both his own persona and its relation to his audience. As Stanley Cavell says of him, "The more deeply he searches for independence from the Puritans, the more deeply in every step and word, he identifies with them." [20] Thus Thoreau's problem, Cavell says, "is not to learn what to say to them; that could not be clearer. The problem is to establish his right to declare it." [21] In light of that problem, his stance as a comic Yankee is, to be sure, partly an overcompensation for the village's view of him as a woods-burner and eccentric loafer, but it is above all his plea to the village to see him as a friendly herald who, if he shocks them with his noise, does so only to waken them to better, wiser ways of life.

The villagers themselves are presented not so much as antagonistic toward Thoreau as skeptical, complacent, and misguided. Although Thoreau seems smugly amused at their naive questions about his life-style, he cares enough about them to write at first a lecture and then a whole book in reply. He addresses the book in general to these curious villagers but more particularly to four distinct audiences. One audience is the "poor students" (4) to whom he can hope to offer guidance in the process of choosing their own way of life. He concedes, however, that the worth of his advice may be severely limited, for "practically the old have no very important advice to give the young" (9). A second audience is "the mass of men who are discontented" (16), who may be seeking an alternative life-style, such as he has to offer. The third audience is "that seemingly wealthy, but most terribly impoverished class of all, who have accumulated dross" (16) and who need to be awakened to problems they do not even think they have. To these three audiences he takes pains to emphasize that his purpose is not to win their imitation in living in a particular place or a certain occupation: "I would not have any one adopt *my* mode of living on any account. . . . But I would have each one be very careful to find out and pursue *his own* way, and not his father's or his mother's or his neighbor's instead" (71, Thoreau's emphases). Nor should we forget that Thoreau was writing to convince yet a fourth audience, himself, that he had indeed found *his* way. As Alfred Kazin says, "he was the first reader he had to convince."[22] It was not only "always the first person that is speaking" (3), but always the "first person"—Thoreau himself—that was listening and reading as well.

An understanding of this relationship between Thoreau and his audiences helps to clarify the other major structural devices he uses in *Walden.* The structure of the book is one intended to unsettle the established attitudes of his readers and to challenge his own convictions as well, based as it is on the conflict between physical and ideal reality and the paradoxes inherent in that conflict.

The first chapter, "Economy," serves as a long prologue to the book proper, one that—like Hawthorne's "Customs House" in *The Scarlet Letter*—does not really begin the progress of the book's "action" (the narrative of life in the woods) but instead establishes themes and motifs on which variations will be played. That Thoreau intended the chapter as prologue is strongly suggested by his numbering its pages separately from the rest of the book in his manuscript of the first version of *Walden*.[23] The purpose of this prologue is essentially to announce the problem by calling into question the materialistic life of his neighbors and to suggest that a more spiritually "economical" way of life might provide a solution. It offers the diagnosis of the disease for which the rest of the book will propose a cure.

The introductory chapter to the book proper is "Where I Lived, and What I Lived For." It begins the narrative by expanding the description of his location and purposes and by continuing the theme of simplicity introduced in "Economy." But it focuses most sharply on the search for ultimate reality—the need to "see" fully and to "front the facts of life," to cut through the mirage of the Milldam's (Concord's business district) materialism and "see only the reality" (96). This theme of vision is supported by the symbolism of morning as both a time of physical awakening and as a state of mind marked by moral and spiritual alertness.

The next fourteen chapters progress by pairs of opposed chapters. Throughout the book Thoreau alternates between chapters that emphasize the ideal and those that emphasize the factual, a structure that imitates the fluctuations of nature itself in ebb and flow, day and night, fall and spring.[24] It is important to notice, however, that Thoreau does not oversimplify these contrasts or make them mutually exclusive. The most factual chapters contain hints of the ideal and vice versa.

"Reading" is an indoor chapter discussing the value of books—what Emerson called "the Mind of the Past"[25]—and of the fine arts. It focuses on the proper use of cultural objects, but it is followed by "Sounds," an outdoor chapter that emphasizes how to "read" the spiritual significance of the sounds of nature, where "much is published, but little printed" (111). Thus the basic opposition and interrelation between ideas and objects is established as a major structural device.

The next two chapters contain a similar opposition. "Solitude" includes Thoreau's affirmation that ideal visitors such as God ("an old settler and original proprietor" [137]) and Nature ("an elderly dame . . . invisible to most persons, in whose odorous herb garden I love to stroll sometimes" [137]) provide better company than human visitors. Thus, he says, "I have a great deal of company in my house; especially in the morning, when nobody calls" (137). "Solitude" is also one of the most mystical chapters, beginning, as it does, with the persona's nearly complete identification with nature: "the whole body is one sense, and imbibes delight through every pore. I go and come with a strange liberty in Nature, a part of herself" (129). "Visitors," however, returns to human society with its hearty personalities such as Alek Therien, as well as its repulsive bores such as "self-styled reformers" (153–54). It is also important to notice that Thoreau welcomes both his ideal visitors in "Solitude" and the human ones in "Visitors" (although he undoubtedly encouraged the departure of the boring reformers as quickly as possible). One type of experience does not negate the other, here or elsewhere in the book, for Thoreau had concluded early in his career that "truth is always paradoxical" (*Writings* 7:153).

The third pair of chapters, "The Bean-Field" and "The Village," also contrasts life in nature to life in human society. Although his account of growing beans seems a most practical, down-to-earth chapter, on closer examination it is a dominantly idealistic chapter in which the beans are symbolic of new opportunities. By learning the facts of bean growing, he was, according to romantic organicism, also learning the secrets of nature's entire system. When he says, "I was determined to know beans" (161), he is not just punning on the popular cliché; he is expressing his earnestness about finding nature's spiritual truths. He finds, however, that his knowledge of beans was perhaps not ideal enough and that next time he would plant "such seeds, if the seed is not lost, as sincerity, truth, simplicity, faith, innocence, and the like" (164). He also confesses that his ideal seeds did not fare as well as his actual bean seeds (from which he made a profit), for "the seeds which I planted, if indeed they *were* the seeds of those virtues, were worm-eaten or had lost their vitality, and so did not come up" (164, Thoreau's emphasis). In admitting this personal failure he also reveals that he is the reader's companion in the search for truth, not a seeker who has already arrived. "The Village," on the other hand, takes us back to town for social criticism of the villagers' misplaced priorities. The village is described as "a great news room" (167) and as a gauntlet to be run by every visitor. It is also the site of his night in jail, which he claims revealed to him the callous side of his usually friendly neighbors.

The fourth pair of chapters contrasts the ideal symbolism of "The Ponds" to the meager life of John Field in "Baker Farm." "The Ponds," the book's central chapter, presents an extended exploration of the central symbol, Walden Pond, as well as some of the neighboring lakes. Walden Pond becomes the meeting point of the thus far contrasted ideal and material impulses of human beings. It is a place where, when fishing at night, Thoreau says he seems able to "cast my line upward into the air, as well as downward into this element which was scarcely more dense. Thus I caught two fishes as it were with one hook" (175), one fish representing the ideal and the other natural fact. Contrasted to Thoreau's mystical fishing in "The Ponds" is John Field's completely ineffectual fishing in "Baker Farm." Thoreau offers his own life-style as an alternative to Field, a poor Irishman who is having difficulty surviving even though he works very hard "bogging." Unable to convince Field with theory, Thoreau extends some practical advice about fishing. Thoreau tells us, however, that Field, "poor man, disturbed only a couple of fins while I was catching a fair string, and he said it was his luck; but when we changed seats in the boat luck changed seats too" (208). Field's inability to relate to nature reveals his inability to perceive the ideal as well.

The fifth pair of chapters is presented ironically, in that "Higher Laws" actually emphasizes humans' lower, animal instincts and "Brute Neighbors" actually presents animals as symbols of the ideal. In the former chapter he reminds us of "an animal in us, which awakens in proportion as our higher nature slumbers. It is reptile and sensual, and perhaps cannot be wholly expelled" (219). On the other hand, he reminds us in "Brute Neighbors" that animals "are all beasts of burden, in a sense, made to carry some portion of our thoughts" (225), and he proceeds to give examples of such symbolic creatures. It is in these two chapters that an undercurrent of uncertainty is felt in a book that otherwise exudes great confidence in humans' ability to direct their own lives.

The sixth pair of chapters contrasts the warmth of his "hibernation" in the cabin during the winter—his storing of physical, intellectual, and spiritual fire for renewal in spring—to the empty, cold, deserted sites of former inhabitants of the Walden Pond woods. He finds little of significance left by the dead slaves and ne'er-do-wells who had lived there as village outcasts. As he says of one such inhabitant, Hugh Quoil, "All I know of him is tragic" (262). Their memory, he says, does not "enhance the beauty of the landscape" (264). But a note of hope in the final chapters anticipates rebirth: "Again, perhaps, Nature will try, with me for a first settler" (264). The comments on "winter visitors," which conclude the chapter, appear to have been a late addition, perhaps intended to expand this hopeful attitude by emphasizing those few friends, such as Alcott and Emerson, who were loyal enough to tramp to the hut even in winter.[26]

The seventh pair of chapters contrasts the essentially factual descriptions of various animals in "Winter Animals"—Thoreau does not load them with symbolic meanings as in "Brute Neighbors"—to further exploration of Walden Pond's symbolic implications in "The Pond in Winter." This chapter contains Thoreau's most complex exploration of Walden Pond's symbolic meaning through his discussion of the search for its bottom and the colors of its ice. "Ice," he notices, "is an interesting topic for contemplation" (297). As he describes the harvesting of the ice, he imagines it being shipped to distant ports as far as India, where "the sweltering inhabitants . . . of Madras and Bombay and Calcutta . . . drink at my well" (297–98) and thus emphasizes the universal connections among all people.

The symmetry of the book is maintained in the last two chapters, with "Spring" bringing full circle the chronological narrative started in "Where I Lived, and What I Lived For" and the "Conclusion" serving as an epilogue to balance the prologue of "Economy." "Spring" fulfills the promise of renewal announced at the beginning of "The Ponds in Winter" when Thoreau says he "awoke to an answered question, to Nature and daylight" (282). It emphasizes resurrection— "Walden was dead and is alive again" (311)—and the organic unity and artistry of nature as represented by the thawing sand in the Deep Cut, which "illustrated the principle of all of the operations of Nature" (308). Finally, the conclusion provides a parallel artistic unifying of the book's many themes, particularly the theme of the need to wake up, to see the deepest reality of life clearly, and to trust in one's ideal self. In one sense, it too is an ironic chapter, for it is not really a conclusion at all—it is instead a commencement, a call to a continual quest: "The life in us is like the water in the river. It may rise this year higher than man has ever known it, and flood the parched uplands; even this may be the eventful year, which will drown out all our muskrats" (332–33).

Interwoven on the skeleton of these contrasting chapters are thematic and symbolic motifs that flesh out Thoreau's thought. The major theme of "Economy," for instance, is simplicity, a condition Thoreau urges us to achieve throughout the book. His neighbors are depicted as having a mistaken simplicity in that "they honestly think there is no choice left" (8) except to immerse themselves in materialism. "The life which men praise and regard as successful is but one kind," he says. "Why should we exaggerate any one kind at the expense of others?" (19). This failure to consider options ironically leads them into a more rather than less complicated life: "The farmer is endeavoring to solve the problem of a livelihood by a formula more complicated than the problem itself. To get his shoestrings he speculates in herds of cattle"(33). Later in "Baker Farm" he offers John Field as the perfect example of such misguided simplicity.

Thoreau's brand of simplicity involves nothing less than a complete reversal of priorities. "The greater part of what my neighbors call good," he says, "I believe in my soul to be bad, and if I repent of any thing, it is very likely to be my good behavior" (10). He undoubtedly has in mind economic as well as moral "good" and "bad" here. An example of such a reversal is his critique of luxury, the goal of so many of his neighbors: "Most of the luxuries, and many of the so-called comforts of life, are not only not indispensable, but positive hinderances to the elevation of mankind" (14). Money is thus at best unnecessary, because it focuses our attention on the material rather than the spiritual—"Money is not required to buy one necessary of the soul," he tells us in the conclusion (329). At worst it is the proverbial root of evil. Insofar as it is done merely to get money, work also becomes unimportant when seen from a spiritual viewpoint. "As for *work*," he suggests, "we haven't any of any consequence" (93, Thoreau's emphasis), and he holds out the option that work should be "not a hardship but a pastime, if we will live simply and wisely" (70). Elsewhere he suggests that working one day and resting six might be a wiser schedule than its more common opposite.

At Walden Pond he explored this contrary concept of simplicity by defining the differences between luxuries and necessities: "It would be some advantage to live a primitive and frontier life, though in the midst of an outward civilization, if only to learn what are the gross necessaries of life and what methods have been taken to obtain them" (11). He defines a necessity as "whatever of all that man obtains by his own exertions, has been from the first, or from long use has become, so important to human life that few, if any, whether from savageness, or poverty, or philosophy, ever attempt to do without it" (12). By this definition he concludes that there are only four necessities—food, shelter, clothing, and fuel—and eventually boils even these four down to only one: heat. Food serves as an internal fuel that creates "animal heat," and the other three provide external means of maintaining that heat (13).

People have turned these necessities into luxuries, however, and have thus unnecessarily complicated their lives. The rich use so much fuel that they "are not simply kept comfortably warm, but unnaturally hot . . . they are cooked, of course, à la mode" (14). Clothing, he argues, has become more fashion than necessity, so that "there is greater anxiety, commonly, to have fashionable, or at least clean and unpatched clothes, than to have a sound conscience" (22).

His idea of necessary housing is "a large box by the railroad, six feet long by three wide, in which the laborers locked up their tools at night" (29). "Every man who was hard pushed," he says, "might get such a one for a dollar, and, having bored a few auger holes in it, to admit the air at least, get into it when it rained and at night, and hook down the lid, and so have freedom in his love, and in his soul be free. This did not appear the worst, nor by any means a despicable alternative" (29). This semicomical coffin is in one sense a criticism of his neighbors' failure to "live." But he adds, emphasizing that this is also a serious way of meeting necessity, "I am far from jesting" (29). His cabin by the pond was only a somewhat larger version of such a box, a model of simplicity in contrast to the increasingly ornate house plans being offered in the popular house pattern books of the day.[27] His furniture was equally simple, consisting of only six modest pieces: a bed, a small table, a desk, and three chairs ("one for solitude, two for friendship, three for society"—[140]).

As for food, he argues that "it would cost incredibly little trouble to obtain one's necessary food, even in this latitude; that a man may use as simple a diet as the animals, and yet retain health and strength" (61). His own diet he describes as consisting primarily of "rye and Indian meal without yeast, potatoes, rice, a very little salt pork, molasses, and salt, and my drink water" (61). Although popular misconceptions of Thoreau have often cast him as a pioneer of vegetarianism in America, the above list, as well as his account of killing and eating a woodchuck ("it afforded me a momentary enjoyment, notwithstanding a musky flavor, [but] I saw that the longest use would not make that a good practice"—[59]), make it clear that he was not a strict vegetarian, although he generally preferred not to eat meat. Nor was he a pioneer even in simplifying his diet. Horace Hosmer tells us that "these food theories were being tested by hundreds of young men besides Thoreau," including Hosmer himself.[28] This fad hardly became general practice, however, so that Thoreau complains, "so far are we from simplicity and independence that, in Concord, fresh and sweet meal is rarely sold in shops, and hominy and corn in a still coarser form are hardly used by any. For the most part the farmer gives to his cattle and hogs the grain of his own producing, and buys flour, which is at least no more wholesome, at a greater cost" (63–64). Once again the system was foolishly complicated.

Considering the ease with which these essentials of life could be obtained in his day, Thoreau questions whether America is making genuine progress in its quality of life by seeking luxuries. He affirms his belief that "civilization is a real advance in the condition of man" (31). But if it is true progress, he says, then better goods—houses, for instance—must be available without being more costly, measuring cost by the amount of time it takes to obtain them. This, he suggests, is frequently not the case. He uses the railroad as an example. Like civilization itself, the railroad is "*comparatively* good, that is, you might have done worse" (54, Thoreau's emphasis), but it is neither faster nor more economical than seemingly slower modes of transportation, because in the day it takes a traveler to earn train fare to go thirty miles, a strong walker can cover the distance by foot at no cost (53). Thus, he says, "if the railroad reached around the world, I think I should keep ahead of you" (53). Considering, as he tells us later in "Where I Lived" and "Sounds," that the railroad is built by exploitation of cheap labor and that its task is not "as heroic and commanding as it is protracted and unwearied" (117), its value as progress is even more doubtful. Although it is unlikely that he would have fared as well against an airplane today, the point about relative cost is interesting even in the twentieth century.

Rather than such dubious material progress, Thoreau urges his readers to consider aiming for true spiritual progress: "Rather than love, than money, than fame, give me truth" (330). "In the long run," he says, "men hit only what they aim at. Therefore, though they should fail immediately, they had better aim at something high" (27). "Economy" very effectively demonstrates how low people generally aim, and the rest of the book attempts to persuade them to raise their sight.

For Thoreau the most practical view of life is the most spiritual. The problem of living is to see reality accurately, *both* physically and spiritually. The crucial question of vision that he poses his audience in "Sounds" is "Will you be a reader, a student merely, or a seer?" (111). The key word is "seer," and like *Walden* itself it has a double meaning. He challenges us to see natural facts more accurately, but he also urges us to be "seers" in the sense of mystical prophet, someone who perceives the spiritual truth contained within nature's facts. The dilemma is described even more precisely in "Where I Lived": "I perceive that we inhabitants of New England live this mean life that we do because our vision does not penetrate the surface of things. We think that *is* which *appears* to be. If a man should walk through this town and see only the reality, where, think you, would the 'Mill-dam' go to?" (96, Thoreau's emphasis). The transcendental answer is, of course, that the Milldam would disappear because the material world is not "real" to one who perceives higher spiritual reality.

But Thoreau's further dilemma, like the reader's, is that he does not really want the Milldam to disappear. As he suggested in *A Week,* he is not enough of a transcendental purist to reject physical reality entirely. In "Sounds" he even has some praise for the commerce represented by the railroad and, by extension, the Milldam: "What recommends commerce to me is its enterprise and bravery" (118). He speaks of commerce as "unexpectedly confident and serene, alert, adventurous, and unwearied," as well as, surprisingly, "very natural in its methods" (119). If he later saw commerce as an activity worse than crime, it was because he saw America's interest in balancing the Milldam's reality with transcendental reality fading fast.

Few could see past the temptations of the Milldam to become true seers able to read "the language which all things and events speak without metaphor" (111). The seer must be able to see physical reality accurately—a task hard enough in itself, as Thoreau's own journal volumes of scientific observations prove—but also to see the symbolic spiritual meaning contained in the physical. Seers must see both kinds of reality, balance them, and by adding their own insights express the meaning of the relationship between the two. In his journal Thoreau depicts the seer (who is the Poet of *A Week*) as a mirror that does not merely reflect images unchanged but modifies them in the act of reflecting: "The poet must bring to Nature the smooth mirror in which she is to be reflected. He must be something superior to her, something more than natural. He must furnish equanimity" (*Writings* 11:183–84).

Thoreau's descriptions of animals present perfect examples of this double vision of nature. The two chapters that focus most fully on animals, "Brute Neighbors" and "Winter Animals," deal with them in opposite ways. The former begins with the comic dialogue in which the "Hermit" leaves his meditation to go fishing with the "Poet," thus apparently abandoning transcendental for physical reality. Immediately after that dialogue, however, Thoreau reminds us that even animals have their transcendental and symbolic meaning and "carry some portion of our thoughts" (225). His symbolic presentation of these animals is much less arbitrary and much more effective than the symbolic catalog of fish in *A Week*, because the meaning now seems to develop more naturally out of the fact. The eyes of young partridges suggest quite naturally "the purity of infancy," but they also express "a wisdom clarified by experience" (227), presumably the experience of achieving their own precarious survival even thus young. The famous ant war stands on its own as a narrative masterpiece and factual observation of nature, but the transition to seeing it as a mock epic of human battle representing humanity's courage and tragic pride is quite natural. The ants become Greek "Myrmidons" (the Greek word means "ants"); a particularly fierce ant becomes an Achilles; and Thoreau comments, "I was myself excited somewhat even as if they had been men. The more you think of it, the less the difference" (230). The "winged cat" about whom Thoreau becomes curious is also described first as a scientific phenomenon but finally as a symbol for the poet's soaring aspirations: "This would have been the right kind of cat for me to keep, if I had kept any; for why should not a poet's cat be winged as well as his horse?" (233).

In "Winter Animals," however, Thoreau presents his animals almost wholly "without metaphor." Although frequently given human traits, they do not clearly represent any higher meaning. The description of the fox hunt, for instance, is compelling narrative, but there is little hint of symbolic import. Nor does he burden with symbolism the descriptions of owls, jays, and rabbits in this chapter. It is as if the onset of winter has chilled the writer's symbolic vision, as if his ability to be a "seer" is in hibernation awaiting the "morning atmosphere" of spring. The facts are carefully and vividly recorded in the belief, expressed in his earliest journals, that "the fact will one day flower out into a truth" (*Writings* 7:18). Later in "Spring," when the "influx of light" fills Thoreau's hut announcing the season, it is accompanied by the arrival not only of the traditional robin but also of geese who settle onto the pond, symbolically suggesting that both natural and spiritual rebirths are occurring.

The double vision that Thoreau seeks, while possible at any chronological time, is symbolically a morning or springtime phenomenon. In "Economy" he complains that most people's "morning work" is mere housekeeping rather than the true seeing that morning light invites (36). Later in "Where I Lived" this invitation is explicit as a main theme: "Every morning was a cheerful invitation to make my life of equal simplicity, and I may say innocence, with Nature herself" (88). For Thoreau morning was not so much a time of day as a state of mind—a state of visual, intellectual, and spiritual alertness: "Morning is when I am awake and there is dawn in me. Moral reform is the effort to throw off sleep" (90). (Note the pun here on Thoreau's name.) Most people, he argues, are never even partially awake intellectually or spiritually. "The millions are awake enough for physical labor," he says, "but only one in a million is awake enough for effective intellectual exertion, only one in a hundred millions to a poetic or divine life. To be awake is to be alive" (90). This statement harks us back to the book's opening address to those "who are said to live in New England" and suggests the probable falsity of the rumor. Although he is Chanticleer crowing to awaken his neighbors to new life, he knows that ultimately they must learn to keep themselves awake: "We must learn to reawaken and keep ourselves awake, not by mechanical aids, but by an infinite expectation of the dawn" (90). His own experience at the pond suggested to him that such sustained awakening, although rare, is possible. "I know of no more encouraging fact," he says, "than the unquestionable ability of man to elevate his life by constant endeavor" (90). It is on that hope that all of *Walden* is based. It is expressed in the conclusion in his desire to speak "like a man in a waking moment, to men in their waking moments" (324) and by his belief that "the sun is but a morning star" (333).

These motifs of morning and light merge quite smoothly with traditional Christian symbols of resurrection, so that by the conclusion of the book Thoreau is no longer the comic outsider or the outcast prophet-preacher, but rather a welcome herald announcing a familiar concept of rebirth in familiar language. As spring arrives, Thoreau tells us that "Walden was dead and is alive again" (311). The spring light suggests that "all things must live in such a light. O Death, where was thy sting? O Grave, where was thy victory, then?" (317). In such a mood and in such light, even the ugliest truths, such as the dead horse decaying on the path to the pond, could seem beautiful. This grand confidence in rebirth makes *Walden,* as Stanley Edgar Hyman says, "a vast rebirth ritual, the purest and most complete in our literature."[29] Thus by finally adapting the village's religious vocabulary to his own ideas, Thoreau is symbolically reintegrated into the village, which he hopes has by now taken his advice and at least started to wake up.

The optimism of this rebirth ritual is not without at least some qualification, however. In a book of paradoxes Thoreau's optimism is also tinged with skepticism. Unlike the early Emerson, Thoreau cannot be accused of oversimplifying life by ignoring its darker side. His darker skepticism is, to be sure, only an undercurrent in *Walden,* but a comprehensive view of the work requires that it be explored, especially because it resides in the book's central symbol, Walden Pond itself.[30] Walden Pond is a much more complex symbol than most casual readers are likely to notice.[31] On the one hand, it clearly supports the optimistic motifs of seeing, light, and morning. On the other hand, there is a mystery about the pond that is unsettling to both Thoreau and the reader.

Thoreau clearly connects the pond to the act of seeing by describing it as both a mirror and an eye. As a mirror, it reflects symbolically the interrelation between the material and spiritual worlds. In "Where I Lived" he speaks of its "smooth reflecting surface" and emphasizes its symbolic reflections: "A lake like this is never smoother than at such a time [an overcast day]; and the clear portion of the air above it being shallow and darkened by clouds, the water, full of light and reflections, becomes a lower heaven itself so much the more important" (86). He emphasizes this same quality again in "The Ponds," where he describes Walden Pond as "a mirror which no stone can crack" that "betrays the spirit that is in the air" (188). His symbolic point is that one need not look afar (to the heavens) for spiritual truth; it can be found close at hand everywhere. "Olympus is but the outside of the earth every where" (85).

The pond reflects objects on the shore as well, and, like the Concord and Merrimack rivers, in this way becomes an art gallery of nature's masterpieces: "Each morning the manager of this gallery substituted some new picture, distinguished by more brilliant or harmonious coloring, for the old upon the walls" (240). The pond thus proves to be "intermediate in its nature between land and sky" (188). Thoreau's hut near the shore becomes, like the seashore at Cape Cod later, a "trivial" ("tri-vial" meaning "three-way" or a crossroads) place where he could view the main elements of nature—earth, water, and sky—at once and where humanity, nature, and God could be united.

The pond thus provided a unique point of view from which the artist could view nature, either from its shore or from the pond itself—in a boat in summer or on the ice in winter. In summer he finds that "the forest has never so good a setting, nor is so distinctly beautiful as when seen from the middle of a small lake amid hills which rise from the water's edge" (185) and in winter such ponds provide "new views from their surfaces of the familiar landscape around them" (271). In both cases the middle of the pond gave the artist centrality in that he could see approximately equidistance all around, and it provided the perspective from nature's details that allowed him to see the whole forest as well as the trees, which enabled him artistically and spiritually to compose and unify the view.[32]

By providing such a point of view, the pond is not only "earth's eye" (186) but also a supplement to the artist's own eyes. Playing on the cliché of the eyes being the windows of the soul, Thoreau suggests that the color of Walden's "eye," which is "blue at one time and green at another" (176), indicates its intermediate position, and its water's "crystalline purity" suggests a symbolic moral purity of nature against which one can "measure the depth of his own nature" (186) and against which the artist can measure the spiritual purity of his or her vision.

In the reflecting eye of Walden Pond, Thoreau saw an analogy for his own role as artist-seer. Both the seer and the pond were poets in their ability to capture the relationship between subject and object and between heaven and earth, and both could reveal the new and beautiful truth it contained. Like God, nature and humanity were creators and revealers of truth. The poet's role was to help others to see that relationship so that they could quit their lives of quiet desperation and become creative seers and reflectors of truth themselves. Thus both the mirror and eye motifs associated with the pond express optimism about people's ability to awaken to the truths around them.

This optimism is subtly undercut, however, by Thoreau's frequent comments on his neighbors' belief that Walden Pond is bottomless. In "Where I Lived" Thoreau announces the search for truth, for "a hard bottom and rocks in place, which we can call *reality*" (98, Thoreau's emphasis), on which to base his life firmly, and he concludes the chapter with the beginning of that search: "here I will begin to mine" (98). But although he does some digging to build his cabin and to plant his beanfield, his search for the foundation of truth involves more diving than mining.[33]

Even before his extended discussion of the search for Walden's depths in "The Ponds in Winter," he hints at it several times. In describing Alek Therien in "Visitors" he finds Therien to be like other humble but honest fellows "who are as bottomless even as Walden Pond" (150), thus suggesting that the depth he seeks is within people as well as in nature. Again in "The Ponds" he briefly says of Walden Pond that "some think it is bottomless" (178) and describes its water as appearing even to him to be "seemingly bottomless" (189). Thus he prepares the reader to consider carefully the detailed and crucial description of his search for Walden's floor.

In "The Ponds in Winter" he recounts at greater length the myths of Walden's bottomlessness, expressing dismay at "how long men will believe in the bottomlessness of a pond without taking the trouble to sound it" (285). These are men who are not yet awake and are thus unable or unwilling to front the facts. Even when they take a weight and a wagon-load of rope to measure the pond, they ignore the evidence, falling victim to their own preconceptions: "while the 'fifty-six' [weight] was resting by the way, they were paying out the rope in the vain attempt to fathom their truly immeasurable capacity for marvellousness" (285). Thoreau, however, easily finds the bottom of the pond "with a cod-line and a stone weighing about a pound and a half" (286). "I can assure my readers," he says, "that Walden has a reasonably tight bottom at a not unreasonable, though at an unusual, depth" (285). The survey map of Walden Pond, which is unfortunately left out of many editions of *Walden,* is thus crucial to Thoreau's meaning, for in recording the depths of the various parts of the pond it verifies that humans are capable of fronting the facts of the natural world regardless of how difficult the task may be thought to be.

Furthermore, the map suggests the possibility of deducing not only natural, but also moral and spiritual principles from these facts, for "the imagination, give it the least license, dives deeper and soars higher than Nature goes" (288). Upon examining the depths recorded on his map, he finds "that the line of greatest length intersected the line of greatest breadth *exactly* at the point of greatest depth" (289, Thoreau's emphasis). He then speculates about whether "this hint would conduct to the deepest part of the ocean as well as of a pond or puddle" and that it may be "the rule also for the height of mountains" (289). Not content to have discovered a natural law, he proceeds to apply this "law of average" to ethics: "draw lines through the length and breadth of the aggregate of a man's particular daily behaviors and waves of life into his coves and inlets, and where they intersect will be the height or depth of his character" (291). This last metaphor is perhaps more clever than it is clear, for he does not discuss in what terms a person's character is to be defined. His main point, however, is that nature contains spiritual and moral principles as well as facts for those who can "see" well enough to find them. Thus the searcher can apparently hope for eventual success in finding the "hard rock" of truth beneath

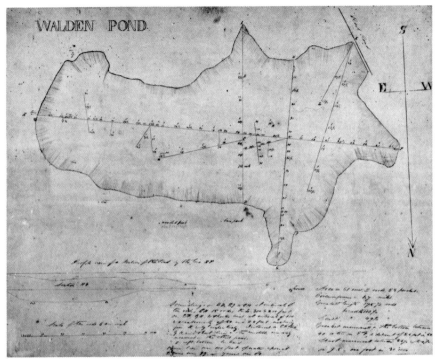

Thoreau's survey map of Walden Pond.
Reproduced courtesy of the Concord Free Public Library.

and within nature's facts if one is open to discoveries such as Thoreau makes in "The Ponds in Winter."

Even as he affirms this confidence in success, however, Thoreau simultaneously undercuts it by apparently approving of the very delusion he has just debunked: "I am thankful that this pond was made deep and pure for a symbol. While men believe in the infinite some ponds will be thought to be bottomless" (287). This statement leaves the reader in a quandry, one best expressed by Walter Benn Michaels: "is he [Thoreau] glad that the pond is *only* deep so that tough-minded men like himself can sound it and discover its hard bottom, or is he glad that the pond is so deep that it deceives men into thinking of it as bottomless and so leads them into meditations on the infinite?" (Michaels's emphasis)[34] Michaels wisely prefers the second explanation, but even it leaves the reader with a problem. For if "be it life or death, we crave only reality" (98), must we ignore physical reality in order to meditate on the infinite, or is Thoreau suggesting that we can have both?

Michaels's view is that Thoreau, by the paradoxes of *Walden,* purposely tries "to show us that we do have choices left and, by breaking down hierarchies into contradictory alternatives, to insist upon our making them."[35] This is an accurate and important observation, as is Michaels's recognition of a "principle of uncertainty"[36] in *Walden* that refuses to let the reader become too comfortable with any one view of reality. This sort of fruitful discomfort is precisely what Thoreau intends. But Michaels stops just short of Thoreau's ultimate purpose when he suggests that he leaves the reader in an impossible predicament ("It's heads I win, tails you lose") in which the only certainty seems to be that there is no certainty.[37]

Thoreau firmly believes that we must search for both kinds of reality. In "Spring" there is a passage that might well be taken as a main theme not only of *Walden* but of all Thoreau's writing: "At the same time that we are earnest to explore and learn all things, we require that all things be mysterious and unexplorable, that land and sea be infinitely wild, unsurveyed and unfathomable by us because unfathomable" (317–18). This is certainly a paradox of the human condition, but Thoreau is not merely reminding us of human fickleness. He is explaining the two elements of true seeing.

First, the seer must be willing thoroughly to "explore and learn all things" in the physical world. Without first fronting such facts, no higher reality is likely to be seen. But perception must not stop with the recording of mere fact. The seer must be aware of the higher (or, in the case of the pond, lower) spiritual truths contained in those facts, truths that, because they emanate from God through nature, are infinite and can never be fully understood. These two types of perception may often occur in sequence, for the seer is likely first to notice nature's beauty and only later apprehend its truths. But Thoreau's goal is a simultaneous perception of the full meaning of both physical and spiritual reality, the fact flowering out into a truth.

Thoreau claims a firmer reality for nature than Emerson does. But he is still very much a transcendentalist in insisting that perception must go through but also beyond nature. In this context, what in "Higher Laws" appears to be mere Victorian squeamishness about diet and sex begins to make sense. Again Thoreau's double vision at first appears to contradict itself: "I found in myself, and still find, an instinct toward a higher, or, as it is named, spiritual life, as do most men, and another toward a primitive rank and savage one, and I reverence them both" (210). He can be "thrilled to think that I owed a mental perception to the commonly gross sense of taste" but on the same page complain "how they, how you and I, can live this slimy beastly life, eating and drinking" (218). The problem is again one of staying spiritually awake, for "the animal in us," he says, "awakens in proportion as our higher nature slumbers" (219). For the person who is spiritually awake, however, "the spirit can for the time pervade and control every member and function of the body, and transmute what in form is the grossest sensuality into purity and devotion" (219). The sensual life is a necessary, if sometimes a regrettable, beginning, but it is only a start toward full "seeing." In "Higher Laws" Thoreau provides his most emphatic warning of the danger of staying on the surface of sensuality and not diving deeper or soaring higher to seek spiritual truth: "Nature is hard to overcome, but she must be overcome" (221). Thoreau is not denying the value of nature; he is warning us (and, since he was occasionally of a mind to fall in love with a shrub oak, himself) about its limitations.

Walden is thus an invitation to an exploration without end. As he says in his journal, "Life is not long enough for one success" (*Writings* 8:316). The universe will always be wider than our view of it (320) and it may be that like the traveler sinking in the bog in *Walden's* conclusion we may find that, while "there is a solid bottom everywhere," one may "have not got halfway to it yet" before one dies (330). One may, however, have several more lives to live after death; Thoreau, at least, seemed confident that he did and faced death cheerfully.[38] It may to some extent be true that he set impossible goals for himself in order not to risk failing to achieve them, but he also deeply believed that the human quest for truth is necessarily incomplete within one lifetime.

Thoreau thus extols the value of the search for truth without promising any foreseeable limits to that search or to the benefits one may derive from it. As he warns the reader in "Economy," "We may not arrive at our port within a calculable period, but we would preserve the true course" (71). It is a course most readers have not yet taken, for "most have not delved six feet beneath the surface, nor leaped as many above it. We know not where we are. Besides we are sound asleep half our time" (332). *Walden* raises many questions, and whatever answers it may seem to suggest are only temporary and partial. Thoreau found the physical bottom of the pond, but he never exhausted its symbolic meaning, nor did he ever find its physical source. "As for the inlet or outlet of Walden," he says, "I have not discovered any but rain and snow and evaporation" (292). (He was only partially right; Walden Pond has since been found to be a natural spring that rises and falls with the water table of the Concord-Lincoln area.)[39]

By the pond Thoreau established a firm base for his own exploration of the infinite, as he advises his readers to do: "If you have built castles in the air, your work need not be lost; that is where they should be. Now put the foundations under them" (324). Such foundations, he warns, can only be found outside the boundaries of everyday life, which is "always on the limits, trying to get into business and trying to get out of debt" (6). The exploration beyond these boundaries often requires sailing by dead reckoning and involves the risk of getting lost, like the two men who got lost on a dark night between the pond and Concord (170–71). Getting lost is, however, part of the search, for "not till we are lost, in other words, not till we have lost the world, do we begin to find ourselves, and realize where we are and the infinite extent of our relations" (171). *Walden* itself is such an exploration. Thoreau's goal in the work is to be *"extra-vagant,"* that is, "to speak somewhere *without* bounds like a man in a waking moment, to men in their waking moments" (324, Thoreau's emphases). It is better to risk getting lost beyond the usual boundaries than to play it safe and stay home, for "a man sits as many risks as he runs" (153). Thoreau believes that such risks can be taken with confidence, however, for "we are constantly, though unconsciously, steering like pilots by certain well-known beacons and headlands, and if we go beyond our usual course we still carry in our minds the bearing of some neighboring cape" (171).

Despite the uncertainty of finding bottom immediately and the probability that one will never find all of the truth in one lifetime, Thoreau opts for faith in the value of the search, a search each person must make essentially alone. True, the Old Settler (God) and the Elderly Dame (Nature) will always be available in the highest sense, and society will always try to insinuate its own values into the search. But as Stanley Cavell says, "The drift of *Walden* is that we *are* alone, *and* that we are never alone—not in the highest and not in the lowest sense" (Cavell's emphases).[40] It is a journey that requires traveling unknown paths beyond the bounds of society, but one that will bring us out right at last.

Thoreau knew the spiritual danger involved in the journey. It was still possible that he was deceived and that his course was not the true one, that "the reptile and sensual . . . cannot be wholly expelled," and that the dead horse on the path is in fact only a dead horse rather than a symbol that "nature is so rife with life that myriads can be afforded to be sacrificed" (318). That he felt he had often given in to the "reptile and sensual" is suggested by his own mea culpa at the end of "Economy": "I never dreamed of any enormity greater than I have committed. I never knew, and never shall know, a worse man than myself" (78). Even when his course seemed the true one, he was aware of the danger of being tempted from it. Fishing and hunting, for instance, he praises as a necessary phase of every boy's (and perhaps every civilization's) education but a phase that must eventually be passed through because it involves the violence toward nature which humanity must transcend. Of his own fishing as an adult he says: "I cannot fish without falling a little in self-respect" (213). Yet he also realizes that "if I were to live in a wilderness I should again be tempted to become a fisher and hunter in earnest" (214). But his stay by the pond gave him enough evidence for optimism to overcome such doubts about himself in *Walden*.

Two other passages from *Walden* deserve special attention as illustrations of his struggle to find and affirm the truth of his experience at the pond. The first is his game of "checkers" with the loon on the pond: "It was a pretty game, played on the smooth surface of the pond, a man against a loon. Suddenly your adversary's checker disappears beneath the board, and the problem is to place yours nearest to where his will appear again" (235). The loon, the animal with whom he identified perhaps more closely than any other, outsmarts him with every dive so that he is forced to admit that "I could not get within half a dozen rods of him" (234). Here is one creature in nature Thoreau cannot fully know. He can only imagine "how surprised must the fishes be to see this ungainly visitor from another sphere speeding his way amid their schools!" (235). The loon can probe firsthand the mystery of Walden's bottom, which Thoreau can only fathom secondhand with a line and sinker, for the loon has "time and ability to visit the bottom of the pond in its deepest part" (235).

The loon in one sense represents the ideal of what Thoreau himself would like to do: get to the bottom of spiritual truth. But at the same time it represents Thoreau's human inability to achieve that goal; the loon is nature's mystery, its wildness incarnate. So there is also something demonic and sinister beneath the silliness of its taunting call: "His usual note was this demonic laughter . . . but occasionally, when he had balked me most successfully and come up a long way off, he uttered a long-drawn unearthly howl, probably more like that of a wolf than any bird" (236). The loon provides "the wildest sound that is ever heard here" and thus makes Thoreau deeply aware of his own human limitations in seeking the "unfathomable" mysteries of nature. It also raises the unsettling possibility that nature is not always a human ally and reserves some truths for itself alone. Overriding such doubts, however, is the essentially jovial kinship between Thoreau and the loon, which suggests nature's ultimate benevolence toward the human quest. The loon seems to enjoy playing the game, even though it will not yet let Thoreau win. Amid the familiar surroundings of Walden Pond, then, Thoreau could at least temporarily discount the loon's demonic and mysterious qualities and opt for affirmation, an affirmation that would be harder to maintain in the less benign wilderness of Maine or on the sands of Cape Cod.

The other key illustration of Thoreau's affirmative attitude in *Walden* is the myth of the artist of Kouroo, who, like Thoreau himself, "was disposed to strive after perfection" (326). Thoreau did indeed believe that one should as long as possible "live free and uncommitted" (84), except in one's commitment to the search for truth. The artist of Kouroo makes such a commitment in attempting to make a staff "perfect in all respects, though I should do nothing else in my life" (326). Like Thoreau, the artist accepts the probability that perfection cannot be achieved in a lifetime. The Kouroo artist's denial of time's importance negates time's influence, endowing him with perennial youth. When he finishes the staff after many centuries, he finds that he has made not only a staff but "a world with full and fair proportions," for "the material was pure, and his art was pure; how could the result be other than wonderful?" (327). This transcendental myth, together with the myth of the wonderful bug that concludes the book, expresses Thoreau's rock-bottom confidence that preserving a true spiritual course beyond the materialistic bounds of one's usual routine can lead to "success unexpected in common hours" (323), even if one must find that success after death.

But *Walden* is also a demonstration of how close to a perfect combination of life and art an artist can come in one lifetime. In writing *Walden,* Thoreau, like the artist of Kouroo was completely committed to his project. He ultimately achieved an artistic unity in *Walden* that derives from its images being so thoroughly a part of Thoreau's own experience that he naturally and necessarily expressed his truths in terms of sunlight, waking, seeing, and exploration. It was these that had given his life new meaning at the pond, and it was with these that he filled his book. As F. O. Matthiessen says of Thoreau: "He had understood that in the act of expression a man's whole being, and his natural and social background as well, function organically together."[41] In *Walden* he achieved this organic unity as nearly perfectly as he would ever do, not by ignoring the dark mysteries within nature and himself, but by fronting the fact that such mysteries exist and by affirming the strength of the human spirit to cope with them.

Chapter Four
Exploring the Sublime in *The Maine Woods*

Although Thoreau saw the Concord woods as a microcosm in which he could "explore and learn all things," he also recognized the danger of becoming too comfortable in such a microcosm. The "true course" could easily become a rut, even at Walden Pond. "I had not lived there a week," he says, "before my feet wore a path from my door to the pond-side" (*Walden,* 323).

To avoid such ruts he advised both his neighbors and himself to explore the infinitely advancing frontiers of nature and of the human mind. It was wise for his neighbors occasionally to go beyond the village's limits to take "the tonic of wilderness—to wade sometimes in marshes where the bittern and the meadowlark lurk" (*Walden* 317). Once they had explored the marshes and swamps around Concord, other more distant places would undoubtedly call them. Thus nature would keep them psychologically and spiritually awake in anticipation of views ever new and wild. The wild became for Thoreau a counterpoint to society's ruts and a symbol for human potential: as long as wilderness existed somewhere, humans could trust that they had not exhausted their potential for achieving harmony with nature and God.

The seer of Walden too felt the need to pursue the "mysterious and unexplorable," to keep crossing those ever advancing borders that seemed to spread around him like ripples on the pond around a thrown rock. He could bemoan the loss of bears and cougars from the Concord woods, but he could also rejoice that "Thank Heaven, here is not all the world. The buck-eye does not grow in New England, and the mocking-bird is rarely heard there" (*Walden,* 320). True, traveling might spiritually be only "great-circle sailing" (*Walden,* 320), and it was possible to explore one's own inner wilderness without ever leaving home. Sometimes, however, a new natural environment seemed helpful, perhaps even necessary, in making new discoveries and in keeping the inner person ever new. As he says in *The Maine Woods,* "not only for strength, but for beauty, the poet must, from time to time, travel the logger's path and the Indian's trail, to drink at some new and more bracing fountain of the Muses, far in the recesses of the wilderness."[1]

Until shortly before his death, Thoreau was either unable or unwilling to pursue the wilderness of the Far West with other American explorers. His youthful plan to go West with his brother had been blocked by John's new job. Then after John's death, Thoreau had economic and emotional responsibilities to his family too strong to allow prolonged absence. Finally later in life he was simply too intellectually and artistically dependent on the Concord environment to leave it for long. Fortunately there was wilderness near at hand in the Maine woods.

Life

Ktaadn.   Thoreau chose the Maine woods as the wilderness to explore both because of its closeness and because of family connections. George Thatcher—a cousin from Bangor, Maine—was an enthusiastic sportsman eager to accompany Thoreau into the wilderness, which he did on Thoreau's first two trips. Thoreau eventually made three trips into the Maine wilderness: the first in 1846, the second in 1853, and the third in 1857.

The first trip was prompted partly by accounts of ascending Mount Katahdin (Ktaadn) in the works of geologist Charles T. Jackson (Emerson's brother-in-law) and in an article in the 5 August 1845 Boston *Daily Advertiser.*[2] But it was also rooted in certain parts of his Walden experiment. Most obviously, a trip to the wilderness would allow him to test the validity of his own attempt at a "primitive and frontier life, though in the midst of an outward civilization" (*Walden,* 11) by experiencing such a life outside the midst of that civilization. The Maine woods also seemed to offer a very practical economic alternative similar to that he was testing at the pond: a good, simple life in nature at little or no monetary cost. As he asks in "Ktaadn," "cannot the immigrant, who can pay his fare to New York or Boston, pay five dollars more to get here,—I paid three all told, for my passage from Boston to Bangor, 250 miles,—and be as rich as he pleases, where land virtually costs nothing, and houses only the labor of building, and he may begin life as Adam did?" (MW, 14). In the Maine woods there were also Indians, the originators of the primitive and frontier life, whom he wished to study firsthand. Finally, his daily encounters with the railroad at the pond made him curious to trace at least one part of

America's economic system, the lumber industry, to its source to see if it was indeed as "alert, adventurous, and unwearied" as it sometimes seemed (*Walden,* 119).

On his first trip Thoreau left Boston by steamer to Bangor on 31 August 1846. In Bangor he met Thatcher and two other businessmen who were going into the wilderness to investigate what damage to their land holdings a recent freshet might have caused. At Oldtown they at first employed as guides an Indian named Louis Neptune and his companion.[3] When the Indians failed to meet them at George McCauslin's farm, Thoreau's party enlisted McCauslin and Tom Fowler, both experienced backwoodsmen, as guides. They traveled by batteau up the west branch of the Penobscot River to the mouth of Abol Stream, and from there on 7 September they hiked cross-country to Mount Katahdin.[4] They chose a direct route up to the south peak (somewhat below the mountain's true peak), a route just east of the Abol Trail rockslide that had been used by the few previous climbers.

They climbed until they could see the plateau below the summit in late afternoon. Thoreau, eager to take advantage of the view, climbed on above the tree line while the others made camp, but he soon returned to find that they had chosen an uncomfortable rock shelf as a campsite. The next morning they started for the summit, but only Thoreau was energetic enough to climb to the tableland below the summit, where he found a chaotic scenery of rocks and clouds that was quite startling. He did not continue on to the actual summit, however, perhaps because of the clouds or perhaps (as he claimed) because he knew his companions were anxious to depart.

Whatever the reason, he rejoined his group for the descent, part of which took them over desolate burnt land. They finished their descent by mid-afternoon. Returning to Tom Fowler's farm the next day, they found Louis Neptune and his friends still recovering from a severe hangover, the result of several days of drinking. After an overnight stay at McCauslin's, the group returned to Bangor, where Thoreau caught a steamer to Boston on 11 September.[5]

Chesuncook. Although the ascent of Katahdin had a great impact on Thoreau, his first trip failed to educate him about logging and Indians. Thus when he returned in September 1853 Thatcher was careful to choose a guide who was both Indian and lumberman so that, as Thoreau tells us, "I might have an opportunity to study his ways" (MW, 93). This guide was Joe Aitteon, the twenty-four-year-old son of the Indian governor. Thoreau and Thatcher set out by wagon from Bangor on 15 September and met Aitteon, who had gone on ahead to make preparations for the trip, at Moosehead Lake the next day.

After riding the length of Moosehead Lake on a steamer, the three set out by canoe for Chesuncook Lake up the west branch of the Penobscot. All the while they kept their eyes alert for moose, which on this trip represented ultimate wildness to Thoreau almost as fully as the mountain had on the previous trip. They did not see a moose until the second day, when Thatcher shot a female at the edge of a meadow. Thoreau made shift to measure the carcass with some knotted cord but later found his measurements to be completely inaccurate. Although Thoreau seems not to have been very distressed at witnessing the shooting of the moose, Aitteon's skinning of the unlucky beast was a different matter. After seeing "the ghastly naked red carcass appearing within its seemly robe" (MW, 115), Thoreau had had enough of moose hunting. The sight, which later haunted him often, deterred him from participating in Thatcher's subsequent hunting; he spent his time botanizing instead.

The three reached Chesuncook Lake on 18 September and spent the evening on the farm of Ansel Smith, a venerable pioneer whose life seemed a more primitive and permanent version of Thoreau's own experiment at Walden. The next day they explored further up the Penobscot and camped with a band of Indians, who at last gave Thoreau the opportunity to observe Indian life closely and to learn some Indian vocabulary. On the nineteenth, awaking to rain, they decided to return to Bangor, which they reached two days later. After spending several days visiting the Thatchers and observing the Oldtown Indians constructing their canoes, Thoreau returned to Concord on the twenty-seventh, feeling that he had at last seen a significant slice of Indian life.[6]

The Allegash and East Branch.   Thoreau took a third trip to the Maine woods in July and August of 1857, accompanied by Edward Hoar, a Concord friend who had wilderness experience recently acquired in California.[7] The two left Concord on 20 July and arrived in Bangor the next day. This time Thatcher chose not to go along, but he enlisted an Indian guide, Joe Polis, for Thoreau and Hoar. On 22 July the two Concordians and their guide (with his canoe) took the stagecoach north to Greenville and Moosehead Lake. The following day they departed up Moosehead Lake with a canoe filled to the brim with supplies. Thoreau soon discovered that Joe Polis was an even better source of Indian lore than Joe Aitteon, so throughout the trip he pestered Polis about Indian words and woodcraft.

This excursion was Thoreau's longest in the Maine woods, taking him from Moosehead Lake to Chesuncook and eventually Chamberlain and Allegash lakes, down Webster Brook north of Mount Katahdin, and then back to Bangor by the east branch of the Penobscot. He arrived back in Oldtown on 3 August after eleven days in the wilderness. On this trip he also received his harshest taste of wildness. Having begun somewhat earlier in the summer than on previous trips, he and his companions were plagued by mosquitoes and black flies. He and Hoar took a wrong turn one day and wandered off miles down a muddy path before Polis could find them, and Hoar got lost one evening and was not found until the next morning. On parts of the trip the rapids were so dangerous that only Polis could shoot them in the canoe while Thoreau and Hoar struggled with the supplies through the dense underbrush along the bank. The hard going gave Hoar such sore feet that they decided not to ascend Mount Katahdin as planned.

The trip provided the fullest test Thoreau had yet had of his own ability to survive the deepest wilderness. The reactions of his companions suggest that he passed the test very handily. Polis liked him well enough to share woodlore freely with him, to challenge him to a portage race in jest, and to trust him with some very difficult and dangerous paddling. Hoar would later write admiringly of "Thoreau's courage and manliness" and vouch for his woodcraft: "nobody who had seen him among the Penobscot rocks and rapids, the Indian trusting his life and his canoe to his skill, promptitude, and nerve, would ever doubt it."[8]

According to his usual practice, Thoreau transformed notes from each of these three trips into lectures and eventually essays. "Ktaadn," the account of his first trip, was given as a lecture at the Concord Lyceum in January of 1848 and was published in five parts in *Sartain's Union Magazine* from July to November 1848.[9] Thus its publication date preceded both *A Week* and *Walden*.

"Chesuncook" was given as a lecture to the Concord Lyceum in December 1853 but was not published until 1858 when James Russell Lowell requested part of the Maine woods material for the *Atlantic Monthly*. Although by then Thoreau had a draft of his essay about the third trip, out of fear of offending Joe Polis he held it back and offered "Chesuncook" instead. "Chesuncook" was published, under protest from Thoreau, in three installments in June, July, and August of 1858. Thoreau's protest concerned Lowell's unauthorized deletion of a statement about the immortality of a pine tree, and the ensuing dispute soured Thoreau permanently on Lowell and led eventually to Lowell's ill-tempered essay on Thoreau.[10]

Because "Chesuncook" was still being revised after Thoreau's third trip, it contains some material from that later trip; and "The Allegash and East Branch" contains some material from notes on the second trip. Although Thoreau offered "The Allegash and East Branch" to *Putnam's* as early as 1858, it was not published until Channing and Sophia Thoreau collected the three essays as a book and published them as *The Maine Woods* through Ticknor and Fields in 1864. Thoreau did not quite finish his revisions of "The Allegash and East Branch" before he died.

Art

Structure. Indications that Thoreau may have planned his Maine woods essays to be printed as a book occur as early as 1858.[11] Whether he might have followed his habit of condensing time as he does in *A Week* and *Walden* if he had lived to put the book together, we can never know. As assembled by his sister and Channing, however, the book stands as an anthology of three separate but related narratives distinct in events and style but unified by theme.

"Ktaadn," by far the earliest of the three, is clearly related by imagery and style to his first two books. As in *A Week,* in "Ktaadn" Thoreau elegizes "mute, inglorious Miltons" (MW, 18), shows special interest in the relation between history and mythology (54), and depicts the climbing of a mountain as a central symbolic episode. "Ktaadn" also has obvious similarities to *Walden* in that it records Thoreau's attempts to extend his experiment with primitive life from the tame beauty of the pond to the actual wilderness and to explore the extreme boundaries of life. Instead of delving to the bottom of the pond, he here seeks truth at the top of Katahdin. Even stylistic echoes of *Walden* creep into "Ktaadn," as when he describes the mountain as "connecting the heavens with the earth" (33) just as the pond did, or when he dwells on "the glassy smoothness" of a wilderness lake (40) and calls a mountain surrounded by lakes "a jewel of the first water" (80), a pun he uses in *Walden* also. There is also the occasional note of personal frustration that we hear as an undercurrent in *Walden* as well.

Comparing his own thoughts and goals to a log jam, he pleads, "O make haste, ye gods, with your winds and rains, and start the jam before it rots" (53). Finally, there is in "Ktaadn" a mixture of fact and philosophy that is much closer to that of *A Week* and *Walden* than to that of its two companion essays.

"Chesuncook" is less philosophical than "Ktaadn" and focuses more on narration, description of the wilderness, and characterization, particularly of Joe Aitteon. Also, as Joseph J. Moldenhauer has noticed, Thoreau's depiction of himself as a narrator with a distinct personality is sharper than in "Ktaadn,"[12] though not as ironic as in *Walden*. Thoreau seems less the wide-eyed tourist and more the trained observer. But he does frequently and effectively depart from objective observation to editorialize about the corruption of the lumber industry and the need to preserve the wilderness.

"The Allegash and East Branch" is even more journalistic in tone than "Chesuncook." Its descriptions of the wilderness are less poetic and more scientific than in either of the previous essays. Typical of this later matter-of-fact approach to nature is his treatment of the act of diving to find bottom. So symbolically crucial to *Walden,* in "The Allegash and East Branch" it receives only this passing comment about Umbazookskus Stream: "The stream, though narrow and swift, was still deep, with a muddy bottom, as I proved by diving to it" (208).

Although Thoreau evokes the facts of the wilderness vividly if not often symbolically in this last essay, it is characterization that dominates. In the description of his stagecoach ride to Moosehead Lake, he presents some of his fellow passengers and their dog, who irritates him by running off and thereby forcing the driver to stop until it can be found. Later Thoreau is smugly amused to note that the dog is finally tied to the top of the stage and is occasionally seen out the window dangling by its neck (though not fatally). There is also a powerfully ironic portrait of another passenger, a frail-looking man who proves to be Maine's most renowned white hunter.

The essay's most fully realized character is Joe Polis, complete with the strengths of his woodlore and his sometimes childlike flaws of superficial devotion to religion and seeming indifference to detail and logic. Thoreau himself shares the spotlight with Polis, however, for this essay gives the fullest view of him actually fronting the facts of the wilderness in survival situations—fighting mosquitoes, shooting rapids, and agonizing over a lost companion. It is a Thoreau we see as fully nowhere else in his writings.

The reader who comes to *The Maine Woods* having first read *A Week* and *Walden* is likely to regret the scarcity of Thoreau's double symbolic vision, especially in the last two essays of the book. It is the least obviously transcendental and most factual of his books. Yet a close reading reveals a sense of wonder and an acknowledgment of nature's darker side that is connected to the other two books while at the same time suggesting a maturer Thoreau, one less frantically trying to juggle the higher and lower laws. He is, as Lebeaux says, "more open to de-illusionment and darkness."[13] He less often nudges facts into flowering truths, but he harbors a subtle hope that the facts of the wilderness can reveal those truths to an observant reader if properly presented. One senses in *The Maine Woods,* as well as in *Cape Cod,* that Thoreau now has less patience with readers for whom nature's truths must always be explained and more respect for those who can detect those truths in his writing on their own.

Themes.   Although *The Maine Woods* has less narrative and stylistic unity than *A Week* and *Walden,* it has a clearer thematic unity. Its main subjects are the lumber industry, the Indians, the moose, and the wilderness of which all of these are a part. Thoreau's single over-riding interest is, as Philip Gura says, "not only in the wilderness itself but in how a man conceives of himself in relation to it."[14] In the course of his three trips he came to see the relation of a white person to the Indian's wilderness as more complex than he at first expected.

He is interested in the logging industry as the source of the lumber that came shooting by Walden Pond on the Fitchburg railroad. As usual, his attitude toward it is ambivalent. "Ktaadn" begins with a condemnation of logging and lumber mills. Amid his summary of the lumber-making process, he exclaims, "Think how stood the white-pine tree on the shore of Chesuncook, its branches soughing with the four winds, and every individual needle trembling in the sunlight—think how it stands with it now—sold, perchance to the New England Friction Match Company!"(5). He then observes bitterly that "the mission of men there seems to be, like so many busy demons, to drive the forest all out of the country, from every solitary beaver swamp, and mountain side, as possible" (5). Later in "The Allegash and East Branch" he reemphasizes this condemnation by comparing lumbermen to "10,000 vermin gnawing at the base of her [the wilderness's] noblest trees" (228).

The lumberman's problem is that he does not follow Thoreau's advice to "get your living by loving."[15] Thoreau complains in "Chesuncook" that "the explorers, and lumberers generally, are all hirelings, paid so much a day for their labor, and as such, they have no more love for wild nature, than wood-sawyers have for forests" (119). They are no better than his neighbors in Concord, blind to the true beauty and value of living trees and too busy cutting them down to wake up to the truth. The lumberer, he observes, "admires the log, the carcass or corpse, more than the tree" (229) and thus blindly chooses death over life.

Nonetheless, in "Ktaadn" Thoreau shows much admiration for his two white guides, George McCauslin and Tom Fowler, two pioneer farmers who have spent most of their lives associated with the lumber industry. McCauslin is presented as a model pioneer: "A man of dry wit and shrewdness, and a general intelligence which I had not looked for in the backwoods" (22). McCauslin and Fowler's batteau proves more stable than an Indian canoe (32), and their skill in handling it is shown to be truly heroic, both by the story of the Fowler boys running the rapids at night to fetch a doctor (77) and by Thoreau's own observations of their skill.

Even the loggers, despite their voracious appetite for trees, are at times heroic. In "Ktaadn" Thoreau describes logging as "an exciting as well as arduous and dangerous business" (42), and he seems to admire the loggers' ability "to navigate a log as if it were a canoe, and be as indifferent to cold and wet as a muskrat" (43). He also expresses a wish to experience the life of lumber explorers, who, in searching for suitable strands of timber to be cut, go into the wilderness in pairs for five or six weeks at a time, living off their provisions and what food they can find or kill. He admires theirs as "a solitary and adventurous life" (101). He is even able to see logging as a courageous endeavor in harmony with nature in that it "depends on many accidents, as the early freezing of the rivers, that the teams may get up in season, a sufficient freshet in spring, to fetch the logs down, and many others" (43).

Thoreau thus has no quarrel with the essential task of the lumber industry and is prepared to admire lumberjacks for their life on the edge of the frontier. After all, he himself had cleared Emerson's land at the pond to get lumber to build his cabin. It is the corruption of the endeavor that he criticizes. If society would build simpler houses, lumber would not be needed in such outrageous quantities. (One wonders whether Thoreau's reaction against his mother's frequent desire for a fancier house might be partially behind his quarrel with logging.)

But the whole process, from standing pine tree to finished house, proves wasteful. In contrast to this wastefulness, Thoreau offers approvingly a description of a simple but typical logger's house and concludes that such "are very proper forest houses, the stems of the trees collected together and piled up around a man to keep out wind and rain: made of living green logs, hanging with moss and lichen" (20).

Also, as in hunting, if the object being killed were viewed with respect, logging could be a truly natural act. But the loggers' failure to appreciate "how the pine lives and grows and spires, lifting its evergreen arms to the light" (21) cuts him off from the recognition that "every creature is better alive than dead, men and moose and pine-trees" and that the pine tree "is as immortal as I am, and perchance will go to as high a heaven, there to tower above me still" (122).[16] Instead of respectful and necessary use of nature, Thoreau saw in logging only greed and the slaughter of living things. In potential, logging was admirable; in practice it was a crime against nature.

In the last two essays he becomes thoroughly opposed to the whole logging endeavor. Despairing of the logger as an ideal of life in the wilderness, he turns instead to the Indian. Recall that Thoreau's interest in Indians dated back to the days when as children he and John played Indians in the woods. After John's death that interest steadily grew. It eventually provided some of his motivation for living a primitive life at the pond, and it continued to tempt him back toward such a life after he left it. In 1855 he writes in his journal, "I sometimes think that I must go off to some wilderness where I can have a better opportunity to play life,—can find more suitable materials to build my house with, and enjoy the pleasure of collecting my fuel in the forest. I have more taste for the wild sports of hunting, fishing, wigwam-building, making garments of skins, and collecting wood wherever you find it, than for butchering, farming, carpentry, working in a factory, or going to a wood market" (*Writings* 13:519–20). Going to the Maine woods was thus his periodic return to an Indian life and an opportunity to compare the real thing to his own adult attempt at playing Indian at Walden Pond.

In going to Maine to study Indians, Thoreau carried with him much mental baggage. As Robert Sayre convincingly argues, "To a great extent, Thoreau was prejudiced, favorably and unfavorably, by the white stereotypes of Indian life. He did not study Indians, in all their variety and social relationships; he studied 'the Indian,' the ideal solitary figure that was the white Americans' symbol of the wilderness and history."[17] Sayre labels Thoreau's attitude as "savagism" and lists the usual stereotypes of such a prejudice: "that Indians were (1) solitary hunters, rather than farmers; (2) tradition-bound and not susceptible to improvement; (3) childlike innocents who were corrupted by civilization; (4) superstitious pagans who would not accept the highest offerings of civilization like Christianity; and, therefore, (5) doomed to extinction."[18] Thoreau, of course, reverses the usual "savagist" preference for Indians wise enough to value Christianity.

Thoreau's first views of the Indian settlement at Oldtown certainly reveal that he shared most of these savagist assumptions. The first Indian he describes is "a short shabby washer-woman-looking Indian" (MW, 6) whom he takes as typical of the Penobscot Indian tribe. The sight prompts him to bemoan the pitiful fate of the Indian: "These were once a powerful tribe. Politics are all the rage with them now. I even thought that a row of wigwams, with a dance of pow-wows, and a prisoner tortured at the stake, would be more respectable than this" (7). Thus he is hardly surprised at Louis Neptune's drunkenness and unreliability. He leaves after his first trip not having had the positive firsthand experiences with Indians he had hoped for. Indeed, this disappointment in the midst of his Walden pond years probably accounts for the scarcity of comments on Indians in *Walden,* where we might expect the Indian to be a prominent model of the "primitive life" he himself was attempting.

Thoreau's prejudices are modified somewhat by his second trip, partially because he had better luck in his guide this time. Joe Aitteon is "a good looking Indian . . . apparently of unmixed blood" (90), who proves to be a reliable guide, thus partially removing the bad taste for Indian guides left by Neptune. But Aitteon is also an Indian who works at the white's logging business and wears lumberman's clothes. (He would die in a log jam some years later.) He also tends to wander off without warning, leaving Thoreau and Thatcher perplexed, and he seems incapable of the foresight Thoreau demonstrates by carrying matches in a watertight container. He sings the whites' songs—"O Susanna" is a favorite—and refuses to go into the wilderness without the whites' provisions: "hard bread, pork, etc" (107).

From Aitteon and the other Indians with whom he camps, Thoreau learns some Indian words and begins to get an accurate look at Indian life, but these experiences do not yet free him of his prejudices. Upon his return to Oldtown, Thoreau notices in the Indians' yards "more introduced weeds than useful vegetables, as the Indian is said to cultivate the vices rather than the virtues of the white man" (146). He then launches into another elegy for "the Hunter Race" similar to the one in "Ktaadn" (146).

In "The Allegash and East Branch" Thoreau makes much more progress toward an unprejudiced, mature view of the Indian, primarily because of the personality of his third guide, Joe Polis. Polis has such a profound effect on him that Emerson lists Polis along with Walt Whitman and John Brown as the three contemporaries Thoreau most admired. Early in the third excursion Thoreau and Polis hit it off so well that they agree to spend the trip exchanging knowledge, and their relationship becomes increasingly close as the trip goes on.

Although Polis is not without some flaws—for instance, his rather superficial Christianity—he nonetheless proves in many ways to be the model Indian Thoreau is seeking. He is an excellent pathfinder who finds his way by self-reliance: "He does not carry things in his head, nor remember the route exactly, like a white man, but relies on himself at the moment" (185). He proves to be the equal of McCauslin and Fowler in shooting rapids, can talk to muskrats, and seems perfectly at home in the wilderness (except for the mosquitoes, which bother him more than they do Thoreau and Hoar because he refuses to use insect repellent). Thoreau is awed by Polis's description of a winter trek on snowshoes across frozen lakes and land alike: "What a wilderness walk for a man to take alone! . . . It reminded me of Prometheus Bound. Here was travelling of the old heroic kind over the unaltered face of nature" (235).

What Thoreau most admires about Polis, however, is his ability to accept the virtues of civilization, reject its vices, and still maintain his Indian identity. Thoreau admiringly describes how Polis first takes a stagecoach to the fringes of wilderness and then proceeds into the forest to make a canoe and complete his hunting: "Thus you have an Indian availing himself cunningly of the advantages of civilization, without losing any of his woodcraft, but proving himself the more successful hunter for it" (201). Furthermore, Polis understands his own relationship to both wilderness and civilization in a way that Thoreau envies. Polis expresses his liking for big cities but then wisely observes, "I suppose, I live in New York, I be poorest hunter, I expect" (197), and Thoreau observes that "he understood very well both his superiority and his inferiority to the whites" (197). After his trip with Polis, Thoreau has a similar sense of his own relation to the Indians.

Polis is one of Thoreau's most fully realized characters, an example of Thoreau's maturing skill at characterization.[19] Lawrence Willson has noticed that in his exhaustive "Indian notebooks" Thoreau gathers quotations that "grow gradually more critical of the concept of the 'noble savage.'"[20] The same progress is evident in his perception of the Indian in *The Maine Woods,* especially in the portrayal of Polis. Thoreau found in Polis a more complex Indian than he had previously envisioned, one less childlike and more cosmopolitan than he had expected.

Nevertheless, Polis exemplifies at least one aspect of the savagist stereotype: the image of the solitary hunter. As such, he represents the Indian that Henry and John had imagined as children playing in the Concord woods. But Thoreau realizes that this aspect of Indian life is only a stage in the development of civilization—a stage it is important to experience and understand but that, like eating meat, must eventually be outgrown. As he says in "Chesuncook," "What a coarse and imperfect use Indians and hunters make of nature! No wonder that their race is soon exterminated" (120).

Thoreau's rejection of the life of the solitary hunter as a modern ideal is also greatly influenced by seeing both his Indian guides and his white companions killing moose. He himself had hunted as a youth and did not condemn hunting as a means of survival.[21] He even recommends it as part of a thorough acquaintance with nature: "to explore a given neighborhood, go and live in it. . . . Fish in its streams, hunt in its forests, gather fuel from its water, its woods, cultivate the ground, and pluck the wild fruits, etc., etc. This will be the surest and speediest way to those perceptions you covet" (*Writings* 16:146). But in the Maine woods he found wanton hunting for sport rather than survival. After seeing Aitteon skin and butcher a moose shot by Thatcher, Thoreau is horrified: "this hunting of the moose merely for the satisfaction of killing him—not even for the sake of his hide, without making any extraordinary exertion or running any risk yourself, is too much like going out by night to some woodside pasture and shooting your neighbor's horses" (119). He finds that even witnessing such slaughter "affected the innocence, destroyed the pleasure of my adventure" (119) and that "nature looked sternly upon me on account of the murder of the moose" (120–21).

Thoreau thus comes to believe that it is neither the logger nor the Indian but rather the poet that makes best use of nature. It is the poet, he says, who understands that "every creature is better alive than dead, men and moose and pine trees" and who "makes the truest use of the pine—who does not fondle it with an axe, nor tickle it with a saw, nor stroke it with a plane" (121). What Thoreau finds the proper use of the wilderness to be, however, has been one of the most perplexing problems for Thoreau scholars.

A crux of the problem is Thoreau's description of climbing Mount Katahdin, an event that has most often been interpreted as seriously weakening Thoreau's confidence in nature's goodness. In summarizing the controversy over this episode, Ronald Hoag cites James McIntosh and Sherman Paul as two representatives of the theory of disillusionment.[22] Hoag, on the other hand, argues that the Ktaadn episode was an affirmation of Thoreau's faith in nature. He says that it provided Thoreau with his fullest encounter with the sublime in nature, a nature so full of meaning that humans can never fully know it. Thoreau's attitude toward the mountain is thus one of reverence, not disillusionment.

There can be little doubt that Thoreau does indeed see Ktaadn as sublime, but Hoag's thesis needs qualifying nonetheless. In a college essay on the sublime, Thoreau quotes Edmund Burke's famous statement that "terror is in all cases whatsoever, either more openly or latently, the ruling principle of the sublime" (*Early Essays,* 93). He continues by adding to the definition Burke's other elements of the sublime—"Mystery, Power, Silence" (*Early Essays,* 93)—only at last to reject terror as the basic element of the sublime in favor of "reverence": "I would make an inherent respect or reverence, which certain objects are fitted to demand, that ruling principle; which reverence, as it is altogether distinct from, so shall it outlive that terror to which he [Burke] refers" (*Early Essays,* 96). "The infinite, the sublime," he concludes, "seize upon the soul and disarm it" (*Early Essays,* 99).

Thoreau's modification of Burke's concept of sublimity is evident at the top of the mountain and in the controversial "Contact!" passage about the descent over the mountain's "burnt land." Thoreau describes the mountaintop as "vast, Titanic, and such as man never inhabits" (MW, 64) and the burnt lands as "vast, drear, and inhuman" (70). The god of Ktaadn, drawn from Greek and Old Testament models, demands reverence. A jealous god, it says sternly to humans, "I cannot pity nor fondle thee here, but relentlessly drive thee hence to where I *am* kind" (64, Thoreau's emphasis). "Pomola [the Indian god of Ktaadn]," he says, "is always angry with those who climb the summit of Ktaadn" (65). Furthermore, Thoreau's reaction to this god also includes a disorientation and disarming of the soul: "the *solid* earth! the *actual* world! the *common sense! Contact! Contact! Who* are we? *where* are we?" (71, Thoreau's emphasis).

But to say that Thoreau's experience on Mount Katahdin is simply a powerfully rendered example of the literature of sublimity consistent with a transcendental reverence for nature does not quite capture the full complexity of the mountain's impact on him. For along with the reverence of the Thoreauvian sublime, these passages clearly contain the Burkean fear that Thoreau not only rejects as sublime but even presents as an enemy of the sublime: "Terror inevitably injures, and if excessive, may entirely destroy its [the sublime's] effect" (*Early Essays,* 96). "Terror," he says, "avoids reflection, though reflection alone can restore to calmness and equanimity" (*Early Essays,* 98).

Thoreau finally composed his description of climbing Katahdin long after the actual event, so that he clearly had opportunity to reflect on it and restore "calmness and equanimity" to it.[23] Yet even in this calm reflection he deliberately includes the element of fear, thus suggesting the deep impact that fear had upon him. The clouds surrounding the summit seem "hostile" (63), so that he beats a hasty retreat back to his companions. Upon crossing the burnt land he says, "I fear bodies, I tremble to meet them" (71). Confrontation with the otherness of the material world, including the human body, clearly inspires not only reverence but fear—fear of perhaps being unable to transcend the physical to achieve spiritual meaning.

This fear is also an undercurrent in other descriptions of the wilderness throughout *The Maine Woods.* He describes the edge of the precipice of Mount Kineo as "a dangerous place to try the steadiness of your nerves" (176). Later when Hoar is lost, Thoreau fears for his safety: "For half an hour I anticipated only the worst. I thought what I should do the next day, if I did not find him, what I *could* do in such a wilderness, and how his relatives would feel, if I should return without him" (259, Thoreau's emphasis). Throughout his trip with Hoar, what particularly bothers Thoreau is the feeling of confinement in the deepest wilderness, the antithesis of the freedom he sought in the wild, for in the "wildest country" he found that "at a hundred rods [from camp] you might be lost past recovery" (275). Imagining having to trek long distances through such wilderness, he says, "It made you shudder" (275). Like Hemingway later, he thus came to appreciate the psychological benefits of "a clean, well-lighted place."

Thoreau's feeling for the sublime wilderness thus includes not only reverence but a nagging sense of fear. One reason for that fear is his full realization of how completely the wilderness can throw one back on physical necessity; in preserving physical safety it is easy to forget one's spiritual goals. Another reason is his recognition that the wilderness can confine or confuse artistic vision as well as free it. On top of Katahdin he finds not a beautiful panorama but an obscure chaos, and along Webster Brook the seer's vision can hardly penetrate the dense forest. Such fears persuade him not to consider the wilderness as a permanent residence. As he says upon completing his Chesuncook excursion, "it was a relief to get back to our smooth, but still varied landscape. For a permanent residence, it seemed to me that there could be no comparison between this and the wilderness, necessary as the latter is for a resource and a background" (155). It was as a resource that he would continue to use the wilderness, as well as as a symbol of "Hope and the future" (*Writings* 5:226).

This hope for the future did not depend on a primitive acquiescence to nature's wilderness but rather on a compromise between civilization and the wilderness. Later in "Walking" he describes his personal compromise: "I feel that with regard to Nature I live a sort of border life, on the confines of a world into which I make occasional and transient forays only, and my patriotism and allegiance to the state into whose territories I seem to retreat are those of a moss-trooper" (*Writings* 5:242). In "Chesuncook" he acknowledges the wilderness as "the raw material of all our civilization," but "a civilized man . . . must at length pine there, like a cultivated plant which clasps its fibres about a crude and undissolved mass of peat" (155). He finds it proper that people should humanize nature. "The farmer," he says in "Walking," displaces the Indian even because he redeems the meadow, and so makes himself stronger and in some respects more natural" (*Writings* 5:230).

The compromise that he suggests for society at large is "to have our national preserves, where no villages need be destroyed, in which the bear and panther, and some even of the hunter race, may still exist, and not be 'civilized off the face of the earth'" (156). Thus all America might live a "border life," enjoying the benefits of civilization while still able to make occasional forays into the wilderness. Thoreau's plea for such national preserves was an inspiration for the creation of America's national park system. If he could see that system today, he would be pleased that it still exists, but he would almost certainly be dissatisfied with the very small portion of wilderness that has been preserved and would remind us even more emphatically that "in Wildness is the preservation of the World" (*Writings* 5:224). But we must remember that he himself believed that few men were suited to live fully in the wilderness. Despite his own considerable woodcraft, he found that he was not. His trips to the Maine woods gave him evidence of what he had suspected as early as *A Week:* that the sublimity of the wilderness was best viewed as a background to civilization, not an alternative to it.

Chapter Five

Exploring Nature's Illusions in *Cape Cod*

Thoreau sought the sublime not only in the Maine woods but also on the shores of Cape Cod. There he found a different and more troubling kind of sublime wilderness, one of desertlike beaches and stormy seas. In *Walden* he looks into the mirror of the pond and sees reflected the truth of human harmony with God and nature, but in *Cape Cod* he looks into the ocean and sees darkness and a frightening bottomlessness. *Cape Cod* is thus even more appropriately a sequel to *Walden* than is *The Maine Woods,* because Thoreau comes to understand that human penetration of nature's mysteries might be much more limited than he had thought it in *Walden.*[1] He learns on Cape Cod what Emerson had warned of earlier in his essay "Experience": "We live amid surfaces and the true art of life is to skate well on them."[2]

Life

Thoreau made four trips to Cape Cod, the first in the fall of 1849. Accompanied by Ellery Channing, he planned to take a steamer from Boston to Provincetown on 9 October. A storm delayed the steamer, however, and news soon arrived that it also had wrecked the brig *St. John* near Cohasset, killing 145 people, mostly Irish immigrants. Thoreau and Channing immediately changed their plans and took a stage to Cohasset. There Thoreau visited Ellen Sewall, who was now married to Joseph Osgood, and with her husband wandered the beach, examining the dead bodies and debris of the wreck and talking to the survivors. After staying the night in Bridgewater, Thoreau and Channing took a train to Sandwich and then a stage to Orleans.

The next day they started on foot and hiked through heavy rain to Wellfleet, where they lodged at the cottage of John Newcomb, an old oysterman to whom Thoreau eventually devoted an entire essay. Newcomb's eccentric stories, together with his wife's suspicions about the honesty of her two guests and the mutterings of their retarded grand-

son, made for a rather bizarre evening. As Thoreau and Channing re-
tired for the night, Mrs. Newcomb locked them in their room, but
they were set free next morning to observe breakfast being cooked
while the oysterman sat by the fire spitting tobacco, which seemed to
land as frequently in the food as in the fire. After Thoreau had repaired
a broken clock for the oysterman, he and Channing resumed their hike
along the beach from Truro to the Highland Light.

That night they stayed with the lighthouse keeper and studied with
interest the rituals of maintaining the light. The next morning they
again hiked the beach, climbed a high sand dune named Mount Ararat,
and eventually arrived at Race Point at the tip of the cape, where they
crossed over to Provincetown for lodging. The next day was extremely
stormy, so they sat on the beach watching the sublime ferocity of the
ocean. After staying a second night in Provincetown, they caught a
steamer back to Boston.

Thoreau quickly worked up a lecture based on this first trip and
delivered it to the Concord Lyceum in January of 1850. This lecture,
his most humorous, proved a great success, so the next summer he
returned alone to the cape to gather more lecture material. On 25 June
1850 he took a steamer to Provincetown. The next day he hiked the
beach, reversing the path of his previous trip, and revisited the Highland Light and the Wellfleet oysterman. He was amused to learn from
the oysterman that after their previous visit he and Channing had been
for a while suspected by the police regarding a bank robbery that had
occurred just after they left. He hiked as far as Eastham and Chatham
and then returned to Provincetown to catch a steamer home.[3]

Thoreau made a third visit to the cape in July 1855. The previous
winter he had felt unusually weak and listless, so perhaps he hoped
that the brisk sea air would be invigorating. Recent news that *Putnam's*
was planning to publish the essays gleaned from his first two trips to
the cape might also have contributed to his renewed interest. This time
he and Channing took a schooner to Provincetown on 5 July. They
stayed in Provincetown that night and the next day, after taking a stage
to North Truro, walked across the cape to the Highland Light. There
they took lodging and stayed for nearly two weeks, during which they
botanized and rambled around the cape. One day when the two went
swimming in a pool created by a recent storm, they found that the
storm had trapped a shark in the pool with them. But all in all it was
a relaxing vacation, and they returned to Boston by schooner on 18
July with Thoreau feeling quite refreshed.[4]

This third visit was the last to be included in the book *Cape Cod* that was later edited by Channing and Sophia Thoreau and published by Ticknor and Fields in 1864. In 1857, however, Thoreau made a fourth trip to the cape which he recorded only in his journal.[5] On 12 June he took the stage from Boston to Plymouth, where he stayed three nights with the Marston Watsons. During his stay he visited "Uncle Ed" Watson on Clark's Island and toured Marston Watson's nursery of trees and shrubs. On the fifteenth the Watsons took him to the beach near Plymouth, where he began his longest walk on the cape. He hiked for three days, reaching the Highland Light on the eighteenth. Along the way he stopped in Wellfleet to visit the oysterman but learned that Newcomb had died that winter. The keeper of the Highland Light was still there, however, so Thoreau spent three days with him. Unfortunately, the weather was wet and foggy, so his walks and botanizing were limited. When the weather cleared on the twenty-first, he hiked to Provincetown, climbing Mount Ararat along the way, and the next day caught a steamer back to Boston.[6]

In addition to Thoreau's first three excursions to the cape, *Cape Cod* also includes material from a beach walk near Hull and from Thoreau's trip to Fire Island in New York in July 1850 to look for the bodies of Margaret Fuller Ossoli and her family, who were drowned in a shipwreck near Long Island. Except for the Fire Island search, all of Thoreau's beach excursions seem motivated by a special attraction to the shore, a sense that the ocean and beach are a more sublime version of Walden Pond. There was for Thoreau an air of mystery, an elusiveness, about the shore that intrigued him. There was also the cape's historical significance as America's first frontier, for he recognized what Frederick Jackson Turner remembered fifty years later: "The oldest West was the Atlantic Coast."[7] On the ever-shifting surfaces of the cape, Thoreau sought the elusive truths both of the Pilgrim past and of nature's present.

Art

Structure.   In *Cape Cod* Thoreau returned to the structure he had used in *A Week* and *Walden,* the condensing of time in his narrative to achieve artistic unity. He originally combined his first two excursions to the cape to unify the lectures and essays that he polished for the 1855 *Putnam's* publication. Later he incorporated additional material from the 1855 excursion. The result is a narrative more tightly woven than *The Maine Woods,* but one with an unusual mixture of tones, for Thoreau combines his observations of nature on the cape with often hilarious character sketches on the one hand and meditations on death and illusion on the other.

The texture of the book is further complicated by the inclusion of sometimes quite lengthy quotations from Thoreau's historical sources. These historical digressions often seem to be spliced into the text with the same awkwardness as were some of the philosophical essays in *A Week,* although careful reading usually reveals their pertinence, as in the account of the Reverend Samuel Treat, whose sublimely frightening fire-and-brimstone sermons are suitable companions for Thoreau as he walks the shore on a sublimely stormy day. Nonetheless, Thoreau himself seems to have been unsure of their effectiveness, at one point even suggesting to his editors at *Putnam's* that some of the historical material could perhaps be deleted.

As in his other books, what most effectively holds these various interests together in *Cape Cod* is Thoreau's persona. *Cape Cod* gives us yet another side of his personality: the curious, naive Yankee tourist. He gawks at the grisly results of a shipwreck, gets sick on clams, eagerly interviews the cape's inhabitants, gets scared by a shark, and frequently stares out to sea like any inlander encountering the sea for the first time. One can almost imagine him carrying a camera around his neck and buying postcards if he were to walk the cape today.

Thoreau seems to have first approached the cape as he did Walden Pond. The trip to the cape was in some ways merely a longer version of his daily excursions in the Concord woods. At the beginning of *Cape Cod* he says that he went "wishing to get a better view than I had yet had of the ocean" and that he had been "accustomed to make excursions to the ponds within ten miles of Concord, but latterly I have extended my excursions to the seashore."[8] At the beginning of the second chapter, Thoreau does the same things he did around Concord—picking up arrowheads and learning the measurements of the land as if by knowing details and distances one somehow began to know and control the landscape itself. On the other hand, Thoreau recognizes his own "greenness" and truly wants to get more than a land-dwelling tourist's view of the cape. "We wished," he says later in the book, "to associate with the Ocean until it lost the pond-like look which it wears to a countryman. We still thought that we could see the other side" (*Writings,* 4:177). One purpose of this tourist's persona is, of course, to entertain the reader. But it also seems at times to mask the profoundly unsettling quality of some of Thoreau's perceptions of the cape.

Themes. Like *Walden, Cape Cod* is a book built upon thematic opposites.[9] Only in recent years, however, have critics begun to recognize the opposing forces that hold the work together in dynamic tension: indoor versus outdoor views, land versus sea, sublime versus picturesque, death versus life, and transcendental certainty versus scientific skepticism.[10] In exploring these oppositions, many recent critics have concluded that in *Cape Cod* Thoreau is able to synthesize a new, more realistic transcendental faith in nature.[11] Others have concluded that the work fails precisely because Thoreau does not find such a synthesis.[12]

Only a few critics have recognized the third alternative that will be explored in this chapter: that Thoreau's inability to resolve opposites in *Cape Cod* is not a weakness but a strength.[13] Although Thoreau is not able to reconcile opposites, domesticate the wilderness of Cape Cod, or reaffirm his transcendentalist faith as fully as he would like to, his ability to recognize his predicament and to accept the cape on its own terms completes a significant shift in his attitude toward nature. Cape Cod, he found, represented the shifting, unsurveyable wilderness of illusions that humans can never fully penetrate in this life. *Cape Cod* is the record of Thoreau's education into this alternative attitude toward nature, but that education occurs slowly and in spite of his reluctance to abandon his optimism.

Despite his Maine woods experience, Thoreau does not seem to have been fully prepared for such a wilderness as Cape Cod. In chapter three, for instance, he savors the detached tourist's thrill of seeing a storm at sea: "On the whole, we were glad of the storm, which would show us the ocean in its angriest mood" (4:40). Such a comment seems all the more shallow because Thoreau has already demonstrated in chapter one the results of the sea's angriest mood. Even before reaching the cape, he and Channing are greeted by the headline, "Death! one hundred and forty-five lives lost at Cohasset" (4:5). Upon visiting Cohasset, he gives a powerfully economical report of the many shipwrecked bodies: "I saw many marble feet and matted hands as the clothes were raised, and one livid, swollen, and mangled body of a drowned girl,—who probably had intended to go out to service in some American family,— to which some rags still adhered, with a string, half-concealed by the flesh, about its swollen neck; the coiled-up wreck of a human hulk, gashed by the rocks or fishes, so that the bone and muscle were exposed, but quite bloodless,—merely red and white,—with wide-open and staring eyes, yet lustreless, dead-lights" (4:6–7).

This scene would certainly be a test for any transcendentalist's optimism, and Thoreau tries hard to pass it. Although he seeks desperately to attach an optimistic spiritual meaning to these dead bodies, his sermon sounds smug and hollow: "Why care for these bodies? They really have no friends but the worms or fishes. Their owners were coming to the New World, as Columbus and the Pilgrims did,—they were within a mile of its shores; but, before they could reach it, they emigrated to a newer world than ever Columbus dreamed of, yet one of whose existence we believe there is far more universal and convincing evidence—though it has not yet been discovered by science—than Columbus had of this" (4:12). This bit of transcendental metaphysics rings false as very few other passages in his writings do.[14] Unlike Emerson at the death of his son, Thoreau does not even grieve that he cannot grieve.

Furthermore, the reader senses that Thoreau does not really believe what his persona says, and the rest of the book supports that impression. As James McIntosh suggests, this first chapter with its theme of death sets up the tone and a major motif for the whole book.[15] Throughout there are repeated references to shipwreck and death, with only token attempts to find transcendental compensation for them. Even if shipwrecks do occasionally "contribute a new vegetable to a continent's stock, and prove on the whole a lasting blessing to its inhabitants" (4:166), such botanical benefits seem small recompense for the dead bodies. Thoreau here sounds too much like Voltaire's ever optimistic Dr. Pangloss, who claims that it is good that Columbus brought syphilis to Europe from America, because if he had not he would not have brought chocolate either.[16] Despite such attempts at optimism, Thoreau could not ignore the apparent antagonism of nature toward humans and their weakness in the face of nature's awesome power.

Thoreau struggles throughout the book to find symbols of permanence to balance the death that he sees as so much a part of life on the cape. Each time he thinks he has found such a sign, however, he finds he must reject it. One such symbol is the unfailing spring at the end of the "Shipwreck" chapter. "The most interesting thing which I heard of, in this township of Hull," he says, "was an unfailing spring, whose locality was pointed out to me, on the side of a distant hill, as I was panting along the shore" (4:15–16). Such a spring was precisely the sort of natural hieroglyphic that he would have made much of in a more transcendental mood, but he completes his sentence by hastily remarking, "I did not visit it" (4:16). His out-of-hand dismissal of a symbol that heretofore would have been attractive to his transcendental persona is one of the first and strongest hints that this book is to be something quite different from his book about the unfailing Walden Pond.

Another seeming symbol of permanence is the lighthouse. At the Highland Light, Thoreau is impressed by its neatness and order, obvious suggestions of permanence in the jaws of the ocean's power: "It was a neat building, with everything in apple-pie order, and no danger of anything rusting there for want of oil" (4:168). Thoreau feels quite secure there for the night: "The light-house lamp a few feet distant shone full into my chamber, and made it as bright as day, so I knew exactly how the Highland Light bore all that night, and I was in no danger of being wrecked" (4:175). He also reports, however, that the lighthouse had in previous years nearly gone dark and, despite improvements in the light's structure, could do so again. The oil allotted the lighthouse was sometimes of poor quality, and previously the windows had been of small, thin panes of glass that a severe storm would sometimes break; thus, "when the mariner stood most in need of their guidance, they had thus nearly converted the lighthouse into a dark lantern, which emitted only a few feeble rays, and those commonly on the land or lee side" (4:169).

Near the end of the book Thoreau returns to this lighthouse image to describe a recently built lighthouse made of iron. Although of stronger material than the Highland Light, this new structure does not seem much more permanent. Thoreau's description of it implies a very fragile and tenuous relation between humanity and the sea:

Here was the new iron light-house, then unfinished, in the shape of an egg-shell painted red, and placed high on iron pillars, like the ovum of a sea-monster floating on the waves,—destined to be phosphorescent. As we passed it at half-tide we saw the spray tossed up nearly to the shell.

A man was to live in that egg-shell day and night, a mile from the shore. When I passed it the next summer it was finished and two men lived in it, and a light-house keeper said that they told him that in a recent gale it had rocked so as to shake the plates off the table. Think of making your bed thus in the crest of a breaker! To have the waves, like a pack of hungry wolves, eyeing you always, night and day, and from time to time making a spring at you, almost sure to have you at last. (4:262–63)

Here in this lighthouse were pioneers braver than any who might go West. Their egg-shell existence is a summary of Thoreau's view in *Cape*

Cod of humans' relation to nature's sublimity, which here contains less reverence and more terror than Thoreau found comfortable. It is clearly not a reassuring symbol of permanence.

A third symbol of flawed permanence for Thoreau is the beach grass that is so important to the ecology of a coastline. Like an "unfailing spring," the beach grass seems to be perdurable. Quoting the local historians, Thoreau describes how, even though virtually covered with sand, it sprouts anew each spring to keep the sand from being blown away completely (4:205). To Thoreau the grass is the anchor that keeps the ship Cape Cod from being destroyed: "Thus Cape Cod is anchored to the heavens, as it were, by a myriad little cables of beach-grass" (4:209). But the anchors, though numerous, are not very strong, and Thoreau is forced to add, "if they should fail, [Cape Cod] would become a total wreck, and erelong go to the bottom" (4:209). Elsewhere in the book he discovers that the cape is indeed disintegrating. In "The Highland Light" he discusses the sea's attack on the cape with the lighthouse keeper, who believes that it is being worn away "on both sides, though most on the eastern. In some places it had lost many rods within the year, and, erelong, the lighthouse must be moved" (4:151). Thoreau himself is not so pessimistic about the cape; his calculations are that "it was not wearing away here at the rate of more than six feet annually. Any conclusions drawn from the observations of a few years, or one generation only, are likely to prove false, and the Cape may balk expectation by its durability" (4:151). Nevertheless, Thoreau could not rid himself of the impression that the sea would eventually conquer the land. He portrays the sea as a cat playing with a mouse—the cape's sandbars—in its jaws (4:155), and at the end of the book he describes the cape as "the edge of a continent wasting before the assaults of the ocean" (4:270).

In his examination of the cape, Thoreau is thrown back time after time upon the elusiveness of its life and landscape, an elusiveness that occasionally pleases him with its continual surprises but more often disturbs him deeply with nature's resistance to human understanding. This is nature not coyly hiding its secrets under leaves in the Concord woods but daring humans to know it if they can or be destroyed if they fail. The tools he used to explore nature in the Concord and even in the Maine woods do not work on the cape. The more elusive the cape becomes, the harder Thoreau tries to measure it. As Thomas Couser correctly comments, "The baffling nature of the Cape . . . accounts for his constant measuring and classifying and for the long digressions into history that clutter the book; he supplemented his naked eye with all the corrective lenses at his disposal—historical sources, local lore, and his skills as naturalist and surveyor. [17] Thoreau's use of these "corrective lenses" is worth a closer look.

Despite all the historical quotations in *Cape Cod,* Thoreau is ultimately disappointed by history's failure to aid him in knowing the cape. Being told, for example, that the cows in Provincetown eat cods' heads, he traces the rumor of fish-eating cows all the way back to Pliny and to the journal of Nearchus (an admiral of Alexander the Great), but after surveying the history of this bovine habit he concludes that "in balancing the evidence I am still in doubt about the Provincetown cows" (4:215). Thoreau is particularly interested in accounts of the cape by its earliest pioneers, the Pilgrims, but he finds their reports to be unreliable. After reading that the Pilgrims found an abundance of fowl and "excellent black earth" on the cape, he reports "*We* saw no fowl there" (Thoreau's emphasis), and "We found that the earth had lost its crust,—if indeed, it ever had any,—and that there was no soil to speak of" (4:253). He concludes that the Pilgrims present far too rosy a view of the cape and that their view was no better—indeed, perhaps worse—than his own "green" view: "I cannot but think that we must make some allowances for the greenness of the Pilgrims in these matters, which caused them to see green. We do not believe that the trees were large or the soil was deep here. Their account may be true particularly, but it is generally false" (4:254–55).

The Pilgrims were not only inaccurate historians but unadventurous pioneers as well. [18] "It must be confessed," he says, "that the Pilgrims possessed but few of the qualities of the modern pioneer. They were not the ancestors of the American backwoodsmen. They did not go at once into the woods with their axes. They were a family and church, and were more anxious to keep together, though it were on the sand, than to explore and colonize a New World" (4:256). History, an illusion itself, could do little to cut through the mirages confronting Thoreau as a modern pioneer exploring the cape's wilderness.

The Pilgrim's descendants, the inhabitants of the cape whom Thoreau met, could also do little to affirm his confidence in humanity's harmonious relation to nature. For the most part, they themselves seem out of tune with nature. Thoreau describes the women as "pinched-up" and hardened by life on the cape, as well as depending too heavily on religion. As a specimen of "a regular Cape Cod man," he describes a "wrecker" (one who scavenges along the beach for artifacts from

wrecked ships) who was "too grave to laugh, too tough to cry; as indifferent as a clam" (4:59). Although the "wrecker" may be in harmony
with the sea's whims, he does not control his own fortune. Thoreau
also finds the inhabitants' religion to be hypocritical and inhumane;
they fail even to provide properly stocked "charity houses" for those
shipwrecked or lost on the wilds of the beach.

But if the lives of these latter-day Pilgrims do not suggest the at-
tainment of an ideal relation to nature, they effectively strip Thoreau
of some of his greenness by forcing him to take a more tragic view of
the sea. In "The Highland Light" he admits that "the stranger and the
inhabitant view the shore with very different eyes. The former may
have come to see and admire the ocean in a storm; but the latter looks
on it as the scene where his nearest relatives were wrecked" (4:160). A
Calvinistic fatalism seems to be the general attitude of cape people, an
attitude expressed with amusing simplicity by the Wellfleet oysterman: "What I gather from my Bible is just this; that man is a poor
good-for-nothing crittur, and everything is just as God sees fit and
disposes" (4:82). Although he seems perhaps too willing to accept the
harsh will of his God, the oysterman's view of the human being as a
"good-for-nothing crittur" is supported by much of what Thoreau sees
of people's struggles on the cape.

What troubles Thoreau even more than the unreliability of history
or the failure of the inhabitants to measure up to his expectations is
the failure of his own perceptions to measure the cape accurately. In
Walden he had suggested that by returning to a proper relation to nature his neighbors could cut through the shams and delusions of materialism to see what really is. But the landscape of Cape Cod suggests
instead that even in nature it might not be possible to separate what
is from what appears to be. As he approaches the cape by stagecoach,
Thoreau finds it deceptively enshrouded in mist. Looking out the
stagecoach window at the town of Dennis, he finds it difficult to believe that he is not already at the shore. He and his fellow travelers see
"rising before us, through the mist, singular barren hills, all stricken
with poverty-grass, looming up as if they were in the horizon, though
they were close to us, and we seemed to have got to the end of land on
that side, notwithstanding that the horses were still headed that way"
(4:25).

This foggy false arrival on the cape is followed by repeated confusion
about distinctions between land and sea. Thoreau often describes the
land as a seascape and the sea as a landscape—a technique not uncom-

mon in other writers of his day, but one that is particularly reflective of his persona's confusion in *Cape Cod*. At one point Thoreau describes the topography of the cape as looking like a "chopped sea" (4:133), and in another he describes the sand dunes as a "tide of sand impelled by waves and wind" (4:204). On the other hand, in more tempestuous moments the sea becomes a "wilderness" and a "jungle" (4:188). To the confusion between land and sea, Thoreau adds confusion between inland and shore scenes. Crossing a "boundless plain, without a tree or a fence," his companion compares it to "the rolling prairies of Illinois" (4:41). The ocean sometimes seems like a pond to Thoreau: it "is but a larger lake" (4:124), and he finds that Massachusetts Bay "is not much deeper than a country pond" (4:124). Part of such confusion is rooted in the Thoreau persona's attempt to domesticate the wildness of the cape, but part of it also seems based on Thoreau's own fundamental difficulty in understanding the cape's reality.

Some of Thoreau's problems in knowing the cape result from his own "greenness," but many others are caused by the nature of the cape itself. A desert in which one can often see to the very horizon uninterrupted by trees, houses or any other landmark, its distant views often make it difficult for Thoreau to judge the reality of objects in relation to the landscape. Thoreau had long understood that distances tend to idealize objects; nevertheless, he is often fooled by objects on the cape, mistaking them for people, and people for them. He often thinks scarecrows are men (4:38), and at one point he mistakes the oysterman's retarded grandson for a scarecrow (4:91). At other times, distances by distorting proportions seem to enlarge the human figure in the landscape: "when in the summer, I saw a family a-blueberrying a mile off, walking about amid the dwarfish bushes which did not come up higher than their ankles, they seemed to me to be a race of giants, twenty feet high at least" (4:134). Other objects are also enlarged by distance. Looking out to sea, he and Channing are "always surprised and disappointed at the insignificance of the mass which had attracted us. As we looked out over the water, the smallest objects floating on it appeared indefinitely large, we were so impressed by the vastness of the ocean, and each one bore so large a proportion to the whole ocean, which we saw" (4:67–68). At other times a distant view across the ocean makes the ships in a mackerel fleet seem more numerous than the fleet at the wharves of a large city (4:198), and the distant clouds to hang low over the ocean "and rest on the water as they never do on land, perhaps on account of the great distance to which we saw" (4:65).

Whether seen over land or sea, however, the reality of distant objects on the cape is frequently open to question, as when Thoreau and Channing see something large and black cast up on the beach behind them too far away to be clear. "As we approached," he says, "it took successively the form of a huge fish, a drowned man, a sail or a net, and finally of a mass of tow-cloth, part of the cargo of the Franklin, which the men who had mysteriously rushed out from the shore's bank loaded into a cart" (4:107). Thoreau follows this incident with the observation that "objects on the beach, whether men or inanimate things, look not only exceedingly grotesque, but much larger and more wonderful than they actually are" (4:107). Here the adjectives "grotesque" and "wonderful" suggest something of Thoreau's ambivalence toward such phenomena. They delighted him by constantly surprising him with their novelty, but they were also somehow perversions of nature that deeply troubled him.

Such phenomena defy both transcendental and spiritual attempts to measure nature. If one learns of God through nature, then one is obliged to know nature accurately. But one cannot measure a continually shifting reality. The topography of the cape frequently causes optical illusions, as in the opening of chapter four describing Thoreau's approach to the beach: "we reached the seemingly retreating boundary of the plain, and entered what had appeared at a distance an upland marsh, but proved to be dry sand covered with beach-grass, the bearberry, bay-berry, shrub-oaks, and beach-plum . . . ; then, crossing over a belt of sand on which nothing grew, though the roar of the sea sounded scarcely louder than before, and we were prepared to go half a mile farther, we suddenly stood on the edge of a bluff over-looking the Atlantic" (4:57). Later, speaking of the land near the Highland Light, Thoreau describes an "elevated plateau" that seems to slope downward "very regularly." But on crossing it, he finds that the plateau is "interrupted by broad valleys or gullies" (4:133). Some of its valleys are "circular, a hundred feet deep, without any outlet," sometimes hiding houses or even whole villages, so that these edifices seem to sink and rise miraculously in the sand before the unsuspecting traveler (4:133). These valleys make Thoreau uneasy when he considers the possibility that "we might tumble into a village before we were aware of it, as into an ant-lion's hole and be drawn into the sand irrecoverably" (4:133). It must have seemed that no eye or instrument could measure such a landscape. Describing the same plateau, he says, "To walk over it makes a stranger such an impression as being at sea, and he finds it impossible to estimate distances in any weather" (4:134).

Such illusions accumulate rapidly near the end of the book, particularly in chapter nine, "The Sea and the Desert," where three occur within three pages. In the first he describes a chain of clear, shallow pools of water that appear to be inclined at a distinct angle to the horizon, thus appearing "to lie by magic on the side of the vale, like a mirror left in a slanting position" (4:191), even though the land is in fact quite level. The second reports Thoreau's erroneous impression that "the inside half of the beach sloped upward toward the water to meet the other" half; "I was not convinced of the contrary till I descended the bank, though the shaded outlines left by the waves of a previous tide but halfway *down* the apparent declivity might have convinced me better" (4:192, Thoreau's emphasis). It is interesting to notice that nature leaves clues that the observer is nevertheless incapable of seeing; humans are not able to decipher all of nature's hieroglyphics. The third illusion is one reported to Thoreau by Emerson, who, while viewing ships at sea through a telescope, thought that the water around the ships was perfectly smooth when in fact the rippled sails of the ships proved that it was undulating (4:192–93).[19] Not only was a trained observer's eye ineffective in measuring such a world, but even such an optical aid as a telescope proved deceptive.

One other kind of illusion requires examination. In *Cape Cod* even light, that transcendental symbol of God's presence that Thoreau uses so effectively in *Walden,* sometimes is illusory and untrustworthy. The lighthouse keeper gives Thoreau such evidence in his accounts of sailors led astray by mistaking a mackerel fisher or a cottager's lantern for the lighthouse light. Even more disturbing is uncertainty about natural light. Thoreau has difficulty adjusting to the sun's rising over the ocean rather than over land. Watching a sunrise in chapter six, he admits that "as yet I still looked at him [the sun] as rising over land, and could not, without an effort realize that he was rising over the sea" (4:104). This dubiety about the sun increases later in "The Highland Light" when the lighthouse keeper tells Thoreau of a "looming" of the sun he had witnessed. Rising to walk on the beach a half hour before sunrise, when he would extinguish the lamps in the lighthouse, the keeper was astonished to see the sun apparently already two-thirds above the horizon. Thinking his clocks must be wrong, he returned to the lighthouse and extinguished the lamps, but the sun remained at the same height for about fifteen minutes and then rose as usual. Thoreau suggests to the keeper two possible explanations for this phenomenon, neither of which is completely convincing (4:173–74). But the possibility of even the sun's being deceptive suggests to Thoreau the need for everyone to trust the lamps of one's own insight more than the light of nature: "He certainly must be a son of Aurora to whom the sun looms, when there are so many millions to whom it *glooms* rather, or who never see it till an hour *after* it has risen. But it behooves us old stagers to keep our lamps trimmed and burning to the last, and not to trust to the sun's looming" (4:174, Thoreau's emphases).

Thoreau's persona's doubts about this central symbol suggest how deeply Thoreau's own ambivalence about such phenomena of light as mirages and illusions runs in *Cape Cod*. On the one hand, as part of the dominant impression of the cape that he wants to give, they sometimes seem to be appropriate transcendental symbols for nature's infinite variety. *Cape Cod* might almost be subtitled "Thoreau in Wonderland," for at various times throughout the book he describes the cape as being "fabulous," "a place of wonder," and a "wonderstrand." "To an inlander," he says, "the Cape landscape is a constant mirage" (4:41). This last passage seems to be adapted from a discussion of mirages in his journal for 9 February 1852: "Men tell about the mirage to be seen in certain deserts and in peculiar states of the atmosphere. The mirage is constant. The state of the atmosphere is continually varying, and, to a keen observer, objects do not twice present exactly the same appearance. . . . The prospect is thus actually a constantly varying mirage, answering to the condition of our perceptive faculties and our fluctuating imaginations" (*Writings* 9:290). He then suggests performing Emerson's experiment of inverting the head between the legs to see instantly a new world and concludes with a discussion of the effects of air on the newness of our perceptions: "I cannot well conceive of greater variety than it produces by its changes from hour to hour of every day. It is a new glass placed over the picture every hour" (*Writings* 9:290–91). Mirages thus become symbols of new worlds available to each of us instantly if we only choose to look. Thoreau's persona probably intends the mirages in *Cape Cod* to serve as such positive symbols as well, just as he intends the dead bodies at Cohasset to be interpreted optimistically.

But even Alice's wonderland had a threatening side to it. A careful examination of Thoreau's mirage passages reveals that the persona's transcendental intentions are offset and even overturned by the concept of mirages as elusive hindrances to Thoreau's understanding of nature. As we have seen, illusions threaten to suck one into the sand or to lure one crashing onto the rocks. They often occur in fog, mist, or haze, all hindrances to accurate vision. They cast doubts upon even the most sacred transcendental symbols, such as light. When interwoven with and juxtaposed to the book's other dominant motifs, death and impermanence, they ultimately create a view of a nature antagonistic to transcendental harmony.

A famous passage in which Thoreau looks for Margaret Fuller's remains on the beach at Fire Island suggests that whatever harmony is possible between humanity and nature may lie only in death. He says that in searching for remnants of a body that someone had marked with a stick, "I expected that I must look very narrowly to find so small an object, but the sandy beach, half a mile wide, and stretching farther than the eye could reach, was so perfectly smooth and bare, and the mirage toward the sea so magnifying, that when I was half a mile distant the insignificant sliver which marked the spot looked like a bleached spar, and the relics were as conspicuous as if they lay in state on that sandy plain, or a generation had labored to pile up their cairn there" (4:107–8). He then describes the unremarkable and inoffensive quality of the individual bones, but soon these few bones take on a sublime union with nature that is blocked to the living man viewing them: "As I stood there they grew more and more imposing. They were alone with the beach and the sea, whose hollow roar seemed addressed to them, and I was impressed as if there was an understanding between them and the ocean which necessarily left me out, with my sniveling sympathies. That dead body had taken possession of the shore, and reigned over it as no living one could" (4:108). Although this passage could be interpreted as illustrating Thoreau's optimism about humans' unity with nature in the afterlife, its implications for the naturalist's desire to unite with nature in this life are clearly very pessimistic, and he seems less willing than in *Walden* to settle for a delayed unity.

Such illusions are enough to make Thoreau recoil from the mystery of the sea's power. In *Walden* he had delighted in proving that Walden Pond was not bottomless, thus demonstrating that people could easily know more of nature than most thought possible. In *Cape Cod*, however, the ocean seems to Thoreau to be more ominously bottomless and unknowable, at least for human purposes:

As we looked off, and saw the water growing darker and darker and deeper and deeper the farther we looked, till it was awful to consider, and it appeared to have no relation to the friendly land, either as shore or bottom,—of what use is a bottom if it is out of sight, if it is two or three miles from the surface,

and you are to be drowned so long before you get to it, though it were made
of the same stuff with your native soil?—over that ocean where, as the Veda
says, "there is nothing to give support, nothing to rest upon, nothing to cling
to," I felt that I was a land animal. (4:123)

Here, then, is Thoreau's reply to his own belief in *Walden* that nature
is knowable. He seems more deeply frightened to realize that perhaps
the only possible union with the ocean is through death than he did in
the parable of the man sinking in the swamp in the conclusion of
Walden.

Instead of harmony with nature, Thoreau finds at Cape Cod an eternal battle between the human being, a land animal, and the sea, a
bottomless wilderness. In the third paragraph of the book, he establishes this relationship by describing the Cape as a boxer: "Cape Cod
is the bared and bended arm of Massachusetts . . . boxing with north-
east storms, and, ever and anon, heaving up her Atlantic adversary
from the lap of the earth" (4:4). This battle, he realizes, has been
fought continually since the beginning of time, and often the land has
lost. After considering the bottomlessness of the ocean, he thinks of
those underwater islands of legend, such as "George's Bank," that lost
their struggle with the sea: "It reminded me, when I thought of the
shipwrecks which had taken place there, of the Isle of Demons, laid
down off this coast in charts of the New World. There must be something monstrous, methinks, in a vision of the sea bottom from over
some bank a thousand miles from the shore, more awful than its imagined bottomlessness; a drowned continent, all livid and frothing at the
nostrils, like the body of a drowned man, which is better sunk deep
than near the surface" (4:124).

The difference between the land wilderness of the American West
and the wilderness of the ocean, however, was that while the West was
certain to be conquered by humans, the ocean never had been and never
would be domesticated. Thoreau says of the ocean,

We do not associate the idea of antiquity with the ocean, nor wonder how it
looked a thousand years ago, as we do of the land, for it was equally wild and
unfathomable always. The Indians have left no traces on its surface, but it is
the same to the civilized man and the savage. The aspect of the shore only has
changed. The ocean is a wilderness reaching round the globe, wilder than a
Bengal jungle, and fuller of monsters, washing the very wharves of our cities

and the gardens of our sea-side residences. Serpents, bears, hyenas, tigers, rapidly vanish as civilization advances, but the most populous and civilized city cannot scare a shark far from its wharves. (4:188)

The imagery of the sea as a monster-filled jungle shows that Thoreau's naturalism in *Cape Cod* is often quite different from the optimistic, transcendental naturalism of *Walden*.

Sherman Paul and Emory Maiden agree that this new kind of naturalism in *Cape Cod* has much in common with the Darwinian naturalism of Stephen Crane, particularly Crane's description of an ocean indifferent to humans in "The Open Boat."[20] Paul thinks, however, that Thoreau hesitated to take the step into Darwinian naturalism, preferring to take refuge in conventional concepts of the sublime: "The forces that they [Darwinian naturalists] would have interpreted naturalistically . . . he interpreted in terms of the sublime. And rather than narrowing his conception of nature, these forces reminded him of the 'Mystery, Power, Silence' at the heart of things and of the reverence and worship which he was powerless to withhold in the presence of the Creator."[21]

Paul is partially right: Thoreau certainly does use the language of sublimity in *Cape Cod*. But the sublimity he presents does not inspire reverence and unity with God; rather it excludes humanity from unity with God and puts the two at odds. Maiden, who examines Thoreau's use of the sublime more fully than Paul, seems more accurate in his assertion that "Thoreau chooses the sublime terminology because it is a kind of descriptive shorthand which carries with it an almost guaranteed recognition by the reader of the type of landscape intended" and that Thoreau does indeed "discover the root of the agonized, diminished modern consciousness" of humans' separation from nature.[22] As Maiden points out, Thoreau is not likely to have made use of Darwin's *The Origin of Species*, which was not published until 1859, but he did know Darwin's account of the voyage of the *Beagle* and was certainly aware of the evolutionary theories in the air in the early 1850s.[23] There is, for instance, a very untranscendental, very Darwinian tone to this description of the beach in *Cape Cod:* "The seashore is a sort of neutral ground, a most advantageous point from which to contemplate this world. It is even a trivial place. The waves forever rolling to the land are too far-travelled and untamed to be familiar. Creeping along the endless beach amid the sun squawl and the foam, it occurs to us that we, too, are the product of sea-slime. It is a wild, rank place, and there is no flattery in it" (4:186).

The shore of Walden Pond had also been a neutral ground from which Thoreau could look one way to the human world and the other way at nature's. There humanity had seemed something more than "the product of sea-slime" and nature had not seemed monstrous. But in *Cape Cod* Thoreau's view of the human relation to God and to nature is often bleak indeed. One metaphor that he uses for humans' place in the universe is that of a bottle cast adrift, suggesting their lack of control over their own destiny: "it seemed to me that man himself was like a half-emptied bottle of pale ale, which Time had drunk so far, yet stoppled tight for a while, and drifting about in the ocean of circumstances, but as destined erelong to mingle with the surrounding waves, or be spilled amid the sands of a distant shore" (4:117). Another more gruesome metaphor is that of humans as dead cods being crunched by a cow. Thinking of the rumor that Provincetown cows ate cods' heads, he says, "I felt my own skull crack from sympathy. What if the heads of men were to be cut off to feed the cows of a superior order of beings who inhabit the islands in the ether? Away goes your fine brain, the house of thought and instinct, to swell the cud of a ruminant animal! (4:214). Clearly in both these metaphors Thoreau is not confident of God's benevolence nor of humanity's godlike potential, as he is elsewhere in his writings.

The dark view of a chaotic, uncontrollable ocean, of a land on which the human being is merely another animal struggling for survival amid nature's indifference, and of a possibly malevolent God was not one with which, as a transcendentalist, Thoreau could be very comfortable. Nor is it the only view of the cape that he presents. There are, to be sure, many descriptions of it as beautiful or picturesque, an attempted balance against the sublimely wild views. But the tame passages are usually followed immediately by a "sublimely dreary" view of the ocean, so that an often irreverent sublimity frequently has the last word.

In adopting a naive, optimistic persona, Thoreau recognized his own reluctance to accept the awesome, uncontrollable sublimity of the cape, and at the beginning of *Cape Cod* he claims that "having come so fresh to the sea, I have got but little salted" (4:3). The evidence of the book following this apology suggests, however, that Thoreau himself as well as his persona was quite thoroughly seasoned by the sea. Near the end, for instance, his persona is sufficiently initiated to be amused by the nautical naivety of some copassengers, men returning home on the same boat with him who are fooled by one such illusion. The men, using the captain's telescope, see two boats in the distance that seem to be maintaining an amazingly consistent distance from each other. But Thoreau has already recognized that one boat is towing the other, and he listens smugly to the captain's dry remark to the men that the two boats probably never would get any nearer to each other (4:265). Thoreau also says that when he arrived home at Concord, "there was still enough sand in my shoes left to sand my pages for many a day; and I seemed to hear the sea roar, as if I lived in a shell, for a week afterward" (4:269). His persona's memory of the lighthouse keepers in the eggshell lighthouse seems to have followed him inland. Thoreau himself also returned to life as a land animal, but the impact of the sea's wildness remained with him. He would continue to measure desperately the objects in the Concord woods, but his measurements could not erase the memory of the immeasurable vastness of the sea.

Thoreau realized at Cape Cod that he had found the first and wildest American wilderness, the Atlantic shore and ocean. In "The Sea and the Desert," he looks out to sea and imagines sailing through the Pillars of Hercules, which in ancient times were thought to be the western boundary of the world, and questioning the inhabitants about what was written on the pillars. "The inhabitants," he says, "shouted *Ne plus ultra* (no more beyond), but the wind bore to us the truth only, *plus ultra* (more beyond), and over the Bay westward was echoed *ultra* (beyond). We spoke to them through the surf about the Far West, the true Hesperia . . . where the sun was extinguished in the *Pacific,* and we advised them to pull up stakes and plant those pillars of theirs on the shore of California, whither all our folks were gone,—the only *ne plus ultra* now" (4:178–79, Thoreau's emphases). There is an unmistakable touch of irony in this passage. California might indeed have been seen as the American Hesperides, but Thoreau knew that it was a pacific (peaceful) and pacifiable wilderness soon to be civilized.

In 1893 Frederick Jackson Turner quoted the census of 1890 as reporting that "there can hardly be said to be a frontier line."[24] The wheel of civilization had rolled on, conquering frontier after frontier on its way to the Pacific, and chasing the serpent and bear ahead of it. For the rest of his life Thoreau continued to use the West as a symbol of wildness that America could readily understand, but he himself preferred to stand in the starting gate of this race westward and look the other way.[25] One could indeed stand on the cape, face the sea, and put all *civilized* America behind one. Thoreau stared out from the eastern shore of America remembering what America had already forgotten— that the first frontier, the first wilderness containing the secret not only of the nation's but of humanity's origin and destiny, was eastward in the illusions of the shore and in the bottomless darkness of the sea.

Chapter Six

The Sauntering Eye: The Nature Essays and the Journal

Whatever shocks Thoreau encountered on the rocky tableland of Mount Katahdin or the stormy shores of Cape Cod, their effect was to temper rather than to undermine his transcendentalism. What ultimately overwhelmed him more than nature's immensity was the infinite variety of nature in the backyards and woods of his own Concord. He "travelled a good deal in Concord" (*Walden,* 4), walking in the woods daily whenever possible. The immediate result of such walks was his multivolume journal filled with observations of nature, a collection of data so rich in detail that it defied organization. Thoreau clearly anticipated using this data for some long-range project that he had difficulty defining. It might have been a "Natural History of Concord" or a comprehensive calendar of the seasons. Whatever he had in mind, the project had not fully taken shape by the time of his fatal illness.

Perhaps it never would have, for Thoreau was not a master of the grand design, and he eventually learned to value facts in their own right rather than as part of such a design. He was at his best capturing brief moments of inspiration and molding them according to whatever organic principle they might contain. Although he never achieved a clear vision of the pattern that he believed lay buried in his journal, throughout his career he mined it for those coherent groups of insights that might work for periodical publication or for lectures. These efforts yielded four nature essays published before his stay at the pond and a group of essays and unified journal sections that in his last years he reworked for publication. Although these nature essays are very uneven, they often contain passages central to our understanding of Thoreau. The journal itself, of course, is essential to a full comprehension of Thoreau because of its detailed record of his intellectual and emotional life.

Life

When Hawthorne first met Thoreau in 1842, he accurately observed that "Mr. Thorow [sic] is a keen and delicate observer of nature—a genuine observer, which, I suspect, is almost as rare a character as even an original poet; and Nature, in return for his love, seems to adopt him as her especial child, and shows him secrets which few others are allowed to witness."[1] In noticing the similarity between Thoreau's eye for detail and a poet's, Hawthorne proved himself to be a keen observer as well, for even when Thoreau's walks resulted only in the recording of dry natural facts, his purpose was always the romantic poet's: to discover the spiritual law within the natural fact.

Both the nature essays and the journal had deep roots in Thoreau's daily walks. His method of walking in the woods he called "sauntering," a word whose etymology he found fascinating. "Sauntering," he says in his essay "Walking," "is beautifully derived 'from idle people who roved the country, in the Middle Ages, and asked charity, under pretence of going *à la Sainte Terre*,' to the Holy Land, till the children exclaimed, 'There goes a Sainte-Terrer,' a Saunterer,—a Holy Lander" (*Writings* 5:205–6, Thoreau's emphasis).[2] Such walks were as much religious exercises as scientific expeditions. They thus required that the walker temporarily renounce all concern for society: "if you have paid your debts, and made your will, and settled all your affairs, and are a free man, then you are ready for a walk" (*Writings* 5:206).[3]

Few were willing to take walking so seriously. Channing, Hawthorne, Emerson, or one of the Concord farmers or sportsmen might occasionally be tolerated as companions, but usually Thoreau preferred to walk alone. Emerson has described the familiar solitary figure that Thoreau cut on such walks: "Under his arm he carried an old music-book to press plants; in his pocket, his diary and pencil, a spy-glass for birds, microscope, jack-knife, and twine. He wore straw hat, stout shoes, strong gray trousers to brave shrub oaks and smilax, and to climb a tree for a hawk's or a squirrel's nest" ("Biographical Sketch," *Writings* 1:xxix).

He walked in all seasons and at all hours of the day. Summer was the most fruitful season for sauntering. Then the light was clearest, ponds and rivers were open for bathing and boating, plants and animals were most numerous and most active, and walking was pleasant at any hour. The other seasons were merely anticipations of summer. "Even in winter," he says, "we are hunters pursuing the summer on snow-

shoes and skates. . . . There is really but one season in our hearts"
(15:164). Spring and autumn were welcome "transition seasons or
states of the atmosphere, which show us thus phenomena which belong
not to the summer or the winter of any climate" (9:105). For sauntering winter was less welcome. The hours of light were too short, and
the teeming life of summer was hidden beneath the snow. Even then,
however, the persistent saunterer could find new points of view by
walking and skating on the ponds and rivers, thus redeeming even the
bleakest season (see *Walden,* 299).

Times of the day were seasons in miniature. His favorite time of day
for sauntering was the afternoon: "In the forenoon commonly I see
nature only through a window; in the afternoon my study or apartment
in which I sit is a vale" (9:57). Like the summer, the afternoon was
best because of its consistent light and centrality. "The after-noon
man," he says, "has an interest in the past; his eye is divided, and he
sees indifferently well either way."[4] Evening, like autumn, he found to
be a time of transition and meditation—"The serene hour, the muses's
hour, the season of reflection!" (11:370–71). It was especially the sunset, "the grandest picture in the world" (10:258), that brought him
out at evening. Like winter, night could smack of death, especially
when it seemed "the mere negation of day" (10:472). At such times,
he felt, "Death is with me, and life far away" (10:472). But night also
had its unique charm. Moonlight provided a softer light, "more favorable to meditation than sunlight" (8:372). It also forced the exercise
of senses other than sight: "Other senses take the lead. The walker is
guided as well by the sense of smell" (5:327). Nighttime walks, with
their return to more primitive senses and their mystery, were as close
as Thoreau could come to sublimity around Concord. So when an urge
for wildness struck him and Maine and Cape Cod were too far off, he
reversed his schedule, sometimes for weeks at a time. The summer of
1851 was one such period when his journal became "selenitic" (9:273).
And morning, of course, was like spring, a time of renewal and hope.
In the morning, the light was also "more trustworthy" (9:354) and
certain facts to be seen at no other time of day revealed themselves.
"Some flowers," he observed, "shut up at noon and do not open again
during the day" (10:216).

Whatever the season or hour, the method of observation was the key
to successful sauntering. "Almost any *mode* of observation will be successful at last," he says, "for what is most wanted is method. . . .
There is wanting constant and accurate observation with enough of

theory to direct and discipline it. But above all, there is wanting genius" (1:388, Thoreau's emphasis). Maintaining a method balanced between accurate objective observation and subjective theory was a touchy business, however.

The choice of which direction to walk, for instance, could be crucial to the success of the saunterer. Thoreau's most frequent choice was southwest from Concord—partly because of the symbolic association of the west with hope and the future, but also because the best hiking country around Concord lay in that direction. Usually he chose a familiar place as a destination for his walk, despite the problem that in doing so he might be too subjective and see only what he expected. He attempted to offset that excessive subjectivity, however, by sometimes striking out on a beeline to the destination, ignoring trails and coping with obstacles as he encountered them. If he followed an established road or trail, he preferred "old, meandering, dry uninhabited roads . . . where travellers are not too often met; where my spirit is free; where the walls and fences are not cared for" (8:322). Often to avoid meeting other people he would "travel chiefly in the fields or pastures parallel with the road" instead of on the road itself (10:132). But always he tried to maintain "a true sauntering of the eye" (10:351), an ability to let his vision wander off the path and catch things by surprise out of the corner of his eye. The saunterer must not "look at nature directly," he thought, "but only with the side of his eye. He must look through and beyond her. To look at her is as fatal as to look at the head of Medusa" (11:45).

When his eyes caught a glimpse of an interesting object, he then had to decide how closely to examine it. Usually he preferred the closest possible inspection, often with the aid of his microscope, which he kept from his days at Harvard. At such times he found that "Nature will bear the closest inspection. She invites us to lay our eye level with her smallest leaf" (5:107). But too much close observation was not healthy either, for he sometimes found that "the habit of looking at things microscopically, as the lichens on the trees and rocks, really prevents my seeing aught else in a walk" (9:336). Such vision could easily become as narrow as that of his spiritually slumbering community.

As a transcendentalist he often found distant views more useful. He agreed with Channing that "the idealist views things in the large" (12:129). He recognized that there could be "some advantage, perhaps, in attending to the general features of the landscape over studying the particular plants and animals which inhabit it" (8:416). Thus he often made a mountain or hilltop the destination of his walks. Arriving late in the afternoon, he would wait there to watch the sunset before returning home. Even such dazzling panoramas, however, presented a problem. Although distance allowed one to idealize nature because one could see it as a unified whole, it obscured nature's less ideal but equally significant details. At one point in his journal Thoreau describes viewing a distant mountain but complains that he is unable to see the "farmhouses, the lonely mills, wooded vales, wild rocky pastures. . . . All these, and how much more, I *overlook*. I see the very peak,—there can be no mistake,—but how much I do not see, that is between me and it!" (10:366, Thoreau's emphasis). He bought a spyglass in Boston in March 1845 (12:166–67), but its novelty soon wore off. In September of that same year he writes that using a spyglass is "a disruptive mode of viewing as far as the beholder is concerned" (13:61), because one concentrates only through the eye; contributions by the other senses are cut off.

He thus found himself wondering, "Who placed us with eyes between a microscopic and a telescopic world?" (12:133). The dilemma seemed unsolvable. He speculated that water reflections might contain an intermediate view between subject and object, between near and distant views, but he never expressed that theory fully in his published works.[5] Eventually he realized that no single view of nature could yield the whole truth of a fact. Charles Feidelson, Jr., expresses Thoreau's dilemma vividly in saying that "Thoreau is extremely aware that what he can present is not absolute experience but a relative fact—'my relation to nature.'"[6] All his nature writing, especially the journal, is an attempt to present this dynamic relationship, to record if not nature, the thing itself, then his own relation to nature in as many of its permutations as possible.

The long-range changes in that relation are most easily seen in his nature essays, which were collected into book form after his death and published as *Excursions,* and in some of his unified fragments of nature writing in the journal. The essays in *Excursions* are interesting because of what Leo Marx calls their "curious 'before and after' effect."[7] The first four essays in this collection were all published before Thoreau's Walden Pond years; the last five were published in the 1860s, some shortly before and some after his death. Even more interesting is the

journal, because it records his thoughts and observations from its beginning (apparently at Emerson's suggestion) on 22 October 1837 to
his last entry on 3 November 1861.

Art

Excursions **and other Nature Essays.** *Excursions* was published
in 1863, as the first posthumous collection of Thoreau's writing. Shortly before his death Thoreau had revised some of his late nature essays
for publication in the *Atlantic Monthly,* and Emerson and Sophia Thoreau added to those late essays some of Thoreau's early pieces to fill out
the volume. The result was a miscellaneous collection unified only by
most of the essays ("The Landlord" is the one exception) being about
nature.[8] Despite this lack of unity, however, this collection does reveal
much about Thoreau's development as a writer and thinker in its contrast between the early and late nature essays.

"The Natural History of Massachusetts," the earliest (1842) of the
essays, is ostensibly a review of a series of zoological and botanical
reports published by the commonwealth of Massachusetts. Thoreau,
however, does very little actual reviewing of the reports. Instead he
uses them as a springboard for his own miscellaneous observations of
nature. In doing so he exhibits his early transcendental tendency to
extract generalities from natural facts. "Nature," he says, "is mythical
and mystical always" (5:125). The goal of the naturalist is thus to
"discern a law or couple two facts" (5:131) and, in doing so, to raise
the facts of nature to the level of myth. The truth within the fact is
always the object of the quest.

In "The Natural History" we see Thoreau beginning that quest with
cheerful confidence that he can improve upon the efforts of the report
writers. In his few sentences of actual reviewing he claims to have
found "several errors" in the report and is confident that "a more prac-
tised eye would no doubt expand the list" (5:130). He is grateful to
the compilers of the reports for their pioneer fact gathering but feels
the need for more interpretation of those facts. He thus substitutes his
own more nearly "mythical and mystical" observations for theirs.

These observations show us in the bud some of the truths that soon
were to flower in his longer works. We find, for instance, a catalog of
birds and fish similar to such catalogs in *A Week.* There are also observations on the origin of the Concord River's Indian name, on civilization's need for a border of wildness, and on the growth of vegetation

as a model for all natural growth—all concepts that appear in *A Week* or *Walden*. But there are a few unique passages that stand on their own in this essay as the equal of his later work. Perhaps the most striking is his extended description of spearfishing at night, with its images of fiery crates used as lanterns tied to the boats and of the fish lurking in the dark waters below. It is, he says with appropriate mythical allusion, "as if he had stolen the boat of Charon and gone down the Styx on a midnight expedition" (5:122). In such a passage we see the kind of vivid truths he finds lacking in the state reports.

The essay ends with a qualified confidence in the value of scientific exploration. Thoreau warns himself as much as the reader that "we do not learn by inference and deduction, and the application of mathematics to philosophy, but by direct intercourse and sympathy. It is with science as with ethics,—we cannot know truth by contrivance and method; the Baconian is as false as any other" (5:131). Robert Sattelmeyer observes of this passage that it is not a rejection of "Baconian" scientific method but a reminder that "no theory of nature or way of representing nature should be mistaken for nature itself."[9] Science is one key to the truths in nature as long as one does not confuse the method with the truth it is used to seek. As Thoreau eventually learned, however, that distinction was sometimes hard to maintain.

Of the other three early essays in *Excursions,* "The Landlord" is not a nature essay but an extended definition of the ideal innkeeper. The other two—"A Walk to Wachusett" and "A Winter Walk"—provide an interesting contrast between two applications of the journey motif. This theme gives the two essays a structural unity that "The Natural History" lacks, but in them Thoreau is still exploring different ways of using it.

"A Walk to Wachusett" is the more literary, less specific, and less successful treatment of the walking motif. Thoreau begins by relating Mount Wachusett to other mountains of literary fame: Homer's "many-peaked Olympus," Virgil's "Etrurian and Thessalian hills," and Humboldt's "more modern Andes and Teneriffe" (5:133). He then includes a poem, one of his best, in praise of Wachusett's "frontier strength" (5:133–35). What follows is a rather tame account of his hike with Richard Fuller through fields of hops, across hot valleys, and up the slopes of Wachusett, with the predictable panoramic view of Massachusetts from the summit as climax. Along the way the two read Virgil and, on the summit, Wordsworth. All the literary allusions warn the reader that the symbolic payoff is likely to be derivative, as indeed it is. Thoreau likens the climbing of the mountain to "human life,—now climbing the hills, now descending into the vales" (5:150), a comparison that had long been a cliché.

Nonetheless, the essay does contain a significant early affirmation of Thoreau's belief in the essential unity behind nature's variety: "man's life is rounded with the same few facts, the simple relations everywhere, and it is bain to travel to find it new" (5:137). That belief in nature's organic unity and thus in the Concord woods as a microcosm of those "same few facts" was what motivated his study of nature for the rest of his life. He would eventually have to change "few" to hundreds and later thousands of facts, but he never lost his belief that there was an essential unity in nature.

"A Winter Walk" also uses the structure of a day's journey as a symbol of human life, but the symbolic ascent of the mountain is replaced by movement from town to woods and back—a stepping beyond the bounds of the villager's usual winter experience. Because Thoreau wishes to take the reader beyond the limits of the usual view of winter as a dead season, he relies heavily on paradox—his verbal equivalent of Emerson's trick of inverting one's head between the knees to get a new point of view—to force the reader into taking a new perspective. He describes the walker's breath as "a crystallized midsummer haze" (5:166), the winter day as "a Scandinavian night" (5:170), and winter as "an arctic summer" (5:170). What is important about winter is not its deathlike chill but the "slumbering subterranean fire in nature which never goes out, and which no cold can chill" (5:167). He compares this "fire" of nature's life stirring silently under the snow and preparing to burst out as new growth in spring to the latent spiritual insight waiting inside every individual. Snow thus becomes a mothering warmth protecting new plants beneath its blanket from the chill of the winter air. It "infolds them deeper in the bosom of nature" (5:182). It also forces the walker to "lead a more inward life" (5:182). For literary support of this paradoxical but affectionate view of snow he offers Homer's description of a snowfall.[10]

"A Winter Walk" is, however, less dependent on literary allusion than is "A Walk to Wachusett," and it strikes a better balance between concrete fact and idealist theory. While "A Walk to Wachusett" is stylistically very close to A Week, "A Winter Walk" reminds us more of the winter chapters of Walden, particularly in its description of pickerel fisherman, its metaphor of a pond as "earth's liquid eye; a mirror in the breast of nature" (5:174), or its use of the fireplace and of smoke to represent inspiration. In "A Walk to Wachusett" and "A Winter Walk" we see Thoreau discovering the patterns behind nature's variety and probing for ways to express them. As Paul suggests, in these two essays Thoreau "began to make walking the explicit symbol of man's life, and he fully employed in the structure of these essays those archetypal patterns of morning and evening, sunrise and sunset, ascent and descent, mountain and plain, woods and village, summer and winter that became the warp and woof of the *Week* and *Walden*."[11]

The symbolism of walking was so central to Thoreau's thought that he frequently returned to it and based one of his most popular lectures on it. "Walking," one of the later essays included in *Excursions,* was originally a lecture composed from his journal for 1850 to 1852 but was not published in the *Atlantic Monthly* until 1862. He added to it over the years and by 1856 had split it into two separate lectures. But in preparing his final essays for the *Atlantic Monthly* he kept the two together.[12] The structural split shows obviously in the published version. The first part contains his essay on "sauntering" and on the virtues of the American landscape. The second part contains his famous essay on wildness. Both themes are central to all his writing and have been discussed elsewhere in this book.

One other crucial aspect of "Walking" deserves mention, however. Dazzled by Thoreau's powerful affirmation of the value of wildness in this essay, many readers are likely to miss its tone of moderation. While praising wildness as a resource, he also admits that it is not without its drawbacks:

Living much out of doors, in the sun and wind, will no doubt produce a certain roughness of character,—will cause a thicker cuticle to grow over some of the finer qualities of our nature. . . . So staying in the houses, on the other hand, may produce a softness and smoothness, not to say thinness of skin, accompanied by an increased sensibility to certain impressions. Perhaps we should be more susceptible to some influences important to our intellectual and moral growth, if the sun had shone and the wind blown on us a little less; and no doubt it is a nice matter to proportion rightly the thick and thin skin." (5:210).

The "natural remedy" to this dilemma, he adds, "is to be found in the proportion which the night bears to the day, the winter to the summer, thought to experience" (5:210).

No doubt these statements demonstrate Thoreau's sensitivity to his neighbors' view of him as personally cold and aloof. But they also contain as clear a statement as we get anywhere in his writings of the balance he sought for himself and for humanity. The dilemma was how to balance an exploration beyond society's bounds with the need for the culture and companionship offered by civilization. He wanted to be free to seek the new visions represented by wildness but not at the expense of being cut off from society permanently. "Undoubtedly," he says, "all men are not equally fit subjects for civilization; and because the majority, like dogs and sheep, are tame by inherited disposition, this is no reason why the others should have their natures broken that they may be reduced to the same level" (5:235). At bottom what he is urging is simply a recognition and tolerance of new points of view, including, of course, his own.

Such tolerance he sees as the first step toward becoming a true seer. "Which is the best man to deal with," he asks, "he who knows nothing about a subject, and what is extremely rare, knows that he knows nothing, or he who really knows something about it, but thinks that he knows all?" (5:240). His goal for himself and mankind is "not knowledge, but Sympathy with Intelligence" (5:240). It is not only in his call for a better balance between wildness and civilization but also in this call for "Useful Ignorance" (5:239) that "Walking" proves to be "the best brief exposition of Thoreau's philosophy."[13]

In the other late essays included in *Excursions* Thoreau seems to be overcompensating for his early transcendental vagueness by too zealous a devotion to facts. "The Succession of Forest Trees" is clearly such an attempt to offset his reputation for airy idealism. Delivered first as a lecture to the Middlesex Agricultural Society at the annual cattleshow in Concord in 1860, it is his first public attempt at "a purely scientific subject" (5:185). In his opening remarks he humorously reveals his own consciousness of being an outsider: "Every man is entitled to come to Cattle-Show, even a transcendentalist" (5:184). He then proceeds to provide an apparently untranscendental theory of how one species of tree supplants another. His key discovery is "that while the wind is conveying the seeds of pines into hard woods and open lands, the squirrels and other animals are conveying the seeds of oaks and walnuts into the pine woods, and thus a rotation of crops is kept up" (5:190). This theory, as some of his own quotations from expert sources suggest, did not originate with Thoreau. But he seems to have been the first to express it thoroughly and systematically. In doing so he apparently anticipated the study of ecology by about eighty years (although he did not use the word *ecology* itself).[14]

But even this scientific treatise has at least two transcendental themes. One concerns the value of seeds—the seeds of trees, but also the seeds of ideas. This symbolic association is much less obvious than in his earlier writings, but there are hints of it. "There is a patent-office at the seat of government of the universe," he says, "whose managers are as much interested in the dispersion of seeds as anybody at Washington can be" (5:187). Thus seeds take on universal significance as ideas planted by the managers of the universe. Later when he says, "I am prepared to believe that some seeds, especially small ones, may retain their vitality for centuries under favorable circumstances" (5:201), his audience can guess that he refers to the tenacity of ideas as well as seeds.

The other tinge of transcendental symbolism in "The Succession" is his concern, seen in all his major works, with humanity's misplaced priorities—particularly the tendency to overlook a natural truth in favor of an artificial one. The process for dispersing seeds that he describes is one visible to anyone interested enough to look carefully. Thus Thoreau invites the farmers "back to [their] wood-lots again" (5:186) to show them what they have overlooked. Indeed, so little aware of their own property are they that "I have several times shown the proprietor the shortest way out of his wood-lot" (5:185). The natural magic of seeds is ignored, he complains, while "farmers' sons will stare by the hour to see a juggler draw ribbons from his throat, though he tells them it is all deception" (5:204). "Surely," he concludes, "men love darkness rather than light" (5:204).

"Autumnal Tints" and "Wild Apples," the other two essays first published in the *Atlantic Monthly,* seem parts of the larger project that Thoreau was struggling to define. Both use a catalog of facts as a structural frame upon which to display some broad transcendental truths.

Although not one of Thoreau's best essays, "Autumnal Tints" is especially interesting as an attempt to regain some of his old balance between fact and truth. The essay is ostensibly a catalog of the autumn leaves according to the order of their appearance, a preliminary and brief part of an anticipated book on "October, or Autumnal Tints" in which he hoped to "get a specimen leaf from each changing tree, shrub, and herbaceous plant" and "outline it, copy its color exactly, with paint" (5:251). Such a book would provide a microcosm of autumn itself. Lacking time to complete such a project, he instead combines factual and poetic accounts of each kind of leaf.

In doing so, he revives the technique he used often in his earlier writings but more rarely in his last years, the technique of organizing his descriptions like landscape paintings. He says of the red maples, for instance, that "different trees being of different colors and hues, the outline of each crescent tree-top is distinct, and where one laps on to another. Yet a painter would hardly venture to make them thus distinct a quarter of a mile off" (5:262). Describing a distant maple swamp, he says that "as I advance, lowering the edge of the hill which makes the firm foreground or lower frame of the picture, the depth of the brilliant grove revealed steadily increases, suggesting that the whole of the inclosed valley is filled with such color" (5:262).

Thoreau fills "Autumnal Tints" with such painterly descriptions and with metaphors of nature as the supreme painter, but as an amateur scientist he also carefully records the precise dates of the peak colors of each kind of tree. Unfortunately this attempt at renewed synthesis of artistic and scientific visions does not quite succeed. He has a tendency to gush a bit over the brilliant colors, and he perhaps underestimates his audience, who are probably not as ignorant of the changing leaves as he seems to suggest.

"Autumnal Tints" has additional significance, however, as Thoreau's prose ode to autumn. It has an elegiac tone that suggests that he is now less interested in the hope of the morning star than in the acceptance of the falling leaf. Like John Keats in his "To Autumn," Thoreau expresses a willingness to accept change and its outcome in death.[15] He says of the autumn leaves, "How beautifully they go to their graves! how gently lay themselves down and turn to mould" (5:269–70). These leaves "teach us how to die" (5:270). Clearly Thoreau found very powerful and personal meaning in the autumn leaves, especially after the death of his father in 1859.

"The Wild Apples" was another essay with great personal meaning for Thoreau. Presented as a comprehensive treatise on the wild apple tree, it is also a transcendental exploration of the trees symbolic meaning for Thoreau personally and for humanity. Thoreau saw the wild apple as the fruit closest to his own temperament, for "the apple emulates man's independence" (5:300) and the wild apples especially are "wild only like myself, perchance, who belong not to the aboriginal race here, but have strayed into the woods from the cultivated stock" (5:301). Of wild apples that taste "acrid and puckery" he says, as he often said of himself, "perhaps they are not fairly ripe yet" (5:310). Perhaps, as Paul suggests, he also meant to contrast his own wildness once and for all to the more civilized sweetness of Emerson's domesticated apples.[16]

The wild apple was also important to him because of "how closely the history of the Apple-tree is connected with that of man" (5:290). This connection is made explicit in the section "How the Apple Tree Grows," in which he presents the wild apple tree's battle for survival against the browsing of cows, with the tree's survival representing humanity's tenacious endurance against fate. Thus Thoreau reverses the usual Christian mythology of apples, for they represent to him the rise rather than the downfall of human beings.[17]

The last piece included in *Excursions* was "Night and Moonlight," a collection of extracts from Thoreau's "selenitic" journal entries compiled by either Ellery Channing or Sophia Thoreau to fill out the volume.[18] These extracts contain some lovely prose poems about the moon, but because they were not put together by Thoreau himself, they are difficult to assess as an example of Thoreau's art, and they have sometimes been omitted from recent reprintings of the nature essays.[19]

At the end of his life Thoreau left several other incomplete attempts to find unity in his myriad notes on nature. His interest in the dispersion of seeds expressed in "The Succession of Forest Trees" led him to begin writing a series of essays on seeds. He was also planning the book-length study of autumn leaves announced in "Autumnal Tints," as well as a series of essays on fruits. That he still hoped to bring order out of his notes was further suggested by his phenological charts of Concord's plants and animals.[20] From these fragments one unified grouping on "Huckleberries" has recently been culled and published,[21] and other such distillations from these manuscripts will be included in the new Princeton edition of the complete works.

The Journal.   The shift in emphasis from generalities to facts in Thoreau's nature writing can be seen even more clearly in his journal. As it developed through the fourteen volumes that eventually filled the Walden edition, it eventually became not only the fullest record of his dynamic relation to nature but also the fullest record of his intellectual and social life.

There is surprisingly little observation of nature in the early volumes of the journal.[22] The first volume of the Walden edition, which covers from 1837 to 1847, is dominated by reflections on and quotations from his reading of various authors and by brief meditations on such generalities as love, bravery, and friendship. In the entries for the late 1830s one finds occasional observations of nature for its own sake, such as the description (on 29 October 1837) of two ducks on Goose Pond who play a sort of hide and seek with Thoreau similar to the loon's checker game in *Walden*. When the ducks reappear after diving, Thoreau observes with gentle amusement their "self-satisfied, darn-it-how-he-nicks-'em air" as they paddle off (*Journal* 1:8). More often, however, these early notes on nature have a heavily allegorical air about them, as in an entry two days earlier in which he describes fog that gives "a sombre aspect" to the landscape and trees that "stand with boughs downcast like pilgrims beaten by a storm." Adding the allegorical level, he continues, "So when thick vapors cloud the soul, it strives in vain to escape from its humble working-day valley, and pierce the dense fog which shuts out from view the blue peaks in its horizon, but must be content to scan its near and homely hills" (*Journal* 1:8).

Such descriptions are consistent with his early Emersonian view of nature as symbol expressed in January 1841: "It is more proper for a spiritual fact to have suggested an analogous natural one, than for the natural fact to have preceded the spiritual in our minds" (*Journal* 1:231). This precedence of spiritual facts over natural prevails at least until his entries at Walden Pond begin to appear in 1845. Then a subtle shift toward reversing the symbol-making process begins, perhaps because of Thoreau's new immersion in the natural facts around his cabin. This reversal is eventually complete and explicit in an entry for 5 September 1851: "All perception of truth is the detection of an analogy; we reason from our hands to our head" (8:463). Later on 1 November 1851 he adds that "a fact truly and absolutely stated is taken out of the region of common sense and acquires a mythologic or universal significance" (9:85). This belief in the inherent significance of facts accounts for the more factual tone of the late *Maine Woods* and *Cape Cod* essays, as well as the late nature essays. Stating the fact truly was now enough; symbol-making commentary had become mostly unnecessary.

Throughout the 1850s we see much of the journal being transformed into what William Howarth calls "a massive compilation of natural history data,"[23] seeds from which Thoreau trusted that truths would flower. At the same time, however, we see him periodically cautioning himself about losing the balance between truth and facts. In 1851 and 1852, for instance, he seems to have been particularly sensitive to the dangers of his increasingly scientific approach to nature. On 18 February 1852 he warns himself that "it is impossible for the same person to see things from the poet's point of view and that of the man of science. The poet's second love may be science, not his first,—when use has worn off the bloom" (9:311). Knowing that Thoreau was thus on his guard against substituting one kind of vision for another, one needs to be careful about attributing too much importance to the shift toward facts in the journal. As Robert Sattelmeyer points out, "there is still about the same amount of reflection and contemplation of ideas in the later journal as the early journal; it only appears to be more scattered because Thoreau now used the journal for the additional purpose of making detailed records of his various natural history observations.[24]

Nonetheless, it seems fair to conclude that in the last decade of his life Thoreau's interest in science did increase, that his method of observing nature was affected by this interest, and that he was to some extent concerned with being taken seriously as a scientist. Consider, for instance, this entry for 13 February 1852: "Color, which is the poet's wealth, is so expensive that most take to mere outline or pencil sketches and become men of science" (9:301). Despite this denigration of scientific pencil sketching, that same year he himself began to use his own primitive pencil sketches in his journal to supplement his verbal descriptions of nature. Science did occasionally sneak into first place in the poet's affections.

The observations of nature in the journal provide a fascinating record of the awesome scope of Thoreau's vision of nature. But the journal, even in his late years, is much more than a collection of notes on nature. It also gives us our most complete view of the many facets of Thoreau's remarkably full life and at times shows us a Thoreau that we see seldom or not at all in his other works. In the brief space available here it is impossible to give a full sense of this variety, but perhaps a few hints will whet the reader's appetite for more.

The journal reveals Thoreau to be an excellent narrative writer, a side of his talent that we see only occasionally in his other writings. He can tell a comic story with the best of them, as in "What Befell at Mrs. Brooks'" (19 March 1856), a hilarious account of how Mrs. Brooks tries to fetch help for her Irish maid who has fallen down the stairs, only to cause a chain reaction of well-meaning passers-by who all fall into mud puddles or down stairs themselves in a made scurry to come to the rescue. It is a story Mack Sennett could have used to good effect in his slapstick comedy films. A similar but more sustained comic anecdote is his story of trying to catch a pig that has escaped from his father's pig pen, another comedy of errors that begins with Thoreau's irritation at being deterred from his afternoon walk in the woods by his father's call for help. Trying to avoid what promises to be a long and arduous hunt for the pig, he suggests that his father "sell the pig as he was running (somewhere) to a neighbor who had talked of buying him, making a considerable reduction. But my suggestion was not acted on" (14:451). The mock epic story of the half-hearted hunt for the pig follows, with the pig at last being captured. But poor Henry must return home somewhat the worse for wear: "wet through and supperless, covered with mud and wheel-grease, without any rare flowers" (14:456).

He also proves to have some talent for serious reportage, as in his account of a powder mill explosion on 7 January 1853. Hearing a distant explosion loud enough to shake his parents' house, he jumps into a wagon and arrives at a scene of horrible devastation. After describing the apparent cause of the explosion, he describes its gruesome results: "Some of the clothes of the men were in the tops of trees, where undoubtedly their bodies had been and left them. The bodies were naked and black, some limbs and bowels here and there, and a head at a distance from its trunk. The feet were bare; the hair singed to a crisp" (10:455). Such a description goes far to dispel any accusation that Thoreau might have tried to escape confrontation with the harsher facts of life.

The journal also reaffirms Thoreau's talent for character sketches, an ability seen occasionally in his other works but nowhere as fully as in the journal. There is the delightfully cantankerous Mary Moody Emerson (Waldo's aunt). One evening (8 January 1852) as Thoreau is reading to her from his own manuscripts, he refers to god in "a merely heathenish sense" and "without any solemnity of voice." Aunt Mary inquires ominously, "Is that god spelt with a little g?" Thoreau adds with relief, "Fortunately it was" (9:179). There is Emerson himself, irreverently described hunting in the Adirondacks (23 August 1858): "Think of Emerson shooting a peetweet (with shot) for Agassiz, and cracking an ale-bottle (after emptying it) with his rifle at six rods! They cut several pounds of lead out of the tree. It is just what Mike Saunders, the merchant's clerk, did when he was there" (17:120).

There are also the Concord townsmen, such as George Minott, Sam Rice, and Bill Wheeler. He describes Minott as "the most poetical farmer—who most realizes to me the poetry of the farmer's life—that I know" (9:41). Sam Rice and his son he portrays as men for whom "life is a long sport" and who "know not what hard times are" (14:27). Wheeler, on the other hand, is the town ne'er-do-well who sleeps in a lean-to in the woods. He is eventually found dead long after the fact, his body "so far decomposed that his coffin was carried to his body and it was put into it with pitchforks" (9:197). But Thoreau wonders whether Wheeler might have been an unappreciated "mighty philosopher, greater than Socrates or Diogenes, simplifying life, returning to nature, having turned his back on towns" (9:196).

This description of Bill Wheeler could as easily be a description of Thoreau himself. Unlike the elusive Wheeler, however, Thoreau purposely left clues in his journal about the conflicts that molded his life, and he frequently used the journal to cope with those personal dilemmas. True, Thoreau was often quite reticent about personal revelations in his journal. As Howarth reminds us, "He left out many episodes from his life: a long-ago romance, the time he nearly died of grief, the night he spent in jail."[25] But there are also some personal problems that he discusses more fully in the journal than anywhere else.

One such problem was his uncertainty about friendship. On 23 February 1841 we see him apparently resigned to a solitary life after his rejection by Ellen Sewall: "Let all our stores and munitions be provided for the lone state" (*Journal* 1:272). But the next year (26 March 1842) finds him feeling defensive (as he frequently did feel) about his solitary lifestyle: "I must confess I have felt mean enough when asked how I was to act on society, what errand I had to mankind—undoubtedly I did not feel mean without a reason—and yet my loitering is not without defence" (*Journal* 1:393). This conflict between his solitary habits and his regret at not relating more warmly to society reappears throughout the journal without being resolved. In 1852 he writes, "If I am too cold for human friendship, I trust I shall not soon be too cold for natural influences. It appears to be a law that you cannot have a deep sympathy with both man and nature. Those qualities which bring you near to the one estrange you from the other" (9:400).

The journal reveals that throughout his life Thoreau was more deeply sensitive to the opinions of his neighbors than his published works suggest. Indeed, we find in the journal (10 February 1852) a longer version of the "mea culpa" that concludes "Economy"; at one point he considered using the passage as the opening epigraph for *Walden*:

Now if there are many who think that I am vainglorious, that I set myself up above others and crow over their low estate, let me tell them that I could tell a pitiful story respecting myself as well as them, if my spirits held out to do it; I could encourage them with a sufficient list of failures, and could flow as humbly as the very gutters themselves; I could enumerate a list of rank offenses as ever reached the nostrils of heaven; that I think worse of myself than they can possibly think of me, being better acquainted with the man. (9:292).

Such a negative epigraph would, of course, have drastically undercut the book's generally optimistic tone and made it quite another book indeed. But that Thoreau could write such a personal indictment, even in his journal, suggests a man more sensitive, more complex, and sometimes more troubled than his readers generally take him to have been.

This same complexity marks journal entries on other personal problems as well. His concerns about losing touch with nature and about his lack of public success as a writer and lecturer find much fuller expression in the journal than in his published works. On such topics the journal is as close as we can come to knowing Thoreau fully. He himself asked on 21 October 1857, "Is not the poet bound to write his own biography? Is there any other work for him but a good journal? We do not wish to know how his imaginary hero, but how he, the actual hero, lived from day to day" (16:115).

This attitude seems to have been the motivating force behind his journal beginning at least as early as 1850, for at about that time we see the journal becoming less a means to an end—material for books and lectures—than an end in itself, the repository for his field notes on nature as well as the artist's studio in which he almost daily tried to mold his facts and thoughts into verbal art. In the journal Thoreau became rather like Funes, the main character in Jorge Luis Borges's story "Funes the Memorious." Borges's character awakes from a blow to the head to discover that he now has total recall, that his brain no longer is able to filter out what sense impressions it does not want to keep. To bring order to a never-ending flood of data, Funes unsuccessfully attempts labyrinthine filing systems, but he eventually dies, like Thoreau, of "congestion of the lungs."[26] The difference between Thoreau and Funes, however, is that Thoreau was able to accept the very process of recording and thinking about natural data as valuable in its own right. The process was "not just a part of life but, in essence, life itself."[27] Writing the journal became the main business of his life, the creation of a very personal verbal reality. As Sharon Cameron suggests, in the journal "Thoreau is not supplementing his experience"; instead "he is writing his life so that it actually comes to comprise alternate—natural—phenomena."[28]

Although after *Walden* Thoreau was never able to distill from the journal as unified and sustained a piece of art, what the journal lacks in artistic unity it compensates for in scope, intimacy, and vitality, so that it ranks with *Walden* as his greatest work.[29] Its length will always deter the hurried reader, but the reader with a sauntering eye who seeks to know Thoreau fully will find that it rewards patient persistence with treasure after treasure left undetected by those unwilling to go beyond the bounds of *Walden* or "Civil Disobedience."

Chapter Seven
The Brave Man as Reformer: *Reform Papers*

When Bronson Alcott said of Thoreau that "Nature, poetry, life—not politics, not strict science, not society as it is—were his preferred themes,"[1] he was essentially accurate in his list of Thoreau's preferences. But politics was nearer to the center of Thoreau's interests than Alcott recognized. All Thoreau's major works and most of his minor ones demonstrate at least implicitly, and most often explicitly, his interest in reform. *A Week,* for instance, contains sharp criticism of the textile industry and of the established church, and *Walden* has as one of its major themes his criticism of the American economic system. His travel books are also peppered with social criticism. The lumber industry is his main target in *The Maine Woods,* and religion takes its lumps again in *Cape Cod.* Even the least of his travel pieces, "A Yankee in Canada," has as its main points of interest his indictments of the Catholic church and the Canadian military. Social and political reform was a logical extension of his transcendentalism and was a concern of his writing throughout his career.

Life

The earliest indications of Thoreau's interest in social and political reform are in his college essays, which address such topics as the danger of conformity and "Barbarities of Civilized States" (*Early Essays,* 105 and 108). But these essays were on assigned topics and contain only vague treatments of their subjects. Thoreau's abiding interest in reform is rooted in his early transcendentalism. Leo Stoller traces Thoreau's concern about reform to the transcendentalist ideal of self-culture transmitted to him from the Unitarians through Emerson.[2] According to this ideal, the highest duty of any person was to perfect the God-like part of oneself, which was part of the universal oversoul. By perfecting oneself, one leavened the whole loaf of humanity. Attempts to reform others were foolhardy if one were not first thoroughly reformed oneself. To do anything but cultivate self-perfection was to hack at the branches but not the roots of evil.

Such premises led Thoreau to a paradoxical approach to reform that sanctioned a program of social action requiring no action upon society.[3] As Thoreau himself says in *A Week*: "It is a great pleasure to escape sometimes from the restless class of Reformers. What if these grievances exist? So do you and I" (*A Week,* 126). His own ideal of "a wise and competent man," as we have seen, is one who "will not meddle with such like matters [as state affairs]" (*A Week,* 130).

Thoreau was thus always a reformer at heart in his own singular way, but to his dying day he was only reluctantly a social activist. Even the Civil War could not shake his emphasis on the primacy of individual reform. As he wrote to Parker Pillsbury concerning the war, "I do not so much regret the present condition of things in this country (provide I regret it at all) as I do that I ever heard of it. . . . I am reading Herodotus & Strabo, Blodgett's Climatology, and Six years in the Deserts of North America, as hard as I can, to counterbalance it."[4]

Despite his ideal of self-culture, Thoreau eventually found that reform might sometimes depend on numbers. His night in jail seems to have been crucial in his recognizing that need. While in jail he came to realize that his neighbors were simply not interested in either his moral perfection or their own and that the state could easily afford to ignore his individual protest as having no impact on the masses. He saw that it was not enough to set a good example and assume that other people would inevitably follow. The others needed to be awakened enough to recognize the problem before they could join the righteous individual in a solution. Thoreau's interest in reform was thus one with his effort in *Walden* to wake his neighbors up and make them seers.

Most of Thoreau's own actions as a reformer have been discussed elsewhere in this book, as have his written attacks on economic, social, and political institutions in his book-length works. His interest in reform, however, was also strongly expressed in brief reviews, lectures, and essays. These so-called reform papers tend to explore three main topics: the characteristics of a true reformer, the individual's relation to America's economic system, and the individual's relation to America's political system.

Art

Early Essays on Reformers.   Early in his career Thoreau had an intense interest in finding a role model for himself, a person he calls "the hero" or "the brave man." His earliest expression of this model is in "The Service," an essay submitted to the *Dial* in 1840.[5] Although it is marred by Thoreau's early problems with organization and a transcendental vagueness of style, it contains his earliest expression of some of the major themes that appear in his major works.

Its soldierly imagery is perhaps surprising to those who see Thoreau as America's patron saint of passive resistance, but—as we shall see—it is typical of the reform papers. He begins by defining the "Qualities of the Recruit" in his own paradoxical way. The recruit is one whose "bravery deals not so much in resolute action, as healthy and assured rest" (*Reform Papers,* 3). He builds "inward and not outward" (4). This brave recruit is "a perfect sphere, which cannot fall on its flat side, and is equally strong every way" (6). At the center of this sphere are the brave man's eyes, the perceivers of truth that enable him to become the seer of *Walden.* Thoreau's brave man is not the soldier of heroic physical action but a man of quiet resolution who subtly and steadily perfects himself, knowing full well—as Thoreau would frequently remind himself—that "the hugest and most effective deed may have no sensible result at all on earth, but may paint itself in the heavens" (16). Like Thoreau's, the brave man's life might develop at a different pace from others.[6]

Thoreau's first published application of this ideal to a contemporary appears in "Herald of Freedom," a notice in the April 1844 *Dial* in which he praises an antislavery journal edited by Nathaniel P. Rogers. Rogers was a leader of the antislavery movement who split from the movement when he became, as Wendell Glick remarks, "convinced that all reform should be accomplished by individual rather than by corporate action" and "began to agitate for the dissolution of all antislavery societies, charging them with infringing upon the individual prerogatives of their members."[7]

In 1841 Thoreau had demonstrated a similar suspicion of group action when a group of transcendentalists invited him to join their utopian community at Brook Farm. He bluntly recorded his reaction to this invitation in his journal: "As for these communities—I think I had rather keep bachelors hall in hell than go to board in heaven" (*Journal* 1: 277). Thoreau thus admires Rogers's independent mind, but also the "pure, youthful, and hearty indignation at all wrong," (*Reform Papers,* 49) that keeps Rogers from getting trapped into narrow support of any one wrong. To Thoreau the true reformer was an individual like Rogers who opposed evil wherever and however it appeared, not the narrow zealot of a single cause. Such a reformer also fought the gloom of evil with a cheerful attitude, not a strident howling. Thoreau describes Rogers as one who fights evil "by other means than sorrow and bitterness of complaint. He will fight this fight with what cheer may be" (50).

Another antislavery reformer singled out for praise was Wendell Phillips, whose lectures to the Concord Lyceum prompted Thoreau to write a letter to William Lloyd Garrison's antislavery journal *Liberator,* where it was published as "Wendell Phillips before Concord Lyceum" on 28 March 1845. Thoreau praises Phillips for some of the same virtues he had praised in Rogers. He describes Phillips as a man of principles, not mere causes: "he was not born to abolish slavery, but to do right" (*Reform Papers,* 61). He also praises Phillips's independence in "deliberating on these subjects, and wisely and bravely, without counsel or consent of any" (60).

In these early short reform pieces, Thoreau no longer insists on the brave man's aloofness from social action as he did in "The Service." He now recognizes individual action as a valid attack on social evil, but he continues to be suspicious of anyone too devoted to converting the world to one point of view. This attitude is expressed most fully in a set of lecture notes on "Reform and Reformers"—written sometime between 1839 and 1845—parts of which were included in *Walden.*[8] In these notes Thoreau contrasts "the Conservative" to "the Reformer." Both, he says, are "sick," but conservatives persist in their sickness, while the reformer is at least convalescent. He acknowledges that the conservative has some virtues, including "courtesy," "practicalness," and "reverence for facts" and, "with a little less irritability, or more indifference" might be the better of the two (*Reform Papers,* 181). Reformers, however, have earnestness on their side, a genuine desire to "heal and reform" the "disorder and imperfection in human affairs" (182) in order "to discover the divine order and conform to it" (182).

The problem, as Thoreau saw it, is that even among reformers there are "few radicals as yet who are radical enough" (182). They attack only "the exposed roots of innocent institutions" ("innocent" perhaps in that such institutions are often so removed from the people that their members are not even conscious of the harm they do) but not the roots of the evil within themselves. Thus, he says, "reform should be a private and individual enterprise" because "the evil may be private also" (183). Thoreau admits that a society can be of some use in achieving reform, but only as long as "it is the individual using the society as his instrument, rather than the society using the individual" (186). There is an implied warning here that a reformer can hardly avoid being pulled down to the common denominator of the group he tries to direct. Although group action might be useful, the reformers' true source of strength must be in their harmony with nature's laws rather than with society's: "let us strive first to be as simple and well as nature ourselves" (191).

Essays on Economic Reform.   Outside of his book-length works, Thoreau wrote little specifically on economic reform. One early and one late piece do, however, focus primarily on economics. The early piece, "Paradise (To Be) Regained," provides a vivid example of Thoreau's characteristic suspicion of misguided reform.

This essay, published in the *United States Magazine and Democratic Review* for November of 1843, is a review of a utopian book entitled *The Paradise within the Reach of All Men, without Labor, by Powers of Nature and Machinery. An Address to All Intelligent Men* by J. A. Etzler. Thoreau finds Etzler's book worth considering because "it entertains large questions" (*Reform Papers,* 19) and expresses faith in the future. Unfortunately, Thoreau feels, Etzler's schemes also have serious flaws, the first of which is that his faith is misdirected. He proposes using machines to harness the powers of nature and thus to eliminate human labor, bending nature to human will rather than shaping the will to the larger forces of nature. Etzler's second fault is that he aims only "to secure the greatest degree of gross comfort and pleasure merely" (45) rather than to achieve the higher goal of spiritual peace. His third fault is that his scheme depends on unreliable tools—"time, men, and money" (40)—and thus ignores the need for self-reliance. "He who wants help," Thoreau says, "wants everything" (42). Finally, even if Etzler's schemes are worth achieving—and Thoreau is willing to admit that ideally "if we were to reform this outward life truly and thoroughly, we should find no duty of the inner omitted" (45)—Etzler still confuses the order in which such reform must be achieved. Inner moral reform must precede outward material change: "A moral reform must take place first, and then the necessity of the other will be superseded" (45–46).

Thoreau's faith in the achievement of such inner moral reform on a large scale faded rapidly in his years after living by Walden Pond. His Concord neighbors did not heed his warning to resist giving up their self-sufficient farm economy. More and more they turned to the city and to cash crops for their living. Nor did America at large show any signs of genuinely attempting to achieve Thoreau's ideal economy rooted in what Stoller describes as "the single homestead based on subsistence agriculture and handicrafts."[9] Instead Americans chose the path of industrialization, with its inevitable destruction of nature and its insatiable appetite for more rather than fewer things.

Thoreau's frustration with this trend is suggested by the changing titles of his most frequently delivered lecture. In December 1854, only a few months after the publication of *Walden,* Thoreau delivered a lecture on one of the main themes of that book under the relatively tame title "Getting a Living." After delivering this lecture twice, however, he must have sensed that his message was falling on unsympathetic ears, for in February 1855 he gave the lecture again under a title that was now a biblical warning: "What Shall It Profit?" By the fall of 1859 he had apparently despaired of his audience and changed the title from a warning to a condemnation: "Life Misspent."[10] Shortly before his death, however, he wrote to the *Atlantic Monthly* authorizing publication of the lecture under its final title, with its bitter pun, "Life without Principle." The lecture was eventually published in the *Atlantic Monthly* in October 1863.

Thoreau's opening remarks in "Life without Principle" suggest a man who already knows that he has little hope of winning the battle to reform his audience but who intends to go down fighting. Tired of audiences who ask that he deliver only ideas with which they will agree, he has resolved to "give them a strong dose of myself . . . though I bore them beyond all precedent" (*Reform Papers,* 155). He no longer finds it worthwhile, as he had in *Walden,* to adopt an agreeable persona to win the audience's ear: "as the time is short, I will leave out all the flattery, and retain all the criticism" (156). This sense of urgency and frustration results in Thoreau's harshest indictment of the American economic system but also in one of the strongest expressions of some of his other basic themes.

As in the chapter "Economy" in *Walden,* Thoreau's main theme in "Life without Principle" is misplaced priorities. He finds that New Englanders mistake getting a living for life itself. "There is no more fatal blunderer," he says, "than he who consumes the greater part of his life getting his living" (16). His neighbors equate living with making money, so that "this world is a place of business. . . . It is nothing but work, work, work. I cannot easily buy a blank-book to write thoughts in; they are commonly ruled for dollars and cents" (156). Because of this overwhelming dominance of greed, Thoreau is no longer willing to give business even a little credit for "enterprise and bravery" (*Walden,* 118). It is unequivocally a damned occupation: "there is nothing, not even crime, more opposed to poetry, to philosophy, ay, to life itself, than this incessant business" (156).

As a distressing example of the commercial influence on American society, Thoreau offers the California gold rush, a "business" enterprise reduced to its essential greed. The horror of the gold rush is that it shows men abandoning all hope of inward self-culture, all hope of taking control of their own destinies. Instead, the "forty-niners" threw themselves at the mercy of sheer luck. He finds it shocking "that so many are ready to live by luck, and so get the means of commanding the labor of others less lucky, without contributing any value to society!" (162). Nor can he console himself that this evil is distant, because he can see similar influences all around him. California "is the child of New England, bred at her own school and church" (166).

Two other implications of the gold rush also distressed Thoreau. First, it involved the grossest abuse of nature itself, men delving into the mountains not to search for the rock bottom of truth as he had suggested in *Walden* but to satisfy the greed at the core of their own being. It is a perfect example that "the ways by which you may get money almost without exception lead downward" (158). Perhaps even more frightening is the symbolic corruption of America's future the gold rush represents. If the West is the symbol of hope for America, then the rapidity with which that hope was being destroyed by greed was appalling. As he recognized in *Cape Cod,* the Pacific West was already becoming pacifiable.

The antidote to greed he prescribes in "Life without Principle" is essentially the same as he had prescribed in *Walden,* but expressed even more urgently. Instead of seeking material riches, people should search for their own inner spiritual wealth. He asks himself "why *I* might not be washing some gold daily, though it were only the finest particles,— why I might not sink a shaft down to the gold within me, and work that mine" (164, Thoreau's emphasis). In such spiritual mining he seeks "a living not merely honest and honorable, but altogether inviting and glorious" (161), a living based on love of truth rather than love of gold. Thus, he says, "You must get your living by loving"

(160). Nor does he ignore the practical economics of such advice. He suggests in all seriousness that "it would be economy for a town to pay its laborers so well that they would not feel that they were working for low ends, as for a livelihood merely, but for scientific, or even moral ends" (159). Thoreau saw no split between ideal and practical economy; the economy most in harmony with God and nature was always the most practical.

Essays on Politics and Slavery. Like his views on the economy, Thoreau's political views were based on his concept of self-culture. Ideally, as he says in "Civil Disobedience," "That government is best which governs not at all" (*Reform Papers,* 63). If everyone made it their business to seek the truth of their own life rather than the gold in their neighbor's pocket or the land on their neighbor's farm, then government would be unnecessary. Such idealism can easily be mistaken for anarchy, as it often is by readers of "Civil Disobedience." Indeed, "Civil Disobedience" is misinterpreted even more often and more extravagantly than *Walden.*

The most frequent error is to see Thoreau as an anarchist proposing the immediate abolition of all government. Vincent Buranelli, for instance, says of Thoreau that "the commitment to personal revelation made him an anarchist."[11] Lewis Van Dusen pushes Thoreau even further down the slippery slope of choplogic to land him among tyrants: "To indulge civil disobedience is to invite anarchy, and the permissive arbitrariness of anarchy is hardly less tolerable than the repressive arbitrariness of tyranny."[12]

Such attacks are based, first of all, on a failure to distinguish among the many different kinds of anarchy, defining it broadly as an intention to destroy all forms of government immediately and to reduce society to a mass of unrestrained individuals.[13] Thoreau, however, was an anarchist only insofar as he was an idealist who believed that people can be connected directly to ideal truth through their own consciences. Should they ever reach utopia, they would naturally be in harmony with each other. But Thoreau himself says in "Civil Disobedience" that he is not speaking of an ideal future, but "practically and as a citizen" (64) and that he asks for "not at once no government, but *at once* a better government" (64, Thoreau's emphasis).

Nor is Buranelli accurate in claiming that Thoreau "instinctively . . . loathes it [government] as such."[14] Although Thoreau might abrogate a specific law that he thought unjust, his very willingness to accept punishment for not paying his tax was a tacit acknowledgment of the validity of the government. Like Socrates he appreciated the necessity and value of government in general while denying its judgments on specifics. He could even accept some government injustice, for "if the injustice is part of the necessary friction of the machine of government, let it go, let it go" (73). But when the government enslaved the minds or bodies of its constituents and demanded that they condone such slavery with their votes and taxes, Thoreau believed that it was time to withdraw his support.

The problem of Thoreau's argument in "Civil Disobedience" is that its effect on the reader is determined immediately and completely by whether or not the reader accepts Thoreau's basic transcendentalist faith in the validity of conscience. If one believes that individual conscience is a more reliable test of a truth than the number of people who support it, than one easily follows Thoreau to his logical conclusion that "any man more right than his neighbors, constitutes a majority of one already" (74) and that justice is more important than law. If, however, one mistrusts the reliability of the conscience, because it may be the tool of the devil as easily as of God, then one must assert law as more important than justice, trust the government to majority rule, and reject Thoreau's entire argument. It is impossible to have it both ways. "Civil Disobedience" thus exposes a basic split in the American mentality, for the tension between these two views has been with us since the Puritans and has not yet been resolved.

Recognizing this split, Thoreau begins "Civil Disobedience" by explaining why government ought not be viewed as supreme. One reason is that "government is at best an expedient" (63)—that is, a convenience, a tool to be used by the many individual consciences from which it derives its power. It is of itself powerless: it "never of itself furthered any enterprise, but by the alacrity with which it got out of its way" (64). Rather "the character inherent in the American people has done all that has been accomplished" (64). Government thus becomes inexpedient when it fails to respond to the people from whom it derives its power. The other reason is that government is unreliable, because it is a "tradition" and as such is more concerned with perpetuating itself than with fulfilling the will of the people. Many of its actions, therefore, are motivated more by self-interest and concern for popular opinion than by concern for justice.

Thoreau acknowledges that the American government does provide some methods to achieve change for the individual who disagrees with it, but he frequently finds these means too unreliable or too slow. Voting, for instance, is not as praiseworthy as Americans like to think, because it is only "a sort of gaming, like chequers or backgammon, with a slight moral tinge to it" (69); hence the voter is "not vitally concerned that right should prevail" (69). "Voting *for the right*," he says, "is *doing* nothing for it. It is only expressing to men feebly your desire that it should prevail" (68, Thoreau's emphases). If the voter's candidate or cause is defeated, that same voter agrees to reverse his or her view of what is right in order to obey the majority. Such an equation of numbers with justice is completely unacceptable to the transcendentalist view that there is "some absolute goodness somewhere" (69).

Other methods of reform besides voting—legislation or petition, for instance—are available, but "they take too much time, and a man's life will be gone" (74). The life referred to here is surely both the life of the reformer and the life of the victim of government-supported injustice. Furthermore, the government's desire to correct its own evils cannot be trusted. Governments are more apt to "crucify Christ, and excommunicate Copernicus and Luther, and pronounce Washington and Franklin rebels" (73) than to welcome them as reformers.

Insofar as a government becomes separated from the will of the people that created it, it is an evil that might then be opposed by appealing directly to the people themselves, but the most discouraging part of Thoreau's experience in prison was what it revealed about his neighbor's unwillingness even to acknowledge, much less to reform, the government's injustice. Looking at Concord by moonlight through the bars of the jail window, Thoreau came to the profoundly sad realization that his neighbors neither knew nor would care if they did know where he was, that he and they might be completely and irreconcilably separated by their different goals: "I saw to what extent the people among whom I lived could be trusted as good neighbors and friends; that their friendship was for summer weather only; that they did not greatly purpose to do right; that they were a distinct race from me" (83).

In "Civil Disobedience" Thoreau is forced to reconsider the power of one individual to leaven the whole loaf of society. He does not abandon his belief in self-culture as a social force, for he persists in believing that "action from principle,—the perception and performance of right,—changes things and relations" (72). But he must consider what the individual can do if society does not follow his example. A person's rock-bottom duty, he decides, is not "to devote himself to the eradication of any, even the most enormous wrong; he may still properly have other concerns to engage him" (71). But one must refuse to contribute to evil with one's vote or obedience: "it is the duty, at least, to wash his hands of it, and, if he gives it no thought longer, not to give it practically his support. If I devote myself to other pursuits and contemplations, I must first see, at least, that I do not pursue them sitting on another man's shoulders" (71). This is a clear recognition of the individual's social responsibility, even if expressed only as negative rather than positive action. Thoreau preferred such noncompliance as his usual approach to social injustice, and on relatively minor issues, such as the poll tax, he found the government unwilling to force the issue.

It is clear even in "Civil Disobedience," however, that Thoreau's concept of self-culture had its limits and that when aroused by an important issue he was willing to oppose the government actively and even violently. In "Civil Disobedience," for instance, he points out the hypocrisy of praising the American Revolution, a violent rebellion, while refusing to acknowledge violence as a valid contemporary force for change. The right to rebel against injustice, he says, includes not only the right "to refuse allegiance" but also "to resist the government," presumably by violence if necessary (67).

This implicit acceptance of violent resistance to injustice is made explicit elsewhere in Thoreau's works, both before and after "Civil Disobedience." On 27 January 1841, for instance, Thoreau and his brother participated, together with Bronson Alcott, in a Concord Lyceum debate on the question "Is it ever proper to offer forcible resistance?" Alcott defended the negative, John and Henry the affirmative.[15] Other evidence that Thoreau could support violent resistance appears in *A Week*, where he protests the Billerica dam's effect on the fish and farmers along the Merrimack River. Taking the side of the fish and farmers, he vows resolutely, "I for one am with thee, and who knows what may avail a crow-bar against that Billerica dam?" (*A Week*, 37). Later, in 1854 in "Slavery in Massachusetts," he makes his advocacy of violence even more explicit regarding slavery: "I need not say what match I would touch, what system endeavor to blow up,—but as I love my life, I would side with the light, and let the dark earth roll from under me, calling my mother and my brother to follow" (*Reform Papers*, 102).

Finally, his approval of John Brown's raid on Harpers Ferry leaves no doubt that he could support violence as a means to end social and political injustice. In "A Plea for Captain John Brown" he condones violent resistance under severe enough circumstances: "I do not wish to kill nor to be killed, but I can foresee circumstances in which both these things would be by me unavoidable" (*Reform Papers,* 133). He also adds this unequivocal approval of Brown's men: "I think that for once the Sharps' rifles and the revolvers were employed in a righteous cause" (133). Of Brown himself he says, "It was his peculiar doctrine that a man has a perfect right to interfere by force with the slaveholder, in order to rescue the slave. I agree with him" (132). A complete reading of Thoreau's works makes it impossible to view him as a patron saint of nonviolence. He certainly preferred other means of resistance and saw violence only as a last resort, but he did not oppose violence on principle as Gandhi did.

Whatever tendency toward violent resistance Thoreau felt seems to have been channeled creatively into his writing. Consider the comparison between scalping and composition in *A Week* ("The talent of composition is very dangerous,—the striking out the heart of life at a blow, as the Indian takes off a scalp"—[329]) or the comparison in *Walden* of thoughts to bullets, which, if not given sufficient room between speaker and hearer, "may plough out again through the side of [the hearer's] head" (141). He returns to this bullet image in "The Last Days of John Brown," where he says that "the *art* of composition is as simple as the discharge of a bullet from a rifle, and its masterpieces imply an infinitely greater force behind them" (*Reform Papers,* 150–51, Thoreau's emphasis).

On the slavery issue particularly, Thoreau appears to have used the pen as his substitute for a gun. "Slavery in Massachusetts," for instance, is a much sharper denouncement of the government than "Civil Disobedience." This essay was written as a speech that Thoreau delivered to a Fourth of July gathering of abolitionists in 1854 following the infamous Anthony Burns affair.[16] Burns was a fugitive slave who was found in Boston by his former owner, arrested, and returned to Virginia despite an unsuccessful rescue attempt by Boston abolitionists. The willingness of the state government to condone slavery by assisting the slaveowner made Thoreau furious. His impassioned speech attacked not just the government in general, but specific officials and institutions. For the governor he could find no excuse. Despite the governor's duty to enforce the laws of the state without violating "the laws of humanity," Thoreau says that "when there is any special important use for him, he is useless, or worse than useless, and permits the laws of the State to go unexecuted" (*Reform Papers,* 94). The judges of the Supreme Court who supported the slaveowners by allowing slavery to continue he describes as "merely the inspectors of a pick-lock and murderer's tools, to tell him whether they are in work-

ing order or not" (98). He also finds the press and the church culpable.
The press "is almost, without exception, corrupt," and the church is
damned by comparison, since the press "exerts a greater and more per-
nicious influence than the church did in its worst period" (99). He
accuses the newspaper of having replaced the Bible as America's most
frequently read work. Nor is Congress spared, for he indicts it as not
only corrupt but foolish. Its Fugitive Slave Law he finds as absurd as a
law that men be made into sausages (96–97).

Amid this offensive against the government, Thoreau stands firmly
on the principles he expressed in "Civil Disobedience": that justice is
more important than legality, that justice depends on the conscience
of the individual not the deliberations of governments, and that just
people have a right—indeed, a duty—to refuse obedience to unjust
laws. What distinguishes "Slavery in Massachusetts," however, is the
vigor of Thoreau's prose. Seldom in his published works do we find
Thoreau's thoughts expressed quite so concisely and forcefully as in this
underrated essay. His sentences are consistently crisp and clear: "The
law will never make men free; it is men who have got to make the law
free. They are the lovers of law and order, who observe the law when
the government breaks it" (98). Even when he turns to transcendental
rhetoric, as he does in the conclusion with the symbol of the water lily
that grows out of foul slime but produces a sweet odor, he drives the
point home with the same sharp vigor. "Slavery and servility," he says,
"have produced no sweet-scented flower annually . . . for they have no
real life: they are merely a decaying and a death, offensive to all healthy
nostrils. We do not complain that they *live,* but that they do not *get
buried.* Let the living bury them; even they are good for manure" (109,
Thoreau's emphases).

About how slavery and servility were to be buried and what was to
happen to blacks afterward, however, Thoreau says relatively little in
any of his antislavery writings. Like many abolitionists, he may have
held views of the blacks' basic inferiority to whites similar to his "savagism" toward Indians. Many abolitionists believed with Harriet
Beecher Stowe that blacks needed to be freed but also that they were
essentially childlike and needed to be protected from exploitation by
the American economic system. Michael Meyer suggests, for instance,
that Thoreau may have considered favorably, as one solution to the
slavery problem, a mass exodus of blacks to Central America.[17] As for
abolishing slavery, Thoreau seems to have given up almost completely
on legislation or court decisions by the time of "Slavery in Massachu-

setts." Although he himself found a pen the most suitable tool for change, he was ready to support someone who could effectively take even stronger measures.

He found such a man in John Brown, whom he met when Brown spoke in Concord in 1857 and 1859. When Brown raided Harpers Ferry and was captured in October 1859, Thoreau immediately leapt to his defense. When even abolitionist newspapers expressed doubts about Brown's wisdom, Thoreau decided that someone needed to speak out in his defense. He announced around town that on 30 October he would read a defense of Brown in the town hall. When the day arrived and the town leaders refused to have the bell rung to announce the lecture, Thoreau rang the bell himself.[18]

The lecture "A Plea for Captain John Brown" was a rapid reworking of his recent journal comments on Brown. The pressure under which he put the lecture together led to a loosely structured but impassioned oration that won the sympathy of many of his listeners. Thoreau thus acquired a reputation as one of Brown's most eloquent defenders. He eventually delivered two other speeches on Brown: the "Martyrdom of John Brown," which he delivered at the memorial service on the day Brown was hanged, and "The Last Days of John Brown," which was written for and sent to the memorial service for the burial of Brown's body in North Elba, New York, in July 1860.

Thoreau's enthusiasm for Brown has puzzled and distressed many critics, because it seems to contradict Thoreau's presumed aversion to both group action and violence. As we have seen, however, by 1859 Thoreau was already disillusioned about society's willingness to heed the example of just individuals seeking to perfect their own lives, and he had never ruled out violence as a means of reform. The Burns case had been the last straw; after it, he was ready to support even extreme and violent action to abolish slavery. He could condone violence in the hands of the just against an otherwise unstoppable evil.

Those who find Thoreau's agreement with Brown's violence upsetting have tended to excuse him by saying that what Thoreau saw in Brown was essentially a transcendentalist, "a man of ideas and principles" (*Reform Papers,* 115), and that he was therefore blind to the horrors of Brown's violence. It is true that what Thoreau admired in Brown was essentially his transcendentalist principles. Brown was a seer who, like Thoreau, wanted to shock America awake. Thoreau describes him in "A Plea" as a man who "had his eyes about him, and made many original observations" (*Reform Papers,* 112). Like Thoreau, he was "a man of rare common sense and directness of speech" (115), who could wield language as a weapon. He was thoroughly independent, willing "to face his country herself, when she was in the wrong" (113). He and his men, like the autumn leaves, "in teaching us how to die, have at the same time taught us how to live" (134), laying themselves down so that a new country might later arise. As Wendell Glick says, Brown fulfilled three of Thoreau's transcendental principles: "he woke man up out of his lethargy; he showed contempt of government; and he set a great personal example."[19]

Thus Harding is quite right in arguing that "there is unquestionably a definite progression in Thoreau's three major statements on the antislavery issue, from 'Civil Disobedience' through 'Slavery in Massachusetts' to 'A Plea for Captain John Brown.' It is a progression of increased resistance to the state as an institution. . . . But it is a progression, not a break with the past."[20] Although Harding is also right in suggesting that Thoreau "was more attracted by Brown's ideals than by his actions,"[21] we cannot deny that Thoreau was strongly attracted to Brown's actions and unequivocally agreed with them. He had said in "The Service" that "the exploit of a brave life consists in its momentary completeness" (16) and had argued that the transcendentalist was at heart a soldier, though a spiritual one. Brown was "the brave man," the spiritual soldier who completed his life by transforming spiritual, bardic rage into righteous, though violent, action. Brown was, in short, the soldier and seer that at heart Thoreau had always been. Thoreau saw his own pen as being as dangerous as Brown's guns, for as he had said in "Slavery in Massachusetts," "my thoughts are murder to the State" (108).

Thoreau had said in *Walden* that if life proved to be mean he wished "to get the whole and genuine meanness of it, and publish its meanness to the world" (91). His own life in Concord and in nature had not proved to be mean, but the government certainly had—and it had become more so as the years went on. So it should not be surprising that Thoreau would publish the government's full meanness to the world and support others who did so, whether they spoke with a pen or a rifle. The gentle seer quite naturally became the angry prophet when people proved unfit for the nature God had created. When Chanticleer's crowing failed, sometimes the roar of a gun was necessary to wake his neighbors up.

Chapter Eight

The Progressions of a Man's Life

In "The Service" Thoreau, looking optimistically to his own future, saw his duty as being to "make life a steady progression and not be defeated by its opportunities" (*Reform Papers*, 15). By the end of his life those who knew him were not always certain that he had achieved that goal. Even Emerson, in his eulogy for Thoreau, regretted that "instead of engineering for all America, [Thoreau] was the captain of a huckleberry-party" and that "he should leave in the midst of his broken task which none else can finish."[1] This Emersonian view that Thoreau was defeated by life's opportunities or, worse yet, failed even to recognize them, persists to some extent today, as does the tendency to see no "steady progression" in Thoreau's life or writings. Readers often discuss "Thoreau's view of nature," for instance, as if that view was precisely the same throughout his career.

If readers have usually been unwilling to acknowledge change in Thoreau's ideas, they certainly have changed their own ideas about him frequently enough. During this century, the public has found diverse but narrow pigeonholes to put him into.[2] Through the 1920s he was viewed almost exclusively as a nature writer. During the thirties he came to be viewed as a model of the simple life whose writing could teach Americans how to make do with less during the depression. During the forties he was castigated as a pacifist who would have been unsupportive of the war effort. During the late forties and the fifties, critics began to recognize him as a literary artist, while the general public slipped back into its view of him as naturalist. Then during the sixties his political views came to the fore as civil rights and Viet Nam war protesters used him to support their views. Finally during the seventies and eighties, critics have come to view him as a subject for postmortem psychoanalysis and as a postmodern writer before his time because of the frequent ambiguity of his language and because of his exploration of the function of language.[3] The general public, meanwhile, seems to have settled into seeing him as an advocate of a pretty but impractical dream of returning to nature.

Thus if Emerson was, as Henry James, Sr., called him, a "man without a handle," Thoreau has proven to be a man with perhaps too many handles.[4] It will be the purpose of this last chapter to try to put these various views of Thoreau into balance and to suggest some of the development—the "progression"—that was indeed there in his life and his writing.

Thoreau and Society

In his social relations Thoreau was first of all a son and brother, second a citizen of Concord, and third an American, and one must be careful not to oversimplify any of these relationships. As a son, he appeared devoted to both his parents, working diligently for his father's business despite the restrictions that such work put on his study of nature and on his writing and apparently accepting with good grace his mother's boarders, as well as her gregariousness and social climbing. As a youth he appears to have been so emotionally tied to his parents that he could not bear to leave them to make his living beyond Concord. Yet it is also clear that he rejected his father's life of quiet desperation as a businessman and that, despite a stronger than usual oedipal affection for his mother, he recognized her limitations as well. Later in his life, when he was asked by Greeley to move to New York, it may have been his regimen in the Concord woods more than family ties that kept him from leaving.

As a brother, Thoreau respected his elder sister Helen, was affectionate to his younger sister Sophia, and was deeply devoted to his brother John. But, as Lebeaux suggests, his relation to John was probably complicated by jealousy toward John's popularity and by guilt about competing with him for Ellen Sewall's hand.[5]

As a citizen of Concord Thoreau seems at first glance to have been a man of extremes. Often he condemns the materialism and insensitivity of his neighbors. But at the same time that sharp criticism is rooted not only in frustration at their inability to recognize their lack of higher goals, but also in genuine affection for them and in the hope that they might improve. As Moller says, "Thoreau was attracted to another image of the village—that of a true *community,* small enough to be fully comprehended, made up of self-reliant, idiosyncratic individuals, whose self-reliance would be nurtured by familiar association and mutual respect" (Moller's emphasis).[6] Although he castigated many of Concord's greedy shopkeepers, landowners, and selectmen, he could also speak appreciatively of villagers and farmers such as Melvin or Minott, who seemed to be suitable inhabitants of such an ideal community.

Even with those he liked, however, he was demanding. For instance, he clearly liked Alek Therien as a "simple and natural man" (*Walden,* 145). Despite Therien's intellectual limitations, Thoreau admired his "positive originality" (*Walden,* 150) and enjoyed conversations with him at the cabin. Yet years later when Therien took to drinking too much and arrived one day at the Thoreau house on business, Thoreau is reported to have told him coldly that he might just as well go home and cut his own throat.[7] Here, as was usually the case, Thoreau's anger at a friend's failure was in proportion to the potential for successful living that he had seen in that friend.

He was not an easy man to get close to. As Emerson put it, "As for taking Thoreau's arm, I should as soon take the arm of an elm tree."[8] Yet there were a number of people both in and beyond Concord who were quite close to him. In Concord there were Ellery Channing, Bronson Alcott, Hawthorne, and Emerson, to name only the most famous of his friends. All of them saw his social limitations: his strict dependence on habit, his love of arguing about even the smallest issues, his veneer of emotional aloofness, and his unwillingness to compromise. But they also saw genius and warmth beneath the rough exterior and loved him even when they could not always like him.

Thoreau too, despite the impossibly high standards of friendship that he expressed, could nevertheless tolerate Channing's flightiness and crass language, look with gentle amusement on Alcott's ludicrously impractical ideas, sympathize with Hawthorne's reticence, and eventually reconcile himself to Emerson's subtle condescension. Beyond Concord, he could put up with Daniel Ricketson's hypochondria and H. G. O. Blake's adulation of him and still keep them as close friends despite their distance in miles.

But perhaps Sam Staples was ultimately right in telling Emerson shortly before Thoreau's death that "very few men in Concord know Mr. Thoreau."[9] Many of those who thought they knew him dismissed him as an atheist. Others respected him but were puzzled by his refusal to conform to the town's standards of success. But those who took the trouble to seek his friendship found it honest and rewarding.

Toward minority groups in the community at large he had his share of provincial prejudices, some benign and some not. As we have seen, he condescended benevolently toward Indians and blacks. But through his experiences in the Maine woods he gradually came to a more realistic assessment of the Indian's way of life. His limited contact with blacks, however, seems not to have been sufficient to give him a realistic view of that race. He was also suspicious of Catholics and at first had little respect for the Irish (the two groups, of course, often overlapped). Through his role as benefactor to Johnny Riordan, a little Irish boy, he eventually developed a higher opinion of the Irish, but his visit to predominantly Catholic Montreal did not raise his opinion of the Catholic religion.

As an American, he was certainly not a patriot in the usual sense of one who is always loyal to the government's actions. As we have seen, he felt little obligation to support the government unless it was properly benefiting its citizens, and he begrudged most of the time he gave to national issues at the expense of his explorations in the woods. On the other hand, he had a clear vision of what he thought America ideally should be: a nation of self-sufficient farmers and craftsmen gathered around villages that would be essentially cultural and educational centers and interfered with as little as possible by the government. He knew well before his death, however, that this vision of America was rapidly fading. The business of America had already become business. So although his attitude toward America was still essentially optimistic during the Walden years and continued to be so, though less firmly, up to the end of his life, much of the writing in his last years has an unmistakably elegiac tone concerning America's economy and its corruption of the wilderness.

Thoreau and Nature

Although one of the most frequent images of Thoreau is as a naturalist, how good a naturalist he really was has often been debated. His scientific observations have found occasional detractors. Fanny Eckstrom, for instance, catalogued his errors as a woodsman and scientific observer in her article on *The Maine Woods,* a book she claimed contains "errors in the estimates of distance, area, speed, and the like, too numerous to mention in detail."[10] She also claimed that "even according to the feeble light of the day, Thoreau was not an ornithologist" because he misidentified at least seven of the thirty-seven birds listed in his appendix to *The Maine Woods.*[11] Although she admits that Thoreau did better as a botanist, she claims that in general his field notes "rarely furnish material for science."[12]

Recently, however, Thoreau has been shown to be a better woodsman and naturalist than Eckstrom supposed. Not only have his woodcraft and scientific observations in the Maine woods been shown to be usually accurate by the standards of his time, but his botanical and meteorological observations have proven useful to modern scientists as well.[13] The National Weather Service, for instance, has added Thoreau's journal notes on Concord's weather to its computerized national data for predicting weather.[14] His theory of plant succession in "The Succession of Forest Trees" is also still acknowledged as valid. Even more remarkable is Thoreau's anticipation of several kinds of scientific study that did not exist as systematic studies in his day. He is considered to be the father of limnology (the study of bodies of fresh water and their fluctuations) based on his detailed notes on streams, ponds, and lakes. He is also acknowledged as one of America's earliest practitioners of ecology and of phenology (the study of climate based on calendars of plant and animal activities as they change through the seasons).[15]

One must be careful, moreover, in measuring Thoreau's success or failure as a scientist against our own definition of such success. Thoreau himself deliberately did not use some of the established scientific methods common in his day—and to some extent in ours—such as killing specimens of birds and other animals in order to study them or attempting to maintain an objective attitude toward the phenomenon at hand. He considered himself a transcendentalist rather than a scientist and insisted on the merging of philosophy and science rather than the separation between them advocated by most scientists of his day. He believed that "the earth; is not a mere fragment of dead history" but "living poetry" (Walden, 308–9). Throughout his life he insisted that the poet and the scientist should be one, and he cautioned himself whenever he sensed that he was overemphasizing one or the other.[16]

In the years before his stay by the pond, he was interested in nature primarily as a source of transcendentalist tropes. That interest continued to some extent throughout his lifetime, but during and after the years by the pond his interest in the phenomena of nature for their own sake as much as for their symbolic value blossomed, so that by 1849 he could write to H. G. O. Blake of his new daily habit of taking long walks in the woods: "almost every afternoon . . . I visit some new hill or pond many miles distant."[17] Eventually through those walks he became more and more convinced of what he had suggested as early as *A Week*: that the physical reality of nature and the ideas it contained were not to be separated. Furthermore, he realized that it was not so much nature as a separate entity but his relation to nature that was of interest and that writing in his journal was a crucial part of maintaining that relation. So although it is probable that Thoreau's interest in scientific approaches to nature did increase over the years, that interest merged with rather than replaced his transcendental approach.

Thoreau and Philosophy

As interesting and important as they are, however, it is neither Thoreau's personality, nor his social activism, nor his contributions to science that account most fully for his value to the modern reader. Underlying all of these aspects of his life was the rock-bottom purpose he faithfully pursued until his death: the search for reality. He was driven by the idealist's belief that there must be some absolute reality somewhere, that in that absolute reality God resided, and that the most basic goal of life was therefore to seek that reality. Everything he did was directed toward achieving that goal himself and urging others to do so in their own way. He explored nature because the most accessible reality seemed to lie there. He criticized institutions and neighbors for allowing themselves to be distracted from reality by illusions such as money or conformity. And he stayed aloof from society in order not to be distracted from the search for reality himself.

Although the goals of his search were those of philosophy, he was not a systematic philosopher. He was, however, a persistent and uncompromising epistemologist, a seeker for knowledge about reality. If read fully, his writing proves valuable to the modern reader not just for the comforting optimism about the goodness of nature and God that so many readers find in it but also for the healthy skepticism—and sometimes pessimism—about any ideas that seemed to offer too neat an end to the search for reality, including many of his own. He forced himself to maintain that "useful ignorance" of which he speaks in "Walking," and always examined an idea from a variety of perspectives before accepting it, no matter how convincing it seemed or how badly he wanted to believe it. Even the concepts of a benevolent nature and a benevolent God—so basic to his transcendentalism—were ones he questioned, and it is this courage in confronting even the most distressing possible realities that is one of his crucial strengths as a thinker.

Perhaps the aspect of his thought that remains foremost in the public's mind is his attempt to live the simple life. Whenever we find our own materialism dissatisfying, we take refuge in his ability to cut through the superfluities of life and get back to economic and spiritual basics. Although few of us can bring ourselves actually to discard many luxuries, we are comforted by Thoreau's having done it. Thoreau's simple life is our philosophical wilderness, an ideal that often tempers our busy lives even if we do not want to commit ourselves to it any more permanently than he wished to live in the wilderness. His example tells us not that all people should live simply by a pond but that each individual should "be very careful to find and pursue *his own* way" (*Walden,* 71, Thoreau's emphasis). As David Shi accurately observes, "Thoreau was fundamentally preaching the advantages of self-culture, not writing a how-to book."[18]

Thoreau knew that finding the reality of one's life was hard enough without pretending to guide others in how to live theirs. Ironically, late in his life, as he saw the increased need for someone to speak out against materialism and social injustice, he also became increasingly skeptical of the individual's ability to have an impact on society. As he wrote to Blake, "To what end do I lead a simple life at all, pray? That I may teach others to simplify their lives?—and so all our lives be *simplified* merely, like an algebraic formula? Or not, rather, that I may make use of the ground I have cleared, to live more worthily and profitably? I would fain lay the most stress forever on that which is the most important,—imports the most to me,—though it were only (what it is likely to be) a vibration in the air" (*Writings* 6:259–60, Thoreau's emphasis). It is this invitation to live, each of us in his or her way, "more worthily and profitably," seeking "that which is most important," that is the crux and the most constant feature of his thought.

Thoreau as Writer

We would not have much of Thoreau's thought, however, if he had not been above all else a writer. Had he simply been a Yankee Diogenes or Socrates and left no written record, we would have comments on him by the other Concord writers. But he would remain only a secondary figure—a disciple of Emerson, one of several American models for the ideal of a simple life, and a minor naturalist and abolitionist. What raises him to the level of a major figure in American culture is his unique struggle with the task of writing.

On this topic too there are widely varying opinions. Richard Bridgman, for instance, suggests that in other major American writers, "one will not regularly encounter mechanically awkward sentences, or ideas evaded or insufficiently thought out" but that in Thoreau's writing one does. From this viewpoint, Thoreau's writing is simply sloppy (Bridgman's word is "unkempt"). On the other extreme, Stanley Edgar Hyman claims that Thoreau "wrote the only really first-rate prose ever written by an American, with the possible exception of Abraham Lincoln."[20]

On balance, one must acknowledge that much of Thoreau's prose is difficult reading. Occasionally his syntax is ambiguous. Usually, though (one must admit not always), this ambiguity is purposeful as an accurate expression of the ambivalence he so often felt about nature. He can construct superbly tight sentences and paragraphs, but beyond individual paragraphs one must often work hard to find the unifying principle of whole essays. This looseness of structure, while it does not make a particularly good model for beginning composition students, does have its own method, however: the organic method of letting content determine form rather than the reverse, which is preferred most often today. It is a method used effectively by most of the writers of nineteenth-century romanticism.

Like any other writer, of course, he had to learn his craft, which we can most clearly see him doing in the journal or in collections of essays, such as *The Maine Woods* or *Excursions*. His early writing often slips into vague abstractions while his later works sometimes seem too matter-of-fact. But he could be, and almost always was, a very, very careful writer, as the seven drafts of *Walden* clearly demonstrate.

The view of Thoreau as a writer of "unkempt" prose seems rooted in a basic misconception about his purpose in writing. As important as his investigation of nature was, his exploration of the language used to express his relation to nature was perhaps even more important. He often saw writing, especially in the journal, more as a continuous probing than as the creation of a finished record. For publication, of course, he had to isolate certain portions of his written explorations, polish them, and to that extent finish them with a specific audience in mind.

But even the two books published during his lifetime went through extensive revision, both before and sometimes after publication. Had he lived longer, those works might very well have continued to change, for the relation to nature that he wrote about continued to change. Certainly the journal was a constant experiment in exploring nature through words. In it, as Sharon Cameron suggests, Thoreau's "reason to record [nature] is not to recall it but to establish a relation to it, with record and relation synonymous to each other."[21] Through the journal he came to understand that writing about his relation to nature was not just a means to an end, but an end in itself. Although he continued to plan the writing of a larger book for which the journal often seems to be the raw material, he did not write it, because the journal naturally evolved into being that book.[22] It also seems likely that he eventually recognized that such a book really could not be completed in one lifetime and that such completion was not finally important compared to the record of the process.

The progression of Thoreau's life as a writer, then, is essentially a gradual shift from writing primarily for publication to writing for exploration. After the publication of *Walden* he continued to publish, of course, but his desire to see his work in print became only sporadic and perhaps motivated as much by financial necessity as by idealism. During his last eight years, supplementing the family income and reassuring himself that the larger world might still be interested in what he was doing often seem stronger motives for seeking publication than the genuine enthusiasm he once had for seeing his words in print.

In 1844, expressing that separation between life and art that was so basic to his early transcendentalism, he wrote, "Writing may be either the record of a deed or a deed. It is nobler when it is a deed though it is noble and rare when it is fine and clear memory impartial—distinct. Its productions are then works of art. And stand like monuments of history" (*Journal* 1:494). In this passage life is superior to art, even when art is "noble and rare." But by 1856 the evidence of the journal suggests that he now saw that his main work—indeed, his life—was his art: "My work is writing . . . no experience is too trivial for me." "This," he says later in the same entry, "is what we sustain life for" (*Writings* 9:121). A year later he writes, "Is not the poet bound to write his own biography? Is there any other work for him but a good journal?" (*Writings* 10:115). Writing his biography and living it had become one. If as a young writer he had hoped that his life would be the poem he would have "writ," by the end of his life his writing had become the life he lived. His art became his life, and it is for that art that ultimately we honor him.

We will not cease mythologizing him as a naturalist, as a political protester, and as a model of the simple life. In all those roles, even when we only partially understand them, he serves admirably as a symbol of Americans' regrets and hopes about their relation to nature, to their own society, and to their own aspirations. But it is also important to acknowledge him as a complex human being whose transcendental optimism was won and maintained only through intense intellectual and psychological conflict throughout his life. Through these conflicts his views changed and progressed—though not as steadily or quickly as he might have wished—toward a merging of his life and art, until he became a writer whose most sustained exploration was not only of nature but also of a language through which to express his relation to nature. For readers willing to explore that lifelong relation with him, the sun is indeed but a morning star.

Notes and References

Chapter One

1. *Collected Poems,* ed. Carl Bode (Baltimore: Johns Hopkins University Press, 1964), 85.
2. In *Walden* he says that "to affect the quality of the day is the highest of arts," *Walden,* ed. J. Lyndon Shanley (Princeton: Princeton University Press, 1971), 90. Further references to *Walden* follow in the text.
3. *The Correspondence of Henry David Thoreau,* ed. Walter Harding and Carl Bode (New York: New York University Press, 1958), 407.
4. Walter Harding, *The Days of Henry Thoreau* (New York: Dover Publications, 1982), 8.
5. Horace Hosmer, *Rememberances of Concord and the Thoreaus,* ed. George Hendrick (Urbana: University of Illinois Press, 1977), 4.
6. Richard Lebeaux, *Young Man Thoreau* (Amherst: University of Massachusetts Press, 1977), 35.
7. Harding, *Days,* 10.
8. Ibid., 12.
9. Ibid., 20.
10. Ibid., 18–19.
11. Hosmer, *Remembrances,* 13.
12. Harding, *Days,* 35.
13. See the table of contents in *Early Essays and Miscellanies,* ed. Joseph J. Moldenhauer and Edwin Moser, with Alexander Kern (Princeton: Princeton University Press, 1975). Further references to this work, designated *Early Essays,* follow in the text.
14. Harding, *Days,* 43.
15. Ibid., 45.
16. Ibid., 49.
17. Ibid., 50–51.
18. See Lebeaux's analysis of Thoreau's postgraduation psychological crisis in the chapter entitled "The Graduate" in *Young Man Thoreau.*
19. Harding, *Days,* 52–53.
20. Mrs. Daniel Chester French, *Memories of a Sculptor's Wife* (Boston, 1928), 94–95.
21. Ralph Aldo Emerson, "The Transcendentalist," in *The Collected Works of Ralph Waldo Emerson,* (Cambridge: Harvard University Press, Belknap Press, (1971), vol. 1, *Nature, Address, and Lectures,* ed. Robert E. Spiller and Alfred R. Ferguson (1971), 201.
22. Emerson, "Nature," in *Nature, Address, and Lectures,* 9.

23. Emerson, "The Transcendentalist," 201.

24. Ibid., 203.

25. Ralph Waldo Emerson, "Self-Reliance," in *Collected Works,* vol. 2 *Essays: First Series,* ed.Joseph Slater, Alfred R. Ferguson, and Jean Ferguson Carr (1979), 29.

26. *The Writings of Henry David Thoreau* (Walden Edition), ed. Bradford Torrey, 20 vols. (Boston: Houghton Mifflin & Co., 1906), 9:250. Further references, designated *Writings,* follow in the text.

27. Ralph Waldo Emerson, *The Heart of Emerson's Journals,* ed. Bliss Perry (Boston, Houghton Mifflin & Co., 1914), 165.

28. Emerson, *Collected Works,* 1:29.

29. F. B. Sanborn, *The Personality of Thoreau,* (Boston, 1903), 69.

30. See Richard J. Schneider, "Reflections in Walden Pond: Thoreau's Optics," *ESQ: A Journal of the American Renaissance* 21, no. 2 (1975):74–75.

31. Harding, *Days,* 24–25.

32. Hosmer, *Rememberances,* 131.

33. Quoted in Harding, *Days,* 104.

34. Hosmer, *Remembrances,* 131.

35. Harding, *Days,* 474.

36. Mary Elkins Moller, *Thoreau in the Human Community* (Amherst: University of Massachusetts Press, 1980), 49.

37. Lebeaux, *Young Man Thoreau,* 141.

38. Quoted in ibid., 144. See also Harding's comments on Thoreau's attraction to nature in *Days,* 104.

39. For a fuller evaluation of Thoreau's poetry, see Richard J. Schneider, entry on Thoreau, in *Critical Survey of Poetry,* ed. Frank Magill (Englewood Cliffs, N.J.: Salem Press, 1982), 7:2896–2904.

40. Lebeaux, *Young Man Thoreau,* 173–74.

41. Harding, *Days,* 136.

42. Sherman Paul, *The Shores of America: Thoreau's Inward Exploration* (1958; reprint ed., Urbana: University of Illinois Press, 1972), 105.

43. Robert Gross, "Culture and Cultivation: Agriculture and Society in Thoreau's Concord," *Journal of American History* 69 (June 1982):54–55.

44. Harding, *Days,* 159–61.

45. Gross, "Culture and Cultivation," 60.

46. *Walden,* 90–91.

47. Quoted in Harding, *Days,* 184.

48. Ibid., 190.

49. Ibid., 195.

50. See Harding's fuller account of Thoreau's incarceration in ibid., 199–208.

51. For a fuller analysis of Thoreau's relation to Emerson during this second stay in the Emerson home, see the chapter entitled "A Sojourner in

Civilized Life Again" in Richard Lebeaux, *Thoreau's Seasons* (Amherst: University of Massachusetts Press, 1984), 64–110.

52. Anonymous newspaper article from the *Worcester Telegram* reprinted in *The Concord Saunterer,* 17, no. 2, p. 4.

53. See J. Lyndon Shanley, *The Making of "Walden"* (Chicago: University of Chicago Press, 1957). Thoreau catalogs what he perceives to be his stylistic weaknesses in *Writings* 13:7–8. His judgment of himself, though perhaps a bit harsh, is essentially accurate.

54. Harding, *Days,* 89.

55. Everett and Laraine Fergenson, "A Personality Profile of Henry David Thoreau: A New Method in Psycho-History," in *Thoreau's Psychology: Eight Essays,* ed. Raymond D. Gozzi (New York: University Press of America, 1983), 95–96.

56. Lebeaux, *Thoreau's Seasons,* 263.

57. For fuller discussion of this study of reflections, see Schneider, "Reflections in Walden Pond."

58. *Reform Papers,* ed. Wendell Glick (Princeton: Princeton University Press, 1973), 63. Further references follow in the text.

59. Harding, *Days,* 73.

60. Harding, *Days,* 317–18.

61. See Michael Meyer, "Thoreau's Rescue of John Brown from History," *Studies in the American Renaissance 1980,* ed. Joel Myerson (Boston: G. K. Hall & Co., 1980), 302 ff.

62. Harding, *Days,* 425.

63. Ibid., 421.

64. Lebeaux, *Thoreau's Seasons,* 326.

Chapter Two

1. Harding, *Days,* 88–93, contains a full account of the boating trip.

2. Linck C. Johnson, Historical Introduction to *A Week on the Concord and Merrimack Rivers,* ed. Carl Hovde, William L. Howarth, and Elizabeth Hall Witherell (Princeton: Princeton University Press, 1980), 433. Further references to this edition follow in the text.

3. Lebeaux, *Thoreau's Seasons,* 199.

4. Ibid., 199.

5. Ibid., 7.

6. Paul, *Shores of America,* 191.

7. Ralph Waldo Emerson, "The Poet," in *Collected Works,* vol. 3, *Essays: Second Series,* ed. Alfred R. Ferguson and Jean Ferguson Carr (1983), 6–7.

8. Ralph Waldo Emerson, *The Letters of Ralph Waldo Emerson,* ed. Ralph L. Rusk, 6 vols. (New York: Columbia University Press, 1939), 3:384.

9. Walter Harding and Michael Meyer, *The New Thoreau Handbook* (New York: New York University Press, 1980), 45. The works referred to by Harding are listed on 81–82.

10. Quoted in Carl Hovde, "Nature into Art: Thoreau's Use of His Journals in *A Week,*" *American Literature* 30 (1958):167.

11. John Conron, *The American Landscape: A Critical Anthology of Prose and Poetry* (New York: Oxford University Press, 1973), xxii–xxiii.

12. In his journal, Thoreau mentions seeing two panoramas, probably "Champney's Rhine" (of the Rhine River) and Samuel Stockwell's panorama of the Mississippi River, both of which were shown in Boston in 1849. See *Writings,* 9:146. See also John Francis McDermott, *The Lost Panoramas of the Mississippi* (Chicago: University of Chicago Press, 1958), 68–69. An example of the stereorama is contained in the reports of the Concord Lyceum: "An Exhibition of the *Stereorama* was given . . . embracing views of scenery and celebrated buildings in this country and Europe." See Kenneth Walter Cameron, *The Massachusetts Lyceum during the American Renaissance* (Hartford, Conn.: Transcendental Books, 1969), pt. 2, 176.

13. Stephen Fink, "Variations of the Self: Thoreau's Personae in *A Week on the Concord and Merrimack Rivers,*" *ESQ: A Journal of the American Renaissance,* 28, no. 1 (1982):29.

14. Ibid., 32.

15. Ibid., 34.

16. Quoted in Bradford Torrey, Introductory Note to *Writings,* 1:xlv.

17. Paul, *Shores of America,* 210.

18. William Drake, "*A Week on the Concord and Merrimack Rivers,*" *Thoreau: A Collection of Critical Essays,* ed. Sherman Paul (Englewood Cliffs, N.J.: Prentice-Hall, 1962), 66.

19. Paul, *Shores of America,* 213.

20. Jonathan Bishop, "The Experience of the Sacred in Thoreau's *Week,*" *Journal of English Literary History* 33 (1966):90.

21. William Blake, "The Marriage of Heaven and Hell," in *English Romantic Writers,* ed. David Perkins (New York: Harcourt Brace & World, 1967), 69.

22. John Keats, Letter to George and Tom Keats, 27 December 1817, in *English Romantic Writers, ed. Perkins, 1209.*

23. Carl Hovde, "Literary Materials in *A Week,*" *PMLA* 80 (March 1965):79.

24. Bishop, "Experience of the Sacred," 90–91.

25. William Wordsworth, *The Prelude,* bk. 14, in *English Romantic Writers,* ed. Perkins, 260–61.

26. See Robert Sayre's discussion of this passage in *Thoreau and the American Indians* (Princeton: Princeton University Press, 1977), 53.

27. Emerson, "Circles," in *Essays: First Series,* 180.

28. Paul, *Shores of America,* 134.

29. Samuel Taylor Coleridge, *Biographia Literaria,* chap. 13, in *English Romantic Writers,* ed. Perkins, 452.

30. Neil Harris, *The Artist in American Society: The Formative Years 1790–1860* (New York: George Braziller, 1966), 3–5.

31. Emerson, "The Poet," 22.

Chapter Three

1. Emerson, *Letters,* 4:460.

2. Harding, *Days,* 340.

3. J. Lyndon Shanley, Historical Introduction to *Walden,* 368–69.

4. Shanley, *The Making of "Walden,"* 24.

5. Lebeaux, *Thoreau's Seasons,* 43.

6. Shanley, *The Making of "Walden,"* 6.

7. Annette M. Woodlief, "*Walden*: A Checklist of Literary Criticism through 1973," *Resources for American Literary Study* 5 (1975):15–58. See particularly entries 37, 39, 62, 89, 131, and 292.

8. Richard and Jean Masteller, "Rural Architecture in Andrew Jackson Downing and Henry David Thoreau: Pattern Book Parody in *Walden,*" *New England Quarterly* 57 (December 1984):483–510.

9. See Woodlief, "Checklist," entries, 62, 165, 228, and 268. See also Harding, *Days,* 334.

10. Lauriat Lane, Jr., "Walden, the Second Year," *Studies in Romanticism* 8 (Spring 1969):191–92.

11. Rosemary Whitaker, "*A Week* and *Walden*: The River and the Pond," *American Transcendental Quarterly* 17 (Winter 1972–73):9–12.

12. Walt Whitman, "Song of Myself," in *Leaves of Grass,* ed. Harold W. Blodgett and Sculley Bradley (New York: New York University Press, 1965), 32.

13. A brief early discussion of Thoreau's comic persona is in Constance M. Rourke, *American Humor: A Study of the National Character* (New York: Harcourt Brace, 1931), 166–68.

14. Quoted by Shanley in Notes on Illustrations, *Walden,* 353.

15. Lauriat Lane, Jr., "Thoreau's *Walden,* I, Paragraphs 1–3," *Explicator* 29 (January 1971):35.

16. *Reform Papers,* 155.

17. Edward L. Galligan, "The Comedian at Walden Pond," *South Atlantic Quarterly* 69 (Winter 1970):21.

18. Ibid., 25.

19. Benjamin Franklin, *The Autobiography of Benjamin Franklin,* in *Anthology of American Literature,* ed. George McMichael et al. (New York: Macmillan Co., 1980), 321.

20. Stanley Cavell, *The Sense of "Walden"* (New York: Viking Press, 1972), 10.

21. Ibid., 11.

22. Alfred Kazin, *An American Procession* (New York: Vintage Books, 1984), 64.

23. Shanley, *The Making of "Walden,"* 11–12.

24. The view of *Walden's* structure presented here is essentially that of Walter Harding in "Five Ways of Looking at *Walden,"* *Massachusetts Review* 4 (Autumn 1962):149–62. This article is reprinted in *Thoreau in Our Season,* ed. John Hicks (Amherst: University of Massachusetts Press, 1966). For a different view of Thoreau's grouping of chapters in *Walden,* see Charles R. Anderson, *The Magic Circle of "Walden"* (New York: Holt, Rinehart & Winston, 1968), 39–56.

25. Ralph Waldo Emerson, "The American Scholar," in *Nature, Addresses, and Lectures,* 55.

26. Shanley, *The Making of "Walden,"* 25.

27. See Masteller, "Rural Architecture," for further discussion of Thoreau's use of house pattern books.

28. Hosmer, *Remembrances,* 53.

29. Stanley Edgar Hyman, "Henry Thoreau in Our Time," *Atlantic Monthly,* November 1946, 140.

30. Richard Bridgman provides a book-length discussion of Thoreau's darker side in *Dark Thoreau* (Lincoln: University of Nebraska Press, 1982).

31. For a fuller discussion of the symbolism of Walden Pond, see Melvin E. Lyons, "Walden Pond as Symbol," *PMLA* 82 (May 1967):289–300.

32. For a fuller discussion of images of circularity and centrality in *Walden,* see Joseph J. Moldenhauer, "Images of Circularity in Thoreau's Prose," *Texas Studies in Literature and Language* 1 (Summer 1959):245–63.

33. Joseph Allen Boone presents a full discussion of Thoreau's images of digging and diving in "Delving and Diving for Truth: Breaking through to Bottom in Thoreau's *Walden,"* *ESQ, A Journal of the American Renaissance* 27 no. 3 (1981):135–46.

34. Walter Benn Michaels, *"Walden's* False Bottoms," *Glyph* 1 (1977):135.

35. Ibid., 147.

36. Ibid.

37. Ibid., 148.

38. Although Thoreau's peaceful death can be accounted for by his philosophy, it may also have been partially due to the side effects of tuberculosis. See Walter Harding, Afterword, *Henry David Thoreau: A Profile,* ed. Harding (New York: Hill & Wang, 1971), 252.

39. Eugene Walker provides the scientific explanation of the pond's rises and falls in "Walden's Way Revealed," *Man & Nature* (1971):11–20.

40. Cavell, *Sense of "Walden,"* 79.

41. F. O. Matthiessen, *American Renaissance* (New York: Oxford University Press, 1941), 175.

Chapter Four

1. *The Maine Woods,* ed. Joseph J. Moldenhauer (Princeton: Princeton University Press, 1972), 156. Further references, designated MW where necessary, follow in the text.

2. Moldenhauer, Afterword to 1983 paperback edition of *The Maine Woods* (Princeton: Princeton University Press), 354–55.

3. Neptune had also been Jackson's guide to Katahdin.

4. J. Parker Huber includes the itinerary of this and the other two Maine woods trips in *The Wildest Country: A Guide to Thoreau's Maine* (Boston: Appalachian Mountain Club, 1981), 2–6.

5. Harding, *Days,* 208–10.

6. Ibid., 309–12.

7. Ibid., 385–92.

8. Quoted in ibid., 371.

9. Ibid., 228–29.

10. James Russell Lowell, *My Study Windows* (Boston: Houghton Mifflin & Co., 1890), 361–81.

11. Moldenhauer, Afterword to *Maine Woods,* 364.

12. Ibid., 366.

13. Lebeaux, *Seasons,* 184.

14. Philip Gura, "Thoreau's Maine Woods Indians: More Representative Men," *American Literature* 49 (November 1977):371.

15. "Life without Principle," *Reform Papers,* 160.

16. This was the passage Lowell deleted from the *Atlantic Monthly* publication of "Chesuncook" without Thoreau's permission.

17. Sayre, *Thoreau and the Indians,* x.

18. Ibid., 6.

19. Donald M. Murray, "Thoreau's Indians and His Developing Art of Characterization," *ESQ: A Journal of the American Renaissance* 21, no. 4 (1975):227.

20. Lawrence Willson, "Thoreau: Defender of the Savage," *Emerson Society Quarterly* 26 (1962):3–4; see also Sayre's discussion of the Indian notebooks in his appendix, *Thoreau and the Indians,* 217–20.

21. For a full discussion of Thoreau's attitude toward hunting, see Thomas L. Altherr, "'Chaplain to the Hunters': Henry David Thoreau's Ambivalence toward Hunting," *American Literature* 56, no. 3 (October 1984):345–61.

22. Ronald Hoag, "The Mark of the Wilderness: Thoreau's Contact with Ktaadn," *Texas Studies in Literature and Language* 24 (Spring 1982):24.

23. Robert C. Cosebey discusses the composition of "Ktaadn" in "Thoreau at Work: The Writing of 'Ktaadn,'" *Bulletin of the New York Public Library* 65 (January 1961):21–30.

Chapter Five

1. Mitchell Robert Breitweiser suggests this relation between *Walden* and *Cape Cod* in "Thoreau and the Wrecks on Cape Cod," *Studies in Romanticism* 20 (Spring 1981):3.

2. Ralph Waldo Emerson, "Experience," in *Selections from Ralph Waldo Emerson,* ed. Stephen E. Whicher (Boston: Houghton Mifflin, 1957), 261.

3. Harding, *Days,* 270–74.

4. Harding, *Days,* 359–64.

5. This material is found in an appendix in the edition edited by Dudley C. Lunt for Bramhall House (New York: 1951).

6. Harding, *Days,* 382–85.

7. Frederick Jackson Turner, "The Old West," in *The Frontier in American History* (New York: Holt, Rinehart, & Winston, 1962), 67.

8. *Writings* 4:31. Further references to this edition of *Cape Cod* will follow in the text.

9. The remainder of this chapter was first published in slightly different form as "*Cape Cod*: Thoreau's Wilderness of Illusion" in *ESQ: A Journal of the American Renaissance* 26, no. 4 (1980):184–96.

10. On indoor versus outdoor see Martin Pops, "An Analysis of Thoreau's *Cape Cod,*" *Bulletin of the New York Public Library* 67 (1963):419–28; on sublime versus picturesque, Emory V. Maiden, Jr., "*Cape Cod*: Thoreau's Handling of the Sublime and the Picturesque" (Ph.D. diss., University of Virginia, 1972), 15–16 and 95; and on transcendental versus scientific, Paul, *Shores of America,* 378–88. See also James McIntosh, *Thoreau as Romantic Naturalist: His Shifting Stance toward Nature* (Ithaca: Cornell University Press, 1974), 216–35.

11. Paul and McIntosh take this view, as do Thomas Couser, "Thoreau's Cape Cod Pilgrimage," *American Transcendental Quarterly* 26 (Spring 1975): 31–36; and John J. McAleer, "Thoreau's Epic *Cape Cod,*" *Thought* 43 (1968):227–46.

12. See Pops, "Analysis of *Cape Cod,*" 428.

13. See Maiden, "*Cape Cod,*" and Lauriat Lane, Jr., "*Cape Cod*: Thoreau's Sandy Pastoral," *American Transcendental Quarterly* 11 (Summer 1971):69–74.

14. See McIntosh's discussion of this passage, *Romantic Naturalist,* 229. See also Maiden, "*Cape Cod,*" 30, and Paul, *Shores of America,* 384, for other interpretations.

15. McIntosh, *Romantic Naturalist,* 218.

16. Francois-Marie Arouet de Voltaire, *Candide, or Optimism,* trans. Robert M. Adams, in *The Norton Anthology of World Masterpieces,* ed. Maynard Mack et al., 4th ed. (New York: W. W. Norton & Co., 1979), 234.

17. Couser, "Cape Cod Pilgrimage," 33.

18. See Lawrence Willson's discussion of Thoreau's attitude toward the Pilgrims in "The Influence of Early North American History and Legend on the Writings of Henry David Thoreau" (Ph.D. dissertation, Yale University, 1944), 222–23.

19. Although Emerson is not mentioned by name in this passage, Thoreau identifies him as seeing this mirage in the journal (*Writings,* 16:15).

20. See Paul, *Shores of America,* 385, and Maiden, *"Cape Cod,"* 114–15.

21. Paul, *Shores of America,* 385.

22. Ibid., 48.

23. Maiden, *"Cape Cod,"* 117.

24. Frederick Jackson Turner, "The Significance of the Frontier in American History," in *The Frontier in American History,* 1.

25. Paul, *Shores of America,* 412, suggests—unconvincingly, I believe— that Thoreau was hesitant to go West because of his reluctance to participate in the economic greed inherent in the westward movement.

Chapter Six

1. Nathaniel Hawthorne, Journal entry, 1 September 1842, in *The Centenary Edition of the Works of Nathaniel Hawthorne* (Columbus: Ohio State University Press, 1972), vol. 8, *The American Notebooks,* ed. Claude M. Simpson, 354.

2. For extended discussions of Thoreau's sauntering see Reginald Cook, *The Concord Saunterer* (Middlebury, Vt.: Middlebury College Press, 1940) and Cook's chapter "The Saunterer" in *Passage to Walden* (New York: Russell & Russell, 1958).

3. Subsequent references to *Writings* in this chapter follow in the text without designation.

4. *Journal,* vol. 1, *1837–1844,* ed. John C. Broderick et al. (Princeton: Princeton University Press, 1972), 69. Further references, designated *Journal* 1, follow in the text.

5. For extended discussion of Thoreau's interest in water reflections, see Schneider, "Reflections in Walden Pond."

6. Charles Feidelson, Jr., *Symbolism in American Literature* (Chicago: University of Chicago Press, 1966), 137.

7. Leo Marx, Introduction to *Excursions* (New York: Corinth Books, 1962), vii.

8. John Hildebidle discusses Thoreau's use of the genre of the natural history essay in *Thoreau: A Naturalist's Liberty* (Cambridge: Harvard University Press, 1983).

9. Robert Sattelmeyer, Introduction to *The Natural History Essays* (Salt Lake City, Utah: Peregrine Smith Books, 1984), xv.

10. Homer, *Iliad* 12.276–89, in *The Iliad of Homer,* trans. Richmond Lattimore (Chicago: University of Chicago Press, 1967), 265–66. James Joyce uses an adaptation of this same passage to conclude his story "The Dead" in *Dubliners* (New York: Viking Press, 1964), 214.

11. Paul, *Shores of America,* 157.

12. Harding and Meyer, *Handbook,* 60.

13. Ibid., 61.

14. Ibid., 59.

15. Lorrie Smith also points out similarities between Keats's poems and Thoreau's nature essays in "Walking from England to America: Re-Viewing Thoreau's Romanticism," *New England Quarterly* 58, no. 2 (June 1985):221–41. But Smith sees "Walking" rather than "Autumnal Tints" as the specific counterpart of Keats's "To Autumn." See 236 ff.

16. Paul, *Shores of America,* 408–9.

17. Kenneth Van Anglen, "Thoreau's Wild Apples and the American Adam," *ESQ: A Journal of the American Renaissance,* 27, no. 1 (1981):30.

18. William Howarth, *The Book of Concord: Thoreau's Life As a Writer* (New York: Viking Press, 1982), 335–36.

19. Sattelmeyer, Introduction to *Natural History,* xxxv.

20. Harding and Meyer, *Handbook,* 75.

21. "Huckleberries," ed. Leo Stoller (Iowa City: The Windhover Press of the University of Iowa and the New York Public Library, 1970).

22. In dealing with the relative scarcity of notes on nature in these early years of the journal, one must remember that Thoreau scissored out many pages from the early journal for use in *A Week, Walden,* and his other writings. See Harding and Meyer, *Handbook,* 74.

Chapter Seven

1. Quoted in Howarth, *Book of Concord,* 180.

2. Leo Stoller, *After "Walden": Thoreau's Changing Views on Economic Man* (Stanford, Calif.: Stanford University Press, 1957), 4.

3. Ibid., 7.

4. *The Correspondence of Henry David Thoreau,* ed. Walter Harding and Carl Bode (New York: New York University Press, 1958), 611.

5. Margaret Fuller rejected "The Service" for publication in the *Dial.* The essay eventually (perhaps when Thoreau resubmitted it) came into Emersons' hands when he became editor. It remained there until Emerson's death and was not published until 1902. See Harding, *Days,* 114–15.

6. A more specific expression of the ideal of the brave man appears in "Sir Walter Raleigh," a lecture written in 1843, but Thoreau was not primarily interested in Raleigh as a reformer.

7. Wendell Glick, "Thoreau and the 'Herald of Freedom,'" *New England Quarterly* 22 (June 1949):197.

8. These lecture notes were not published as a separate essay until they were included in the Princeton edition of *Reform Papers*.

9. Stoller, *After "Walden,"* 28.

10. Wendell Glick, Textual Introduction to "Life without Principle," in *Reform Papers*, 369.

11. Vincent Buranelli, "The Case Against Thoreau," *Ethics*, 67 (July 1957):264.

12. Lewis H. Van Dusen, Jr., "Civil Disobedience: Destroyer of Democracy," *American Bar Association Journal* 55 (February 1969):123–26, reprinted in *Writing and Reading across the Curriculum*, ed. Laurence Behrens and Leonard J. Rosen (Boston: Little, Brown & Co., 1985), 368.

13. The problems of labeling Thoreau an anarchist are discussed by Richard Drinnon in "Thoreau's Politics of the Upright Man," in *Thoreau in Our Season*, ed. Hicks, 154–68.

14. Buranelli, "Case," 264.

15. See the report on the Concord Lyceum debate in the *Yeoman's Gazette*, reprinted in *Massachusetts Lyceum*, 155.

16. Harding, *Days,* 317–18.

17. See Michael Meyer, "Thoreau and Black Emigration," *American Literature* 53 (November 1981):380–96.

18. Harding, *Days,* 416–17.

19. Wendell Glick, "Thoreau and Radical Abolitionism," (Ph.D. diss., Northwestern University, 1950), 168.

20. Harding, *Days,* 418.

21. Ibid., 418.

Chapter Eight

1. Ralph Waldo Emerson, "Biographical Sketch," in *Writings,* 1:xxxvii and xl.

2. A full account of the pendulum swings of Thoreau's reputation can be found in Michael Meyer, *Several More Lives to Live* (Westport, Conn.: Greenwood Press, 1977).

3. See particularly the books by Cavell and Cameron for close readings of Thoreau's exploration of the function of language.

4. Quoted in Henry James, Jr., *Notes of a Son and Brother* (New York: Charles Scribner's Sons, 1914), 185.

5. See Lebeaux's section of *Young Man Thoreau* entitled "Rivals for the Hand of a Maiden," 114–40.

6. Moller, *Thoreau in the Human Community,* 89–90.

7. Quoted in Ralph Waldo Emerson, *Collected Works,* vol. 15, *The Jour-*

nals of *Miscellaneous Notebooks 1860–1866,* ed. Linda Allardt et al. (1982), 239.

8. Ralph Waldo Emerson, *Collected Works,* vol. 10, *The Journals and Miscellaneous Notebooks 1847–1848,* ed. Merton M. Sealts, Jr. (1973), 343.

9. Quoted in Emerson, *Journals and Notebooks 1860–1866,* 246.

10. Fannie Hardy Eckstrom, "Thoreau's *Maine Woods,*" *Atlantic Monthly,* July–August 1908, 245.

11. Ibid., 246.

12. Ibid., 246.

13. Mary P. Sherwood, "Fanny Eckstrom's Bias," *Massachusetts Review* 4 (Autumn 1962):64.

14. Walter Harding, "Walden's Man of Science," *Virginia Quarterly Review* 57 (Winter 1981):49.

15. Ibid., 55–56.

16. Robert Sattelmeyer and Richard A. Hocks claim Coleridge as a source for Thoreau's interest in yoking science and philosophy. See "Thoreau and Coleridge's *Theory of Life,*" *Studies in the American Renaissance 1985,* ed. Joel Myerson (Charlottesville: University Press of Virginia, 1985), 269–84.

17. *Correspondence,* 250–51.

18. David Shi, *The Simple Life* (New York: Oxford University Press, 1985), 149.

19. Bridgman, *Dark Thoreau,* xiii.

20. Hyman, "Thoreau in Our Time," 138.

21. Cameron, *Writing Nature,* 148.

22. Ibid., 82.

23. Howarth, *Book of Concord,* 10.

24. Sattelmeyer, Introduction to *Natural History,* xx–xxi.

25. Howarth, *Book of Concord,* 5.

26. Jorge Luis Borges, "Funes the Memorious," in *Labyrinths: Selected Stories and Other Writings,* ed. Donald A. Yates and James E. Irby (New York: New Directions, 1964), 66.

27. Lebeaux, *Seasons,* 112.

28. Sharon Cameron, *Writing Nature: Henry Thoreau's Journal* (New York: Oxford University Press, 1985), 4.

29. Cameron, ibid., 22, pushes this comparison with *Walden* even further by suggesting that "if the works are to be considered hierarchically, it may be the *Journal* which Thoreau understood to be the primary work, for it is *Walden* which is splintered from the *Journal,* not the other way around."

Selected Bibliography

PRIMARY SOURCES

The standard collection of Thoreau's works is the 1906 Walden edition listed below. This is gradually being superceded, however, by the editions of individual works and of the journal being published by the Princeton University Press. Those volumes of the Princeton edition available at the time of this writing are listed below.

1. Prose

A Week on the Concord and Merrimack Rivers. Edited by Carl Hovde, William Howarth, and Elizabeth Hall Witherell. Princeton: Princeton University Press, 1980.

The Correspondence of Henry David Thoreau. Edited by Walter Harding and Carl Bode. New York: New York University Press, 1958.

Early Essays and Miscellanies. Edited by Joseph J. Moldenhauer and Edwin Moser, with Alexander Kern. Princeton: Princeton University Press, 1975.

Journal. Vol. 1, *1837–1844,* edited by John C. Broderick et al. Princeton: Princeton University Press, 1972.

Journal. Vol. 2, *1842–1848,* edited by Robert Sattelmeyer. Princeton: Princeton University Press, 1984.

The Maine Woods. Edited by Joseph J. Moldenhauer. Princeton: Princeton University Press, 1972.

The Natural History Essays. Introduction by Robert Sattelmeyer. Salt Lake City, Utah: Peregrine Smith Books, 1984. (Includes "Huckleberries.")

Reform Papers. Edited by Wendell Glick. Princeton: Princeton University Press, 1973.

The Variorum "Civil Disobedience." Edited by Walter Harding. New York: Twayne Publishers, 1967.

The Variorum "Walden." Edited by Walter Harding. New York: Twayne Publishers, 1962.

Walden. Edited by J. Lyndon Shanley. Princeton: Princeton University Press, 1971.

The Writings of Henry David Thoreau (Walden Edition). Edited by Bradford Torrey. 20 vols. Boston: Houghton Mifflin & Co., 1906.

2. Poetry
Collected Poems. Edited by Carl Bode. Baltimore: Johns Hopkins University
   Press, 1964.

3. Translations
Translations. Edited by Kevin P. Van Anglen. Princeton: Princeton University
   Press, 1986.

SECONDARY SOURCES

1. Bibliographies
In addition to the items below, ongoing bibliographies of Thoreau material
and criticism are published quarterly in *The Thoreau Society Bulletin* and yearly
in the *PMLA Bibliography.*

Harding, Walter, and Michael Meyer. *The New Thoreau Handbook.* New
   York: New York University Press, 1980. The most complete selected
   and annotated bibliography of Thoreau's life and works. Partially su-
   percedes Walter Harding's *A Thoreau Handbook* (New York: New York
   University Press, 1959), which is still useful because it is comprehensive
   for the years prior to 1959.
Leary, Lewis. "Henry David Thoreau." In *Eight American Authors,* edited by
   James Woodress, 129–71. Rev. ed. New York: W. W. Norton & Co.,
   1971. A useful brief bibliographical essay.
Meyer, Michael. "Henry David Thoreau." In *The Transcendentalists: A Review
   of Research and Criticism,* edited by Joel Myerson, 260–85. New York:
   Modern Language Association of America, 1984. The most recent bibliographical essay on Thoreau. Conveniently organized and a good place
   to start.
Woodlief, Annette M. *"Walden*: A Checklist of Literary Criticism through
   1973." *Resources for American Literary Study* 5 (1975):15–58. A comprehensive listing of significant criticism of *Walden.*

2. Books
Anderson, Charles R. *The Magic Circle of "Walden."* New York: Holt, Rinehart, & Winston, 1968. A thorough study of the imagery in *Walden.*
Bridgman, Richard. *Dark Thoreau.* Lincoln: University of Nebraska Press,
   1982. Presents a controversial view of Thoreau as essentially cold and
   pessimistic. Bridgman is unsympathetic to Thoreau but provokes recon-
   siderations of his position as a historical figure and a writer.
Buell, Lawrence. *Literary Transcendentalism: Style and Vision in the American
   Renaissance.* Ithaca, N.Y.: Cornell University Press, 1973. Includes an

excellent discussion of Thoreau's writing style in the context of New England transcendentalism.

Cameron, Kenneth Walter. *The Massachusetts Lyceum during the American Renaissance.* Hartford, Conn.: Transcendental Books, 1969. Reprints nineteenth-century records of lyceum programs in Concord and other Massachusetts towns.

Cameron, Sharon. *Writing Nature: Henry Thoreau's Journal.* New York: Oxford University Press, 1985. The first close reading of Thoreau's journal as a literary work in its own right rather than as raw material for other works. Contains some interesting insights, but perhaps not enough to justify the reader's plowing through the author's impossibly difficult prose.

Canby, Henry Seidel. *Thoreau.* Boston: Houghton Mifflin, 1939. An early biography containing material not available in the Salt biography. Still useful but contains some questionable dabbling in Freudian commentary.

Cavell, Stanley. *The Senses of "Walden."* New York: Viking Press, 1972. The best close reading of *Walden,* difficult but rewarding.

Channing, William Ellery. *Thoreau: The Poet-Naturalist.* Boston: Roberts, 1873. Contains interesting firsthand anecdotes of Thoreau by his closest friend.

Christie, John A. *Thoreau as World Traveler.* New York: Columbia University Press, 1965. Demonstrates how Thoreau uses geography to provide both symbols and structures for his writing.

Cook, Reginald. *Passage to Walden.* New York: Russell & Russell, 1958. A good introduction to Thoreau's interest in nature.

Emerson, Edward Waldo. *Henry Thoreau as Remembered by a Young Friend.* Boston: Houghton Mifflin, 1917. Perhaps the single best source of personal anecdotes about Thoreau as remembered by Ralph Waldo Emerson's son.

Feidelson, Charles, Jr. *Symbolism and American Literature.* Chicago: University of Chicago Press, 1953. Makes an important distinction between Thoreau's use of symbolism and Emerson's.

Fleck, Richard F. *Henry Thoreau and John Muir among the Indians.* Hamden, Conn.: Archon Books, 1985. An interesting comparison of these two famous American naturalists, including some previously unpublished selections from Thoreau's "Indian notebooks."

Garber, Frederick. *Thoreau's Redemptive Imagination.* New York: New York University Press, 1977. The best extended discussion of Thoreau's works as related to international romanticism.

Gozzi, Raymond, ed. *Thoreau's Psychology.* Lanham, Md.: University Press of America, 1983. A collection of essays exploring Thoreau from various psychological perspectives.

Gura, Philip F. *The Wisdom of Words: Language, Theology, and Literature in the New England Renaissance.* Middletown, Conn.: Wesleyan University

Press, 1981. Includes an important discussion of Thoreau's interest in language theory.

Harding, Walter. *The Days of Henry Thoreau*. New York: Dover Publications, 1982. The standard biography of Thoreau. Essential for any student of Thoreau's works.

————, ed. *Henry David Thoreau: A Profile*. New York: Hill & Wang, 1971. A collection of essays on various aspects of Thoreau's life and writings.

————, ed. *Thoreau: Man of Concord*. New York: Holt, Rinehart, & Winston, 1962. A collection of comments on Thoreau by his contemporaries.

————. *Thoreau's Library*. Charlottesville: University of Virginia Press, 1957. Contains a useful list of books Thoreau owned.

Hicks, John, ed. *Thoreau in Our Season*. Amherst: University of Massachusetts Press, 1966. Perhaps the best single collection of essays on Thoreau, with emphasis on Thoreau as a social and political reformer.

Hildebidle, John. *Thoreau: A Naturalist's Liberty*. Cambridge: Harvard University Press, 1983. An extended discussion of Thoreau's use of the genre of the natural history essay.

Hosmer, Horace. *Remembrances of Concord and the Thoreaus*. Edited by George Hendrick. Urbana: University of Illinois Press, 1977. Contains vivid reminiscences by a student who attended the Thoreau brothers' school.

Howarth, William. *The Book of Concord: Thoreau's Life As a Writer*. New York: Viking Press, 1982. Discusses Thoreau's journal, with emphasis on what it reveals about Thoreau's life in Concord and his aspirations as a writer.

————. *The Literary Manuscripts of Henry David Thoreau*. Columbus: Ohio State University Press, 1974. Attempts to list all known manuscripts of Thoreau's writing.

Huber, J. Parker. *The Wildest Country: A Guide to Thoreau's Maine*. Boston: Appalachian Mountain Club, 1981. A helpful gathering of maps and information about Thoreau's three excursions to the Maine woods, nicely illustrated.

Johnson, Linck C. *Thoreau's Complex Weave: The Writing of "A Week on the Concord and Merrimack Rivers" with the Text of the First Draft*. Charlottesville: University Press of Virginia, 1985. Argues for unity in *A Week* and contains a reconstruction of Thoreau's first draft.

Lane, Lauriat, Jr., ed. *Approaches to "Walden."* San Francisco: Wadsworth, 1961. A collection of essays representing a variety of critical approaches to reading *Walden*.

Lebeaux, Richard. *Thoreau's Seasons*. Amherst: University of Massachusetts Press, 1984. An excellent psychological interpretation of Thoreau's life during and after the Walden Pond years.

————. *Young Man Thoreau*. Amherst: University of Massachusetts Press, 1977. An Erikonsian psychological interpretation of Thoreau's life prior to his stay by Walden Pond.

Lowell, James Russell. *My Study Windows.* Boston: Houghton Mifflin, 1890. Contains Lowell's infamous criticism of Thoreau's achievement.

McIntosh, James. *Thoreau as Romantic Naturalist: His Shifting Stance toward Nature.* Ithaca, N.Y.: Cornell University Press, 1974. Demonstrates that Thoreau could see nature as both benevolent and threatening.

Marble, Annie Russell. *Thoreau: His Home, Friends, and Books.* New York: Crowell, 1902. Another source of interesting reminiscences of Thoreau.

Matthiessen, F. O. *American Renaissance.* New York: Oxford University Press, 1941. Contains the first major discussion of Thoreau as a literary artist.

Meltzer, Milton, and Walter Harding. *A Thoreau Profile.* New York: Crowell, 1962. A useful collection of biographical essays.

Meyer, Michael. *Several More Lives to Live: Thoreau's Political Reputation in America.* Westport, Conn.: Greenwood Press, 1977. Surveys changes in Thoreau's reputation up to the 1970s. Emphasis is on his political views, but his reputation as a naturalist is also discussed.

Moller, Mary Elkins. *Thoreau in the Human Community.* Amherst: University of Massachusetts Press, 1980. Suggests that Thoreau was a lover of humanity, not a misanthrope.

Paul, Sherman. *The Shores of America: Thoreau's Inward Exploration.* 1958. Reprint. Urbana: University of Illinois Press, 1972. The fullest single study of Thoreau's intellectual and artistic development.

—, ed. *Thoreau: A Collection of Critical Essays.* Englewood Cliffs, N.J.: Prentice-Hall, 1962. A useful and widely available collection of previously published essays on Thoreau's various works.

Porte, Joel. *Emerson and Thoreau: Transcendentalists in Conflict.* Middletown, Conn.: Wesleyan University Press, 1965. Emphasizes Thoreau's attraction to the physical rather than the mystical side of nature.

Richardson, Robert D. *Myth and Literature in the American Renaissance.* Bloomington: Indiana University Press, 1978. Contains a significant clarification of Thoreau's use of mythology.

—. *Henry David Thoreau: A Life of the Mind.* Berkeley: University of California Press, 1986. A biography of Thoreau which emphasizes how his writing is influenced by his wide reading and by cultural events. An excellent aid to placing Thoreau in the context of his time.

Rourke, Constance. *American Humor: A Study of the National Character.* New York: Harcourt, Brace, 1931. Contains a brief but important early recognition of Thoreau as a humorist.

Ruland, Richard, ed. *Twentieth Century Interpretations of "Walden."* Englewood Cliffs, N.J.: Prentice-Hall, 1968. A widely available collection of previously published critical essays on *Walden.*

Salt, Henry S. *The Life of Henry David Thoreau.* London: Richard Bentley, 1890. The earliest full biography of Thoreau, mostly superceded by Canby and Harding.

Sanborn, Franklin B. *The Life of Henry David Thoreau.* Boston: Houghton Mifflin, 1917. A biography largely superseded by Canby and Harding but still of some interest for Sanborn's firsthand knowledge of Thoreau.

Sayre, Robert. *Thoreau and the American Indians.* Princeton: Princeton University Press, 1977. The fullest discussion of Thoreau's attitude toward American Indians.

Seybold, Ethel. *Thoreau: The Quest and the Classics.* New Haven: Yale University Press, 1951. A significant discussion of Thoreau's use of classical literature.

Shanley, J. Lyndon. *The Making of "Walden."* Chicago: University of Chicago Press, 1957. The pioneering study of Thoreau's manuscripts of *Walden* showing how the book developed through successive revisions and expansions.

Stoehr, Taylor. *Nay-Saying in Concord.* Hamden, Conn.: Archon Books, 1979. Discusses the views of Thoreau and other Concord writers on social and political issues.

Stoller, Leo. *After Walden: Thoreau's Changing Views on Economic Man.* Stanford, Calif.: Stanford University Press, 1957. The first major study of Thoreau's economic views.

Stowell, Robert F. *A Thoreau Gazeteer.* Princeton: Princeton University Press, 1970. Contains maps and pictures of the places Thoreau lived and visited.

Tanner, Tony. *The Reign of Wonder: Naivety and Reality in American Literature.* Cambridge: Cambridge University Press, 1965. Includes an interesting discussion of Thoreau's unique mode of vision by one of the best British critics of American literature.

Wagenknecht, Edward. *Henry David Thoreau: What Manner of Man?.* Amherst: University of Massachusetts Press, 1981. A good general introduction to Thoreau, organized by topics rather than by chronology.

Wolf, William J. *Thoreau: Mystic, Prophet, Ecologist.* Philadelphia: Pilgrim Press, 1974. Discusses Thoreau's view of God with emphasis on his mysticism.

3. Articles

Altherr, Thomas L. "'Chaplain to the Hunters': Henry David Thoreau's Ambivalence toward Hunting." *American Literature* 56, no. 3 (October 1984):345–61. Demonstrates Thoreau's paradoxical attitudes toward hunting.

Bishop, Jonathan. "The Experience of the Sacred in Thoreau's *Week." Journal of English Literary History* 33 (March 1966):68–91. Views *A Week* as a literary analog of transcendental mystical experience.

Boone, Joseph Allen. "Delving and Diving for Truth: Breaking through to Bottom in Thoreau's *Walden." ESQ: A Journal of the American Renaissance*

27, no. 3 (1981):135–46. Explores Thoreau's use of images of digging and diving in *Walden*.

Breitweiser, Mitchell Robert. "Thoreau and the Wrecks on Cape Cod." *Studies in Romanticism* 20 (Spring 1981):3–20. Discusses the imagery of wreckage in *Cape Cod* and how it reflects a somber side of Thoreau's view of nature.

Coseby, Robert C. "Thoreau at Work: The Writing of 'Ktaadn.'" *Bulletin of the New York Public Library* 65 (January 1961):21–30. Traces Thoreau's composition of his first Maine woods essay.

Couser, Thomas. "Thoreau's Cape Cod Pilgrimage." *American Transcendental Quarterly* 26 (Spring 1975):31–36. A brief but sensible discussion of *Cape Cod*.

Eckstrom, Fannie Hardy. "Thoreau's *Maine Woods*." *Atlantic Monthly,* July-August 1908, 16–18, 242–50. The most influential early assessment of *The Maine Woods*.

Emerson, Ralph Waldo. "Thoreau." *Atlantic Monthly,* August 1862, 239–49. Appears as a "Biographical Sketch" in the Walden edition of Thoreau's works and is often reprinted.. Accurately sees many of Thoreau's strengths while ultimately judging his life a disappointment. See also Joel Myerson's new edition of this essay in *Studies in the American Renaissance 1979*, 17–92. Boston: Twayne Publishers, 1979.

Fink, Steven. "Variations of the Self: Thoreau's Personae in *A Week on the Concord and Merrimack Rivers*." *ESQ: A Journal of the American Renaissance* 28, no. 1 (1982):24–35.

Galligan, Edward L. "The Comedian at Walden Pond." *South Atlantic Quarterly* 69 (Winter 1970):20–37. A study of Thoreau's use of humor in *Walden*.

Glick, Wendell. "Thoreau and the 'Herald of Freedom.'" *New England Quarterly* 22 (June 1949):193–204. Discusses how Thoreau's early newspaper review reveals the beginnings of his interest in social action.

Gross, Robert. "Culture and Cultivation: Agriculture and Society in Thoreau's Concord." *Journal of American History* 69 (June 1982):42–61.

Gura, Philip. "Thoreau's Maine Woods Indians: More Representative Men." *American Literature* 49 (November 1977):366–84. A significant discussion of Thoreau's depiction of Indians in *The Maine Woods*.

Harding, Walter. "Walden's Man of Science." *Virginia Quarterly Review* 57 (Winter 1981):45–61. An excellent reassessment of Thoreau's abilities as an amateur scientist.

Hoag, Ronald. "The Mark of the Wilderness: Thoreau's Contact with Ktaadn." *Texas Studies in Literature and Language* 24 (Spring 1982):23–46. Argues that Thoreau's experience on the mountain was an affirmation rather than an undermining of Thoreau's transcendentalism.

Hovde, Carl. "Literary Materials in *A Week*." *PMLA* 80 (March 1965):76–83. Shows how Thoreau used literary source material in *A Week*.

————. "Nature into Art: Thoreau's Use of His Journals in *A Week*." *American Literature* 30 (1958):165–84. Demonstrates how Thoreau used his journal in the writing of his first book.

Hyman, Stanley Edgar. "Henry Thoreau in Our Time." *Atlantic Monthly,* November 1946, 137–46. Still one of the best assessments of Thoreau as a literary artist.

Lane, Lauriat, Jr. "Thoreau's *Walden*, I, Paragraphs 1–3." *Explicator* 29 (January 1971):35. A close examination of Thoreau's use of wordplay in the opening paragraphs of *Walden*.

————. "Walden: The Second Year." *Studies in Romanticism* 8 (Spring 1969):183–92. Discusses the effect on *Walden* of Thoreau's experience during his second year by the pond.

Lyon, Melvin E. "Walden Pond as Symbol." *PMLA* 82 (May 1967):289–300. A good discussion of *Walden*'s most important symbol.

McAleer, Joseph J. "Thoreau's Epic *Cape Cod*." *Thought* 43 (1968):227–46. The best early (pre-1970) assessment of *Cape Cod* as literary art.

Meyer, Michael. "Thoreau and Black Emigration." *American Literature* 53 (November 1981):380–96. An interesting investigation into Thoreau's attitudes toward blacks.

————. "Thoreau's Rescue of John Brown from History." In *Studies in the American Renaissance 1980*, edited by Joel Myerson, 301–16. Boston: G. K. Hall & Co., 1980. Reassesses Thoreau's admiration of John Brown's violent rebellion.

Michaels, Walter Benn. "*Walden*'s False Bottoms." *Glyph 1* (1977):132–49. A significant essay on the problem of Thoreau's paradoxical attitudes in *Walden*.

Moldenhauer, Joseph J. "Images of Circularity in Thoreau's Prose." *Texas Studies in Literature and Language* 1 (Summer 1959):245–63. An important study of Thoreau's imagery.

Murray, Donald M. "Thoreau's Indians and His Developing Art of Characterization." *ESQ: A Journal of the American Renaissance* 21 no. 4 (1975):222–29. Discusses how Thoreau's skill at characterization progressed through the three *Maine Woods* essays.

Schneider, Richard J. "Reflections in Walden Pond: Thoreau's Optics." *ESQ: A Journal of the American Renaissance* 21, no. 2 (1975):65–75. Relates Thoreau's study of optics to his literary art.

————. "Thoreau and Nineteenth-Century American Landscape Painting." *ESQ: A Journal of the American Renaissance* 31, no. 2 (1985):67–88. Discusses Thoreau's familiarity with the visual arts, as well as the similarities between Thoreau's views of nature and those of American landscape painters.

Smith, Lorrie. "Walking from England to America: Re-Viewing Thoreau's Romanticism." *New England Quarterly* 58, no. 2 (June 1985):221–41.

Contains some useful comparisons of Thoreau to British romantic writers.

Van Anglen, Kevin. "Thoreau's Wild Apples and the American Adam." *ESQ: A Journal of the American Renaissance* 27, no. 1 (1981):28–37.

Wells, Henry. "An Evaluation of Thoreau's Poetry." *American Literature* 16 (May 1944):99–109. An early but fair assessment of Thoreau's poetry.

West, Michael. "Scatology and Eschatology: The Heroic Dimensions of Thoreau's Wordplay." *PMLA* 89 (October 1974):1053–64. An important study of Thoreau's use of wordplay.

Willson, Lawrence. "Thoreau: Defender of the Savage." *Emerson Society Quarterly* 26, no. 1 (1962):3–4. Suggests that Thoreau gradually lost many of his biases toward Indians.

Index